Prison Writing in the Twentieth Century

Prison Writing in the Twentieth Century

A Literary Guide

Julian Murphet

EDINBURGH
University Press

Edinburgh University Press is one of the leading university presses in the UK. We publish academic books and journals in our selected subject areas across the humanities and social sciences, combining cutting-edge scholarship with high editorial and production values to produce academic works of lasting importance. For more information visit our website: edinburghuniversitypress.com

Edinburgh University Press Ltd
The Tun – Holyrood Road
12(2f) Jackson's Entry
Edinburgh EH8 8PJ

Typeset in 11/13pt Adobe Sabon by
Cheshire Typesetting Ltd, Cuddington, Cheshire, and
printed and bound in Great Britain

A CIP record for this book is available from the British Library

ISBN 978 1 3995 1396 8 (hardback)
ISBN 978 1 3995 1398 2 (webready PDF)
ISBN 978 1 3995 1399 9 (epub)

Contents

Acknowledgements

The author would like to thank Benjamin Madden and Clare Charlesworth for stimulating conversations about much of the material discussed herein, and for all the students at the University of Adelaide who have engaged with this material. Andrew van der Vlies is owed credits for improving the chapter on Ruth First. Sean Pryor and Mark Byron helped with the material in the chapter on Ezra Pound. Conversations with Ruth Jennison over the years have sharpened my understanding of Rosa Luxemburg, Angela Davis, George Jackson and many others.

The staff at EUP has been courteous, professional and helpful throughout. Particular thanks to Michelle Houston and Susannah Butler for their generous support in the early stages before moving on to other pastures, and to Elizabeth Frazer, Emily Sharp and Fiona Conn for their work steering the project to completion. Camilla Rockwood is an eagle-eyed copyeditor, deserving of many thanks. And the team at Newgen, Angela Butterworth and Aidan DeVore, did a sterling job on the cover.

My sincerest thanks to the great Turkish artist Gülsün Karamustafa for her permission to use her *Prison Paintings 15* (1972) on the cover of this book. Thousands of yet-to-be written urgent words are latent in its austere pigments.

Thanks on the home front are due to Tamlyn Avery and Gabriel Lusty, for such excellent company and larks.

To every human being imprisoned and vilified for their political beliefs, their articulate public statements on behalf of peace, solidarity, justice and love, or for the simple fact of being alive and unaccepting of the wretched lot assigned to them and their kind by regimes of control, we all owe an immeasurable and unpayable debt. This book is offered in the spirit of abolition: of all gaols, work camps, detention centres, offshore island-prisons, concentration camps, and all the other walls thrown up around human liberty.

Introduction

I

This book is offered as a contribution to the literary scholarship of texts written by political prisoners – of one description or another – in the 'long' twentieth century, stretching from Oscar Wilde's two-year sentence to hard labour in the 1890s to Behrouz Boochani's seven-year detention on Manus Island more recently.[1] It is neither criminological nor sociological in its orientation; rather, it proposes a specifically literary investigation into the properties and varieties of a particular subgenre of life-writing (sometimes in a lightly fictionalised mode) concerning the imprisonment of men and women for broadly political reasons. Although its method is principally to dwell, critically and intimately, with the individual texts themselves,

---

[1] For major contemporary literary scholarship on prison writings, see Michelle Kelly and Claire Westall, eds, *Prison Writing and the Literary World: Imprisonment, Institutionality and Questions of Literary Practice* (London: Routledge, 2021); Andrea Brady, *Poetry and Bondage: A History and Theory of Lyric Constraint* (Cambridge: Cambridge University Press, 2021); Monika Fludernik, *Metaphors of Confinement: The Prison in Fact, Fiction, and Fantasy* (Oxford: Oxford University Press, 2019); Caleb Smith, *The Prison and the American Imagination* (New Haven: Yale University Press, 2009); Philip Edward Phillips, ed., *Prison Narratives from Boethius to Zana* (New York: Palgrave Macmillan, 2014); Jason Haslam, *Fitting Sentences: Identity in Nineteenth- and Twentieth-Century Prison Narratives* (Toronto: University of Toronto Press, 2005); Ruth Ahnert, *The Rise of Prison Literature in the Sixteenth Century* (Cambridge: Cambridge University Press, 2013); Sean Grass, *The Self in the Cell: Narrating the Victorian Prisoner* (New York: Routledge, 2003); and Thomas S. Freeman, 'The Rise of Prison Literature', in William J. Sheils and William Sherman, eds, 'Prison Writings in Early Modern Britain', *Huntington Library Quarterly* 70.2 (June 2009): 133–46.

looking to details of style, voice, mood and tone for information about many of the most pressing political and aesthetic qualities of modern prison writing, there is also a larger argument at play as regards the historical transformations of the carceral institution itself, in several national contexts, as the century matured. In this introduction, I will first justify my methodology and the nature of my investigations; then outline the main lineaments of this larger argument, as it weaves its arterial way through the chapters that follow.

As far as the approach taken by this study is concerned, while it shares the abiding concern of most critics engaged in this field – the sense that, as H. Bruce Franklin aptly puts it, 'Writers scribbling away in their cells or in limited prison libraries tell us most of what we know about these dark fortresses of gloom and terror. They disclose the nasty, brutish details of the life within'[2] – it also departs from this overwhelmingly epistemological attitude by insisting that the style and voice of prison texts do rather more than 'disclose' the institutions they inscribe. Indeed, what I will want to show is that details of tone and mood, imagery and rhetoric not only add to our pool of information about the 'obscene' space of prison life; they create a veritable force-field of literary energy that holds that space at arms' length, allowing for new and untold imaginative capacities to flood the carceral gloom and thence enter into our world. As Michelle Kelly and Claire Westall point out in their important study, 'bridges between the "inside" and the "outside" are important for any conception of prison and its effects. Prison writing is one such bridge.'[3] It is a bridge woven of perceptions and feelings as much as concepts. Far from merely cataloguing the evils of penal solitude and servitude, prison writing attains peaks of expressive and pathic intensity of which few other genres are capable.[4] Perhaps only war writing can vie with prison writing's structural privileging of everything with which literature is typically not comfortable: boredom, reiteration, solitude, despair, trauma and terror.[5]

---

[2] H. Bruce Franklin, ed., *Prison Writing in 20th-Century America* (New York: Penguin, 1998), xi.

[3] Kelly and Westall, eds, *Prison Writing and the Literary World*, 22.

[4] Monika Fludernik's ambitious undertaking in *Metaphors of Confinement* is to compile a thorough tropology and symbology of prison literature from the medieval through to the contemporary periods. It shows how deeply literary the genre of prison writing has always been.

[5] See, on the relations between prison writing and war writing, Ben Stubbs, *Creative and Non-Fiction Writing during Isolation and Confinement: Imaginative Travel, Prison, Shipwrecks, Pandemics, and War* (London: Routledge, 2022).

It will be my argument that, because prison writing springs from a situation uniquely spartan, nay denuded, in its phenomenological and social diversity, and subject to matchless degrees of repetition and routine, on the one hand, and shock and violence on the other, its literary qualities must be forged almost entirely out of self-generated materials: memory (including the memory of literary texts), otherwise repressed sensory domains (sound and smell particularly), the 'poor, bare fork'd' body of the incarcerated individual, the minor worlds of insect and avian visitants, political rhetoric as a nourishing spiritual resource, and the generally dissociated, spatio-temporally alienated subjectivity of penal life. I will turn to a finer itemisation of these paradigmatic categories of prison literature in the chapters ahead; but here I simply wish to affirm the methodological decision to track them as they appear in the texts to hand, to attend to them in their actual realisation in prose and verse. For what finally matters is not the simple increase in the yield of knowledge afforded by these texts, but the further evidence they give of the astonishing resilience, strength and resourcefulness of the human being in its efforts to surmount, in writing, everything that can be levelled against it in the way of torture and horror. It is out of this resistance that something like our 'immortal' dimension can be seized, particularly insofar as it articulates with a broader political horizon.[6]

Each chapter begins with a more or less lengthy quotation as a representative illustration of its subject text's governing techniques and vocal qualities. This allusion to the method of Auerbach's *Mimesis* is not merely derivative;[7] rather, it posits a deeper claim about the developmental arc of prison writing across the previous

---

[6] Alain Badiou writes: 'The stories told by survivors of torture forcefully underline the point: if the torturers and bureaucrats of the dungeons and the camps are able to treat their victims like animals destined for the slaughterhouse, with whom they themselves, the well-nourished criminals, have nothing in common, it is because the victims have indeed become such animals. What had to be done for this to happen has indeed been done. That some nevertheless remain human beings, and testify to that effect, is a confirmed fact. But this is always achieved precisely through enormous effort, an effort acknowledged by witnesses (in whom it excites a radiant recognition) as an almost incomprehensible resistance on the part of that which, in them, *does not coincide with the identity of victim*. This is where we are to find Man, if we are determined to *think* him [*le penser*]: in what ensures, as Varlam Shalamov puts in his *Stories of Life in the Camps*, that we are dealing with an animal whose resistance, unlike that of a horse, lies not in his fragile body but in his stubborn determination to remain what he is – that is to say, precisely something other than a victim, other than a being-for-death, and thus: *something other than a mortal being.*' Badiou, *Ethics*, translated by Peter Hallward (London: Verso, 2001), 11–12.

[7] Erich Auerbach, *Mimesis* (Princeton, NJ: Princeton University Press, 2003).

century – that it progresses closer and closer to a certain achieved style, and away from another one, with various evolutionary leaps and setbacks along the way. Just as Auerbach wanted to show the stylistic growth of realism out of myth, magic and romance, so I want to demonstrate the development of a specific kind of political memoir style out of the older integuments of moral and stoical introspection which had governed prison writing for centuries up to the end of the nineteenth.[8] The evolutionary span may be far tighter than Auerbach's, but its various mutations and negations are all the more startling for their all having taken place within the century in question. Without this patterned evolution, which can only be observed in details of style, voice and tone that require close reading, it is unimaginable that Behrouz Boochani, for instance, should have written a document (like *No Friend but the Mountains*) as radically free from those sanctimonious and sentimental proclivities that Oscar Wilde's *De Profundis* was still obliged to indulge a century or so before. But this tale of development and change is rooted in deeper, objective structures which now require some elucidation.

II

Although the spectacular campaigns of prison expansion and privatisation that have taken place in the USA since the 1980s are the most pressing contemporary development in the history of the institution,[9] there is a longer, global story that usefully frames that flagrant metastasis of mass detention in the world's dominant economy and provides a broader explanatory matrix for what 'prison' has come to mean today, in any number of contexts around the world.[10]

---

[8] This part of my argument is developed further in the first chapter, on Oscar Wilde. See in particular Philip Edward Phillips, 'Boethius, the Prisoner, and *The Consolation of Philosophy*', in Phillips, ed., *Prison Narratives from Boethius to Zana*, 11–34; W. B. Carnochan, 'The Literature of Confinement', in Norval Morris and David J. Rothman, eds, *The Oxford History of the Prison* (Oxford: Oxford University Press, 1995), 427–55; Joanna Summers, *Late-Medieval Prison Writing and the Politics of Autobiography* (Oxford: Oxford University Press, 2004).

[9] See Angela Davis, *Are Prisons Obsolete?* (New York: Seven Stories Press, 2003), Loïc Wacquant, *Prisons of Poverty*, expanded edition (Minneapolis and London: University of Minnesota Press, 2009), and Ruth Wilson Gilmore, *Golden Gulag: Prisons, Surplus, Crisis, and Opposition in Globalizing California* (Berkeley: University of California Press, 2007).

[10] For some sense of this spread, see Johan Fuhrmann and Stefan Baier, eds, *Prisons and Prison Systems: Practices, Types, and Challenges* (New York: Nova, 2013); Judah Schept, *Progressive Punishment: Job Loss, Jail Growth, and the Neoliberal Logic*

At the end of the nineteenth century, as we know from Foucault's work, the prison was in the process of evolving into the modern disciplinary institution it would stabilise into – in the Auburn model particularly – in the north-eastern USA: a reformist penitentiary space for the transformation of unruly proletarian bodies into atomised assemblages of docile and penitent workers primed for the industrial age. Isolated, silenced and put to work, prisoners were to assimilate the Protestant work ethic as a by-product of the 'reformatory' process of the prison itself, which went to work on the soul of the incarcerated subject precisely by separating him from his comrades and subjecting him to work disciplines borrowed wholesale from the factories nearby.

Yet alongside this story runs another, parallel one, which will ultimately be absorbed into the same apparatus over the course of the twentieth century. This is the converging story to which we bear particular witness in the texts covered in this book: the story of modern political detention. We can get some initial idea about it in considering the fate of political dissidents and nihilists in Russia in the late nineteenth century.[11] Rather than treat them as common criminals, the Tsarist judiciary conferred the sentence of 'katorga' (forced labour and internal exile) on political terrorists. Forced exile to Siberia, a sentence surviving from the seventeenth century, was the preferred treatment of refuseniks and revolutionaries.[12] This punishment deliberately separated political prisoners from common criminals, in a strategy that accepted a certain categorial difference as the price to pay for a minimisation of any possibility of wide-scale prisoner radicalisation. Spells in Siberian exile were thus part of the rite of passage for many Russian revolutionaries: Trotsky, Stalin and Lenin all served significant sentences there, under police observation

---

of *Carceral Expansion* (New York: New York University Press, 2015); John Pratt, *Punishment and Civilization: Penal Tolerance and Intolerance in Modern Society* (London: Sage, 2002); Devah Pager, *Marked: Race, Crime, and Finding Work in an Era of Mass Incarceration* (Chicago: University of Chicago Press, 2007); Michelle Alexander, *The New Jim Crow: Mass Incarceration in the Age of Colorblindness* (New York: The New Press, 2010); James Kilgore, *Understanding Mass Incarceration: A People's Guide to the Key Civil Rights Struggle of Our Time* (New York: The New Press, 2015).

[11] See, however, the discussion in Nicholas Bujalski, 'Narrating Political Imprisonment in Tsarist Russia: Bakunin, Goethe, Hegel', *Modern Intellectual History* 18.3 (2021): 681–707.

[12] Alan Wood, *Russia's Frozen Frontier: A History of Siberia and the Russian Far East, 1581–1991* (London: Bloomsbury, 2011); Zhanna Popova, 'The Two Tales of Forced Labour: Katorga and Reformed Prison in Imperial Russia, 1878–1905', *Almanack* 14 (2016): 91–117.

and isolated from the party organisation, but prolific in their writing and theorising nonetheless.

In one form or another, political dissidents of the first half of the twentieth century broadly accepted that periods of detention and incarceration were an inevitable consequence of their commitments. Neither was this always an altogether disagreeable prospect. As we shall see, Rosa Luxemburg tended to look on her prison terms as welcome periods of respite from the ardours of party work, allowing her to turn to theory and research.[13] Soldiers of the IRA knew well to expect the time they might serve at Her Majesty's pleasure in sordid Belfast jails, indemnified – between 1971 and 1976 – by the status of prisoner of war from any stain on their characters and indeed ennobled by it in the popular nationalist imagination. In her prison memoir *117 Days* (1965), Ruth First notes this about the sanguine attitude of imprisoned communists and ANC activists prior to the full consolidation of apartheid:

> Those held in prison pending political trials, or during the 1960 State of Emergency and the days of the 1961 Mandela strike, had emerged from a spell of community jail life with morale marvellously unimpaired. Every new stretch of prison for a group of political prisoners gave birth to a new batch of freedom songs. Jail spells had not broken us; they had helped to make us.[14]

First's text, however, marks a significant historical transition in South African politics that we will consider more closely in Chapter 7 – the moment at which this robust enclave of political prisoners detained within a penitentiary or in exile becomes an impossibility. And, in one way or another, that moment is the same one we will see amplified and distributed across various critical sites of the carceral twentieth century: the closing of the gap between political and general prison populations, the folding in of prisoners held for political reasons under the general legal rubric of criminality, and the consequent disclosure of the overarching political function of the prison itself.

Here we may indeed turn to the USA prison system as the exemplary and inspirational model for a modern world of nation states looking more and more towards biopolitical containment as the ulterior purpose of detention as such – not the USA of the late

---

[13] See Chapter 3, below.
[14] Ruth First, *117 Days: An Account of Confinement and Interrogation under the South African 90-Day Detention Law*, Kindle edition (London: Virago, 2010), 153.

twentieth century, however, but of the century prior, when, after the Emancipation Proclamation, millions of Black Americans were liberated from bondage only to be virtually re-enslaved through the revanchist Black Codes of the post-secessionist South.[15] As Angela Davis wrote during her own detention by the California justice system, 'After the Civil War, the Black Codes, successors to the old slave codes, legalised convict labor, prohibited social intercourse between Blacks and whites, gave white employers an excessive degree of control over the private lives of Black workers, and generally codified racism and terror.'[16] More specifically, Black sharecroppers were newly subject to a cynical regime of criminalisation (for 'vagrancy, absence from work, breach of job contracts, the possession of firearms, and insulting gestures or acts'[17]) that situated them squarely within a regime that can best be described as carceral through and through. If, as Foucault writes, 'the universality of the carceral lowers the level from which it becomes natural and acceptable to be punished',[18] then this is nowhere truer than for Black Americans after slavery, for whom *it is normal to be criminal and normal to be punished*. The 'universality of the carceral' is not a metaphor or a striking critical conceit; it is the element in which Black Americans are henceforth obliged to act and move, as their everyday lives are translated into routine transgression. If you cannot prove your address (which is to say, remain fixed on the property of the landlord for whom you toil all year long), or if you show up late to work, or swap glances with a white woman on the street, your criminal body will be made subject to a new discipline of value-extraction through unpaid labour, held indefinitely against all its putative rights as a 'citizen' of the democratic state. The time you serve will make it permanently impossible for you to exert your 'democratic right' at the ballot box. And it will therefore redouble the degree to which you are harassed and punished anew. Prison, then, works to normalise the innate criminality of entire sectors of the population: it is a key instrument in demographic control and biopolitical command over the most disenfranchised communities of colour. It is, to be succinct, racist.[19]

---

[15] See H. Bruce Franklin, *Prison Writing*, 4–8.

[16] Angela Y. Davis and Bettina Aptheker, eds, *If They Come in the Morning: Voices of Resistance* (University Park: Pennsylvania State University Press, 1971), 21.

[17] Angela Y. Davis, *Are Prisons Obsolete?* (New York: Seven Stories Press, 2003), 28.

[18] Michel Foucault, *Discipline and Punish: The Birth of the Prison*, translated by Alan Sheridan (London: Penguin, 1991), 303.

[19] See Dylan Rodríguez, *White Reconstruction: Domestic Warfare and the Logistics of Genocide* (New York: Fordham University Press, 2021).

James Whitman writes that 'when the Nazis set out to build a racist order, they turned to America first to see what sort of models they could find',[20] and three of the models at the forefront of their policy-making were (1) the Jim Crow prison and prison lease system of the US South, (2) the concentration camps used by US forces for interred Filipino POWs during the Philippine-American War of 1899–1902, and (3) Washington's blatantly racist immigration restrictions against Chinese and Japanese migrants in the 1920s. The US had wrought a legal and juridical emblem that held a fascination for all subsequent capitalist regimes predicated on innate racial inequalities and exerted a powerful influence on subsequent prison policy worldwide. As Kelly and Westall paraphrase Breyten Breytenbach, 'there is an international continuity to the manner in which modern carceral spaces function and are experienced, and there is also an international or worldly continuity evident within prison writing'.[21] What matters is that we understand this continuity properly. In the prison texts considered in the chapters that follow, we find Alexander Berkman surrounded by Black and Jewish inmates in Western State Penitentiary, Pennsylvania; Ezra Pound coming face to face with Black America for the first time in his life at the US Army Detention Training Center in Pisa; Primo Levi incarcerated as a Jew with other Jews at Auschwitz III; Ruth First exchanging gestures and signs with Black prisoners and recounting their stories in Johannesburg prisons; Angela Davis grappling with the structural logic of Black incarceration in the USA; Ngũgĩ wa Thiong'o explaining the residual racist detention policies of the neocolonial Kenyan regime; Bobby Sands excoriating the racist anti-Catholic nationalism of the British State in a Belfast prison; to mention only the most odious instances. The explicit and outright use of 'correctional facilities' to serve political ends – in rendering *de facto* race and class hierarchies in the populace *de jure* at the level of apprehension and sentencing – goes hand in hand with an outward-facing posture of enlightened democratic liberalism. Criminalisation thus becomes a central and determining mechanism of the modern state's management of its population and the containment of dissident political energies, offered as a showcase of its evolving reformist agenda as regards crime and punishment.

[20] James Q. Whitman, *Hitler's American Model*, Kindle edition (Princeton, NJ: Princeton University Press, 2017), 140.
[21] Kelly and Westall, eds, *Prison Writing and the Literary World*, 23.

It is this story that modifies and inflects Foucault's story of 'carcerality' as a general law of modernity, and of the prison as an exemplary space of the production of docility through disciplinarity.[22] To be precise, what I am arguing is that *that* general tendency – which can look very much like a social strategy of depoliticisation and pacification – needs to be rethought as a political instrumentation of the underlying principles of racial capitalism in a global mode of production.[23] The prison is simultaneously (theoretically) the space in which docility is produced out of refractory bodies in line with prevailing industrial expectations and techniques, and (practically) where race is openly inscribed on the body politic as a lesion or fault line in the presumption of equality before the law.[24] And, as this extraordinary double standard becomes normalised and exported during the twentieth century, what happens is that it no longer matters to separate political and general prisoners: the Nazi policy of 'racialising' communism (as a Jewish plot and disease) is implicit already within this new configuration of the carceral apparatus. To be a political dissident is itself a form of racialised criminality and can be punished as such by the normal methods, for the prison system is already predisposed to rationalise its irrationality by applying the self-same concept, 'crime', to every divergent type of activity it exists to incapacitate.[25] The political prisoner is a 'Jew', or a 'Negro', inasmuch as she has failed to understand or coincide with her biopolitical function in the new state – she is always and already the one for whom existing per se is a criminal activity. And indeed, *every* prisoner is implicitly racialised to the extent that they are positioned outside the legitimate realm of civil society, denied rights and identified with their felony, now become existential rather than legal.[26] As a prisoner wrote after the Charlottesville race riot of 2017: 'prison is a real-life example of the world that white supremacists want to return to.

---

[22] See the various contributions to Dominique Moran, Nick Gill and Deirdre Conlon, eds, *Carceral Spaces: Mobility and Agency in Imprisonment and Migrant Detention* (Farnham: Ashgate, 2013).

[23] See Ruha Benjamin, ed., *Captivating Technology: Race, Carceral Technoscience, and Liberatory Imagination in Everyday Life* (Durham, NC: Duke University Press, 2019), Michael J. Coyle and Mechthild Nagel, eds, *Contesting Carceral Logic: Towards Abolitionist Futures* (London: Routledge, 2022) and the contributions to Joy James, ed., *Imprisoned Intellectuals: America's Political Prisoners Write on Life, Liberation, and Rebellion* (Lanham: Rowman & Littlefield, 2003).

[24] See Brett Story, *Prison Land: Mapping Carceral Power across Neoliberal America* (Minneapolis: University of Minnesota Press, 2019).

[25] See Joe Sim, *Punishment and Prisons: Power and the Carceral State* (London: Sage, 2009).

[26] See Rodríguez, *White Reconstruction*.

The only difference between prison in 2017 and a segregated 1950s is the fact that whites are often the minorities behind bars.'[27]

This is why the status of 'political prisoner' has never existed in the USA, and why elsewhere in the latter half of the twentieth century that category has tended to be rescinded. In a system where the prison is instrumentalised as a legal-juridical cover for blatant political ends, the category cannot be allowed to stand. As the warden tells Alexander Berkman in the latter's *Prison Memoirs of an Anarchist*, 'We have no political prisoners in a free country!'[28] It is, then, precisely as a reflex of the rhetoric of 'freedom' that the distinct category of political prisoner must be resolved into a straightforward matter of criminality. Because you are free (to protest, to organise, to speak, to dissent), it cannot be your political activities that have landed you where you are. As Margaret Thatcher said apropos of the Irish Republican prisoners in the Maze Prison, channelling Gertrude Stein, 'Crime is crime is crime. It is not political. It is crime and there can be no question of granting political status.'[29] Angela Davis remarks about Black incarceration rates in the USA: 'In this country [. . .], where the special category of political prisoners is not officially acknowledged, the political prisoner inevitably stands trial for a specific criminal offense, not for a political act. Often the so-called crime does not even have a nominal existence.'[30] Abbie Hoffman was recorded (by the FBI), during an event in support of the NYC Panther 21, saying that 'all prisoners are political prisoners', which is the direct correlative of suppressing the category in the first place.[31] As he elaborated: 'All trials in America are political trials. All prisoners are political prisoners. Ninety per cent of the people in jail are black. Ninety per cent are young. Ninety per cent haven't had a fucking trial.'[32]

It is in just this sense that, as the twentieth century aged, it became increasingly dubious to distinguish between 'criminals' on the one

---

[27] Jerry Metcalf, 'Prison is a Real-Life Example of the World White Supremacists Want', *The Marshall Project* (24 August 2017), https://www.themarshallproject.org/2017/08/24/prison-is-a-real-life-example-of-the-world-white-supremacists-want.

[28] Alexander Berkman, *Prison Memoirs of an Anarchist*, edited by Jessica Moran and Barry Pateman (Chico, CA: AK Press, 2016), 358.

[29] Margaret Thatcher, press conference ending a visit to Saudi Arabia, 21 April 1981.

[30] Davis, *If They Come in the Morning*, 22.

[31] Abbot H. Hoffman quoted speaking on 1 April 1970, in Federal Bureau of Investigation HQ File 176–34, section 7 of 10, Report April 13, 1970.

[32] Hoffman, quoted in Sonny Kleinfield and Peter Frishouf, 'Hoffman, Dharuba Speak at Square Rally; 180 March on Med School, Disrupt Speech', *Washington Square Journal* (2 April 1970).

hand and detained political dissidents on the other – the prison captures something essential in the extent to which states are prepared to criminalise and punish everything that contests their logic and their subservience to the dictates of racial capitalism. Criminal codes have their origins in racialised and class-based interests exposed by political dissidents housed alongside thieves, drug addicts and prostitutes. Earlier justifications of the system implode and, in the wreckage, a new cynical reasoning prevails.

Thanks to various tectonic shifts in the underlying logic of capital accumulation, the earlier insistence on docility and industrial plasticity has given way to the blandishments of 'risk' and 'flexibility' that accompany the post-Fordist ascendancy. Prisons are no longer required to do what they were designed to do and can be repurposed to accommodate a range of new socioeconomic desiderata. As the rate of profit begins its apparently terminal underlying decline from the 1970s onwards, what this means in the US in particular is that the prison can shake off the calyx of its older Protestant rationale and become openly what it has always been, namely an organised wing of racial capitalism itself. With the society in general confronting a 'permanent army of the unemployed',[33] racialised through and through, prison becomes the self-evident place in which to force that army into submission while feeding off its extorted labour. If 'the courts, the jails, and the prisons are now generally acknowledged to be key links in a system by which youthful delinquents are transformed into hardened criminals', then that feedback loop simply helps to justify the wildfire expansion and privatisation of the system itself.[34] 'Thanks to a bipartisan law-and-order consensus, millions of African Americans were policed, prosecuted, and banished behind prison walls' in the last two decades of the twentieth century.[35] This more than 500 per cent growth of the US prison-industrial complex since the sharp shocks of the neoliberal turn has triggered a worldwide reconceptualisation of the carceral landscape and of the function of prisons more generally – a reconceptualisation that goes hand in hand with a momentous expansion of camp life for refugees and asylum seekers in a context of incessant war. Under conditions of general disequilibrium and rising inequality, human displacement and forced migration ramify the global carceral system with new and

[33] James Boggs, *Pages from a Black Radical's Notebook: A James Boggs Reader*, edited by Stephen Ward (Detroit: Wayne State University Press, 2011), 302.
[34] Boggs, *Pages from a Black Radical's Notebook*, 230.
[35] Destin Jenkins and Justin Leroy, *Histories of Racial Capitalism*, Kindle edition (New York: Columbia University Press, 2021), loc. 1698–1700.

unpredictable growths in camp and prison populations. Add to this the persistent pressure of ethno-nationalist territorial struggles and ideological campaigns against belligerent ethno-fascist regimes, and we have a perfect storm for the hardening and expansion of prison infrastructures around the planet: in Erdoğan's Turkey (frontline for the mass of Middle Eastern refugees seeking harbour in Europe, with a brutal stranglehold on Kurdish freedom fighters), in China, in Israel, in Egypt, in Brazil, in Russia, in India, in Iran, in Eritrea, in Belarus, in Zimbabwe – in a vast and ever tightening noose around the dispossessed and displaced, the poor and the dissident, the prison-industrial complex has swollen to over ten million inmates, a full third of whom have not even faced a trial.[36] This incarcerated population joins the 90 million displaced people on our planet today, more than a quarter of whom are refugees – many living in camps scattered around the world. In this context, the previously exceptional status of 'political prisoner' is statistically dwarfed and recast within the more significant category of the *politically detained*, a category that covers, in one way or another, the vast majority of these intolerable numbers of the unhoused.[37]

III

So it is that the strange integration of the moral and the legal, the punitive and the reformatory, the penal and the disciplinary that marked the prison at the end of the nineteenth century, gave way over the twentieth to a pervasive cynical reasoning about the 'carceral archipelago' that now stretches across a globalised space of integrated flows and channels.[38] The earlier accent on penitence, cloistral reform and quiet submission has been summarily abandoned in favour of a straightforwardly political deployment of the infrastructure and bureaucracy of containment to secure – not docility or subjective conformity – but domination pure and simple. This rise and rise of the *penal* within the structure of the *carceral* defines our present conjuncture. But what must interest us here are the

---

[36] See the World Prison Brief website, which has detailed and current data on the global prison population: https://www.prisonstudies.org/.

[37] UNHCR website: https://www.unhcr.org/figures-at-a-glance.html.

[38] The relationship between commercial and carceral logistics is deep and developing. For some initial findings, see Iolanthe Brooks and Asha Best, 'Prison Fixes and Flows: Carceral Mobilities and their Critical Logistics', *Environment and Planning D: Society and Space* 39.3 (January 2021), https://doi.org/10.1177/0263775820984791.

consequences of this for the material and ideological preconditions of writing itself, as perhaps the most volatile feature of prison detention around the world.

In the broad arc of this transformation of the prison from a space of shameful isolation to a widely contested punitive regime, something equally significant happens to the 'spiritual' (which is to say, intellectual and imaginative) capacities engendered by its violent grasp on the incarcerated subject. As Michelle Kelly and Claire Westall put it, the general tendency is towards a situation in which prisons become 'sites of creativity and resistance', rather than of inward reflection or silent self-recrimination.[39] The structural transformation of the prison's social role coincides with a modification of the subjective stance of the prisoner, from stoical expressions of fortitude and prototypical scenographies of religious conversion, to overtly political organisation, solidarity and critique. In other words, prison writing was obliged by virtue of the rapidly evolving circumstances of the social institution that underwrites it to alter its modes and forms, moving distinctly away from moral discourse towards sociological and political anatomies of the prison system. This is not to say that, here and there, strong echoes of the long legacy of contrition, reform and reflexive stoical self-reliance do not ring across the corpus of twentieth-century prison writing (as, for instance, in Pound's *Pisan Cantos*, the *Autobiography of Malcolm X* or George Jackson's *Soledad Brother*); only that this has now become a relatively minor aspect of a now preponderantly political genre of autobiographical discourse.

In short, the increasingly political instrumentation of the prison around the globe over the last 130 years has tended to produce a reflexively political tradition of literary work by prisoners, in which residual ideas about the penitentiary or reformatory qualities of incarceration have either been dismantled or displaced. Prison sentences are experienced directly as exercises of state power rather than moral assessments of character or just legal punishments of criminality, and as a result the time-honoured tendency towards silence and shame has been supplanted by the urgent need to communicate the existential, psychological and physical torture of involuntary incarceration as explicit evidence of the state's unworthiness to wield such power in the first place. What the history of twentieth-century prison writing teaches is precisely the opposite of what the history of twentieth-century incarceration was designed to accomplish, namely

[39] Kelly and Westall, eds, *Prison Writing and the Literary World*, 22.

the supreme authority of the state to determine what is thinkable and sayable within the context of imperial racialised capitalism. It teaches that the prisoner is the site, not of a nihilation of the Cause for which she has been imprisoned, but of *the bankruptcy of the state's monopoly of violence*. Prison writing is the genre in which, exemplarily, state violence is refashioned into emblems of its own horror, which then circulate in the public sphere as tokens of a subjective refusal of the general terms of engagement. Far from contrite or apologetic, prison writing has been, for the last century or so, the privileged genre for adamantine avowals of a subjective fidelity to what goes beyond the state, beyond the law, beyond civil society. Indeed, regardless of national context or immediate political circumstances, prison writing has tended to affirm a *meta-political solidarity* with a certain 'post-capitalism' that prison – precisely due to its suffocating foreclosure of horizons and networks within the open shop of racial capitalism – paradoxically makes visible amidst its punitive architecture. It is as if every political prisoner of the twentieth century has glimpsed within that penal gloom the sparks and gleams of a new international formation rooted in the existential void of the gaolhouse.

Let us turn to two examples of what I mean from texts that will be considered more closely in the chapters that follow. In the closing section of her *Memoirs from the Women's Prison* (1986), Nawal El Saadawi reflects on the experience of being liberated from one Egyptian prison only to discover herself in another, more insidious, global one:

> Writing: such has been my crime ever since I was a small child. To this day writing remains my crime. Now, although I am out of prison, I continue to live inside a prison of another sort, one without steel bars. For the technology of oppression and might without justice has become more advanced, and the fetters imposed on mind and body have become invisible. The most dangerous shackles are the invisible ones, because they deceive people into believing they are free. This delusion is the new prison that people inhabit today, north and south, east and west.[40]

Throughout the text, as Nawal forges new links of alliance between secular and religious, political and general prisoners at the Women's Prison, Cairo, the sense develops that, rather than being a site of

---

[40] Nawal El Saadawi, *Memoirs from the Women's Prison*, Kindle edition (London: Zed Books, 2020), 200.

political opacity and dissipation, the prison focuses and enhances political sensibilities and solidarities. Designed to isolate, demoralise, dehumanise and dissociate the incarcerated subject, prison instead forces an allegorical reckoning with the larger social machinery that depends upon it to do this work. Forced to wear the physical, directly violent 'shackles' with which the state subjugates its delinquent bodies, prisoners are then far better equipped to descry the reality of Blake's 'mind-forg'd manacles' across late capitalism's innumerable sites of technological and ideological enclosure. Nawal's dialectical sensitivity to the 'delusion' and 'deceit' of the neoliberal rhetoric of freedom and human rights is sharpened by her intimate acquaintance with its ubiquitous *other scene*: the torture chamber, the isolation cell, the steel bars of the human zoo.

It is here that she espouses a *new international* predicated on the transcendental homelessness that prison stamps upon its inmates – the sharply felt rift between the subject and any proper place in the national social space fomented by time served inside. The proximity between detention and exile, a frequent theme of this genre of writing, obliges Nawal to observe:

> Today I live outside my homeland. Futilely I seek a place free of the structures of patriarchy and class. I search for true justice, true peace, but to no avail. Dangers threaten thousands, no, millions in the world – the dangers of death, war, and hunger – and the danger I live is no more than a part of these perils. (203)

The 'place' she is seeking in this violently fractured world is finally not geographical, but literary. And she finds it precisely through the labour of textual production and circulation – in the new utopia of prison writing:

> Since childhood a dream has inhabited my imagination: I write my words and people read them – today, tomorrow, the day after. When does not matter, for people will read them. Those are the people who make a homeland, and my homeland has become those people. (204)

This is the sense in which contemporary prison writing refuses the habitual sequestration of political struggles in and for the state and heralds the new horizon of a homeland-to-come constituted by human beings already too deeply marked by state violence to accept it as a legitimate frame of reference. Prison has the tendency to eject the political imagination from the boundaries of the nation state, into this utopia of an anonymous international community of readers, where writing commits its energies to a future unconstrained by law or norms – where writing is *criminal* in an ontological sense, and fugitive as a matter of course.

In his own prison memoirs, *Wrestling with the Devil* (first published as *Detained* in 1982), Ngũgĩ wa Thiong'o recounts the words of a fellow political prisoner who greets him shortly after arriving at Kamĩtĩ Maximum Security Prison, in Nairobi. The friend says: 'I am glad they brought you here. The other day – in fact a week or so before you came – we were saying that it would be a good thing for Kenya if more intellectuals were imprisoned. First, it would wake most of them from their illusions. And some of them might outlive jail to tell the world.'[41] Again, the emphasis falls on the advantages to political intellectual production of a stint behind bars. And what Ngũgĩ is moved to write is of the highest interest to us in this context:

> The act of imprisoning democrats, progressive intellectuals, and militant workers reveals many things. It is first an admission by the authorities that they know they have been seen. By signing the detention orders, they acknowledge that the people have seen through their official lies labeled as a new philosophy, their pretensions wrapped in three-piece suits and gold chains, their propaganda packaged as religious truth, their plastic smiles ordered from abroad, their nationally televised charitable handouts and breast-beatings before the high altar, their high-sounding phrases and ready-to-shed tears at the sight of naked children fighting cats and dogs for a trash heap, that all have seen these performances of benign benevolence for what they truly are: a calculated sugarcoating of the immoral sale and mortgage of a whole country, its people and resources, to Euro-American and Japanese capital for a few million dollars in Swiss banks and a few token shares in foreign companies. (24)

It is not only that the view from behind prison bars focuses with laser intensity the writer's critical political gaze on his 'New' Kenyan jailers and the plutocrats they serve; it is that the situation described is transposable to any number of other national formations in the neocolonialist web. The subsumption of a local comparador bourgeoisie within international capitalism's supply chains and profit margins has the consequence, all over the planet, of militant workers and dissident intellectuals being sentenced to prison terms in accordance with the penal logic of containment itself. In order to function

---

[41] Ngũgĩ wa Thiong'o, *Wrestling with the Devil: A Prison Memoir* (London: Vintage, 2018), 19.

smoothly, racial capitalism incarcerates its critics, hoping to break them the while, transform them into yea-saying lackeys through the violent 'ritual symbolism' of political detention (25). This 'calculated act of psychological terror' is properly aimed at the 'struggling millions' who are expected to balk at its 'psychological siege' of their political drives (26). But in Ngũgĩ's fiercely dialectical prose, such strength is always weakness.

> Recourse to imprisonment, with or without a trial, is above all an admission by the ruling minority that people have started to organize to oppose the plunder of the national wealth and heritage. It fears that the people might rise in arms, and therefore acts to forestall such an uprising, real or imaginary.
>
> Thus detention and imprisonment more immediately mean the physical removal of progressive intellectuals from the people's organized struggles. (25)

The 'might of the state' is thus always an indication of its internal contradictions and inherent weakness as a monopoly of the 'ruling clique' (32) posing as a universal. The detained serve as sacrificial lambs for the 'struggling millions' they represent; and, if they write, their writing is charged with an intense allegorical capability: 'A narration of prison life is nothing more than an account of oppressive measures in varying degrees of intensity and the individual or collective responses to them' (106). All trace of moral discourse has fallen away, and if self-pity or the merely individual do rear their inevitable heads, the dialectic is always primed to resume its rhythmic alternations. 'There was another side to my detention: the growing anti-imperialist consciousness among peasants, workers, university lecturers, and students, and I was the sacrificial lamb! Thought for despair? No! I am part of a living history of struggle. And without struggle, there is no movement, there is no life' (131).

We are light years away, in this language, from the kinds of speech associated with pre-twentieth-century prison writing. The terrible gaze inward, the searching confessions, the shame and self-disgust, the spiritual search for individual fortitude and salvation, the stoical concessions to fortune and favour, the sentimental recollections of lost loves and lost opportunities: all evaporate at the merest touch of a properly political sensibility, now installed by fiat according to the very logic of detention itself. What this book seeks to track, across the full circumference of that century's duration, are the intercalated signs of this momentous reversal – tonal, vocal, rhetorical, narrative, stylistic, imagistic – that has redefined prison writing in ways that have yet to be accounted for, yet to be acknowledged. If it makes some headway in the progressive clarification of the place and role of writing in relation to the large-scale transformations in the carceral system itself, it will have justified its composition.

Chapter 1

The Symphony of Sorrow: Oscar Wilde's *De Profundis*

All this took place in the early part of November of the year before last. A great river of life flows between you and a date so distant. Hardly, if at all, can you see across so wide a waste. But to me it seems to have occurred, I will not say yesterday, but today. Suffering is one long moment. We cannot divide it by seasons. We can only record its moods, and chronicle their return. With us time itself does not progress. It revolves. It seems to circle round one centre of pain. The paralysing immobility of a life, every circumstance of which is regulated after an unchangeable pattern, so that we eat and drink and walk and lie down and pray, or kneel at least for prayer, according to the inflexible laws of an iron formula: this immobile quality, that makes each dreadful day in the very minutest detail like its brother, seems to communicate itself to those external forces the very essence of whose existence is ceaseless change. Of seed-time or harvest, of the reapers bending over the corn, or the grape-gatherers threading through the vines, of the grass in the orchard made white with broken blossoms, or strewn with fallen fruit, we know nothing, and can know nothing. For us there is only one season, the season of Sorrow. The very sun and moon seem taken from us. Outside, the day may be blue and gold, but the light that creeps down through the thickly-muffled glass of the small iron-barred window beneath which one sits is grey and niggard. It is always twilight in one's cell, as it is always midnight in one's heart. And in the sphere of thought, no less than in the sphere of time, motion is no more. The thing that you personally have long ago forgotten, or can easily forget, is happening to me now, and will happen to me again tomorrow. Remember this, and you will be able to understand a little of why I am writing to you, and in this manner writing.[1]

---

[1] Oscar Wilde, *De Profundis and Other Prison Writings*, edited by Colm Tóibín (London: Penguin, 2013), 88–9.

In *De Profundis*, the greatest flowering of nineteenth-century prison writing and in many ways the culmination of a centuries-old tradition, Oscar Wilde presses the rhetorical advantages of the epistle form to establish some existential divisions between the life outside Reading Gaol and what passes for life behind the 'iron-barred window'. Addressed to his lover and, according to Wilde, the author of his ruin, Lord Alfred Douglas, the lengthy letter wields the second-person pronoun as a talisman of their broken intimacy – occasioned by the young man's careless disregard for consequences – and to dramatise the chasm between the outsider whom it nominates and those nameless of the first-person plural who now provide the only intimacy left to the age's greatest social butterfly. To 'you', in this passage, time is properly linear; it moves as a river, sundering past from present, bearing one merrily into an open future. 'You' are thus able to forget the sins of yesterday and range freely in the dimension of thought, blithely indifferent to the stings of conscience that might otherwise afflict the guilty and infamous; for as the seasons change and one year follows another, so the mind at liberty is free to rear-range its memories to suit the temper of its needs. Behind the walls of prison, however, time is annulled and 'motion is no more'. Trapped on their dreadful treadmill, the inmates experience at all moments the same 'paralysing immobility', the 'immobile quality, that makes each dreadful day in the very minutest detail like its brother'. In place of movement, progress, change, 'we' know only stasis, repetition, empty revolution around the fixed point of what is no longer memory at all, but the eternal recurrence of shame. 'For us there is only one season,' it 'is always twilight', and the bars and bricks have become a very tomb of the soul. This is the insistent movement of Wilde's prose in *De Profundis*: the transformation of an objective incarceration into a spiritual ordeal of the highest, most tragic order.[2] The missive 'from the depths' is written in the accents of the damned, pressed into the living hand of one who has strayed, as a Dantesque *memento mori*. Out of time and out of place, 'we' occupy the eternal midnight of the heart; while 'you', dancing to the music of time, are challenged to glimpse cold eternity from within the warm embrace of transience.

Wilde is not incapable of registering the harsh, objective aspects of a prison existence, 'a life, every circumstance of which is regulated

---

[2] Wilde 'seems to consider the development of his soul – *i .e.*, spiritual development – as the main purpose of his prison experience. For him, spiritual development parallels closely the kind of personal development he repeatedly refers to as "self-realization".' Molly Robinson Kelly, 'Reading Oscar Wilde's Spirituality in *De Profundis*', REM 68.3 (Summer 2006): 213 [210–27].

after an unchangeable pattern, so that we eat and drink and walk and lie down and pray, or kneel at least for prayer, according to the inflexible laws of an iron formula'. But his interest lies elsewhere, in the mortal depths of Bosie's soul and in the writhing torment of his own. His is, for all its scandalous legal specificity and historical-material determination, not finally a physical ordeal but a spiritual one. As he writes most exactly on this score:

> I have got to make everything that has happened to me good for me. The plank-bed, the loathsome food, the hard ropes shredded into oakum till one's fingertips grow dull with pain, the menial offices with which each day begins and finishes, the harsh orders that routine seems to necessitate, the dreadful dress that makes sorrow grotesque to look at, the silence, the solitude, the shame – each and all of these things I have to transform into a spiritual experience. There is not a single degradation of the body which I must not try and make into a spiritualising of the soul. (104)

With these words, Wilde effectively brings to an apotheosis one august tradition of prison writing and clears the slate for the emergence of another – one that will flourish out of the ashes of his life in altogether different accents from these stirring spiritual appeals to the Good. Most shocking about these appeals, of course, is their stark negation of the rhetorical pose and persona of the gay 'Oscar' he had presented to the world, a negation best exemplified in the letter's thrice-repeated refrain: 'The supreme vice is shallowness. Whatever is realised is right.' Prison has, in that sense, had the extraordinary effect of making Wilde the writer sincere, and serious, and true; and his letter is a long *mea culpa* indited as much to himself as to Douglas – recanting neither his own individualism, his agnosticism, nor his aestheticism, but apologising roundly for the insincerity of his hitherto merely superficial morality.

Dante recurs as the text's most saluted *maestro* (twelve times explicitly, but a tutelary presence on every page), for Dante is the supreme artist of the sublimation of personal griefs and grudges into cosmological profundities. The infernal prison is, for Dante, like exile, a figure for those sentences the individual must read upon himself in the eternal present of guilt: 'I blame myself terribly. As I sit here in this dark cell in convict clothes, a disgraced and ruined man, I blame myself. In the perturbed and fitful nights of anguish, in the long monotonous days of pain, it is myself I blame. I blame myself . . .' (47 – the phrase echoes a further four times in the following four pages). The physical prison is merely an afterthought to this one, on which the poet turns the lock in order to be alone with his inexorable (if not inexpiable) culpability. The great test of the Inferno, of course, is whether or not the damned can learn to feel this awful pang of remorse; prison is the space of a trial so awful it cannot be undertaken anywhere else. 'All trials are trials for one's life, just as all sentences are sentences of death' (158). The house of detention is their *topos*; and judge, jury and executioner are all one, whom Freud will call the Superego.

Wilde is not immune to the temptations of pathos in his situation, and indeed indulges them as a matter of course; as when, recreating the mortifying humiliation of standing in prison garb on a railway platform for half an hour *en route* to Reading as the crowd gathered and jeered and spat, he writes: 'For half an hour I stood there in the grey November rain surrounded by a jeering mob. For a year after that was done to me I wept every day at the same hour and for the same space of time' (133). He frequently meditates on his catastrophic decline in fortune, as one who, placed at the very zenith of a national culture and revered as a genius – 'I had genius, a distinguished name, high social position, brilliancy, intellectual daring' (100) – is then plunged into 'Failure, disgrace, poverty, sorrow, despair, suffering, tears even' (113), obliged to play first violin in his own 'Symphony of Sorrow' (61). But it is in the nature of his rhetoric and the tradition to which he understands himself to be contributing here that all of this is transformed into an inner theatre of spiritual testing and fortification. The pathos of self-pity is transubstantiated by the moral seriousness of the prose into a temptation to be overcome: 'each and all of these things I have to transform into a spiritual experience', as he says (104), very much including morbid introspection and recrimination.

The tradition in question is the venerable one of Christian-Stoic prison writing, running in a long line descending from Boethius, through the later medieval and Renaissance poets and scholars who found themselves serving time on the wrong side of power, to John Bunyan's Puritan allegory and beyond.[3] It is a rich and powerful tradition of writing, verily a language-game of its own, which undertakes to 'transform prison experience into spiritual exercise and the habit of meditation', as W. B. Carnochan writes.[4] Wilde inherits

---

[3] See Joanna Summers, *Late-Medieval Prison Writing and the Politics of Autobiography* (Oxford: Oxford University Press, 2004).

[4] W. B. Carnochan, 'The Literature of Confinement', in Norval Morris and David J. Rothman, eds, *The Oxford History of the Prison* (Oxford: Oxford University Press, 1995), 446 [427–55].

this 'rich stoic and Christian tradition that figures the world and the body itself as a prison more substantial than any cage', and rings the changes on it appropriate to a non-believer and contrarian without squandering a moment of its powerful drive and tropology.[5] As Ruth Ahnert explains in her excellent study of some of the major flowerings of this tradition:

> Religious prisoners were confident that their cause was validated by a stoic endurance of imprisonment and execution. Rather than appealing for freedom, Catholic prisoners' writings reflected their private devotions and prayers; and Protestant prisoners sought to encourage their co-religionists at home and in exile, to teach and guide them on doctrinal issues, and to ensure unity of belief. Unsurprisingly, these circumstances and impulses resulted in works of literature that covered a vast range of genres and forms: from trial narratives to Psalm translations, dialogues, religious polemics, pastoral guidance, poems, love lyrics, humanistic translations, prayers and meditative guides, letters of appeal, letters modelled on St Paul's, marginalia, and graffiti.[6]

What, then, is Wilde's cause if it is not doctrinal? In the absence of any 'belief' ('Religion does not help me,' he writes. 'The faith that others give to what is unseen, I give to what one can touch, and look at,' 103), the cause must be as it has always been: *aesthetic*, only now aesthetics itself is made into an arena for spiritual growth and evolution. Prison convinces Wilde that life itself is lived in the key of the aesthetic, and that a progress through the valley of thorns must lead to greater depths and shades of beauty. It is, he writes, 'as though my life, whatever it had seemed to myself and to others, had all the while been a real Symphony of Sorrow, passing through its rhythmically-linked movements to its certain resolution, with that inevitableness that in Art characterises the treatment of every great theme' (61). What emerges, then, is a defence of the incarcerated experience of degradation, shame and loss as moments of the belated growth of a soul. 'And exactly as in Art one is only concerned with what a particular thing is at a particular moment to oneself, so it is also in the ethical evolution of one's character. I have got to make everything that has happened to me good for me' (104).

---

[5] Ronald Bush, 'Poetic Metamorphosis: Ezra Pound's *Pisan Cantos* and Prison Poetry', *Rivista di Letterature d'America* XXIX.126–7 (2009): 46 [37–60].

[6] Ruth Ahnert, *The Rise of Prison Literature in the Sixteenth Century* (Cambridge: Cambridge University Press, 2013), 3.

His self-presentation as a martyr is offered in the hope of over-coming the shame, of transmuting it into the spiritualisation of a self too mired in the sensual and frivolous. 'To reject one's own experiences is to arrest one's own development. To deny one's own experiences is to put a lie into the lips of one's own life. It is no less than a denial of the Soul' (105). His language here is virtually identical to that of the great Christian martyrs of yore: Sir Thomas More, John Frith, Edward Seymour and the rest, all of whom sought to reclaim their catastrophes as stations of the cross leading to salvation.[7] As Joanna Summers has written about the late medieval prisoners who sealed their experience in words, so it is virtually unchanged for Wilde at the end of the nineteenth century: their texts 'share a sustained concern with the careful inscription of an incarcerated narrator-author, an evident petitionary element, and the tendering of an identity that is highly persuasive to its prospective audience, often employing the situation of imprisonment – its alleged wrong-fulness and the author's virtues in enduring it – in the service of such persuasion'.[8] If Wilde transposes the religious into the aesthetic, he nevertheless leaves intact the sacred rhetorical language of the form of the Christian-Stoic prison epistle, with its accent on privation, humility, temptation and fortitude.

> And, though at present you may find it a thing hard to believe, it is true none the less that for you, living in freedom and idleness and comfort, it is more easy to learn the lessons of Humility than it is for me, who begin the day by going down on my knees and washing the floor of my cell. For prison-life, with its endless privations and restrictions, makes one rebellious. The most terrible thing about it is not that it breaks one's heart – hearts are made to be broken – but that it turns one's heart to stone. One sometimes feels that it is only with a front of brass and a lip of scorn that one can get through the day at all. And he who is in a state of rebellion cannot receive grace, to use the phrase of which the Church is so fond – so rightly fond, I dare say – for in life, as in Art, the mood of rebellion closes up the channels of the soul, and shuts out the airs of heaven. Yet I must learn these lessons here, if I am to learn them anywhere, and must be filled with joy if my feet are on the right road, and my face set towards the 'gate which is called Beautiful', though I may fall many times in the mire, and often in the mist go astray. (112)

---

[7] For example, Seymour, the Earl of Somerset, wrote simply the day before his execution in the Tower of London: 'be not wise in thyne owne conseyte but fere the lord and fle from euele'; in Ahnert, *Rise of Prison Literature*, 44.

[8] Summers, *Late-Medieval Prison Writing*, 3.

So it is that Wilde crowns a great and noble tradition of prison literature in *De Profundis*. He even goes so far, in pages that must count
among the most moving and trenchant of any literary recounting of
the life of Jesus, to create a parallel between his suffering and the
Passion itself, and to paint a picture of Christ the Artist (114–29) –
a picture so extraordinary, indeed, that 'I dare say one has to go to
prison to understand it. If so, it may be worth while going to prison'
(128).[9] But we begin to sense, already, the stirring and itching of
another, nascent register in the interstices of Wilde's great apotheosis
of the Christian-Stoic tradition – the one that admits, with a flaring
of the nostrils and a flush of the cheeks, that 'prison-life, with its
endless privations and restrictions, makes one rebellious'. Even as
the stoic quells this incendiary streak, with the lashings and gruel of
Humility, it insists on flaring out, and it is one of the most striking
qualities of this letter that it cannot quite constrain its native Irish
rebelliousness in the hairshirt of an assumed English martyrology.

One of his allegorical personifications is different from the others,
which have roots deep in Christian culture. This one is distinctly
nineteenth-century in flavour. 'Many men on their release carry their
prison along with them into the air, hide it as a secret disgrace in
their hearts, and at length like poor poisoned things creep into some
hole and die. It is wretched that they should have to do so, and it is
wrong, terribly wrong, of Society that it should force them to do so.
Society takes upon itself the right to inflict appalling punishments
on the individual, but it also has the supreme vice of shallowness,
and fails to realise what it has done' (106). 'Society', then, insists
on being a participant in this spiritual drama, and each time it
intrudes, it tends to rewire the rhetorical circuit board. 'I claim on
my side that if I realise what I have suffered, Society should realise
what it has inflicted on me' – this is not a sentence imaginable in the
Christian-Stoic tradition, and it inflects the martyr's lamentation into
the register of a very different language-game, the much more recent
one called *critique*. For the better part of sixty long pages, to be sure,
that critical energy and fury is spent on the unworthy form of Lord
Alfred Douglas and his wretch of a father – both allegorical representatives of 'Society' who nevertheless, through the sheer exhaustive detail of their individual failures, tend to substitute for it. These
excoriations and indictments are, in their vituperative unworthiness

---

[9] See the discussion of Wilde's account of Christ in Jason Haslam, *Fitting Sentences:
Identity in Nineteenth- and Twentieth-Century Prison Narratives* (Toronto: University
of Toronto Press, 2005), 100–8.

of their author, a shallow screen behind which a more fitting jer-emiad lies latent. Occasionally it shows through. 'The prison-system is absolutely and entirely wrong. I would give anything to be able to alter it when I go out. I intend to try,' he writes (131). What Colm Tóibín calls Wilde's 'Irish disrespect for the law' (xxiii) is registered in the prisoner's account of those 'inflexible laws of an iron formula' that we noted in our opening passage, in his remark, 'That the law should decide, and take upon itself to decide, that I am one unfit to be with my own children is something quite horrible to me' (98), and in his self-characterisation as 'a born antinomian. I am one of those who are made for exceptions, not for laws' (103).[10] It comes to a head in his extraordinary critical summation: 'Reason does not help me. It tells me that the laws under which I am convicted are wrong and unjust laws, and the system under which I have suffered a wrong and unjust system' (104). Here lie in embryo the dominant notes of much twentieth-century prison writing: the critical rejection of the law, the prison system, 'Society' itself as injurious to the wellbeing of humanity and unjust in their current configurations, insofar as they have imprisoned *this* individual, *this* reasoning man whose reason is made futile. These notes are undeveloped here for the reasons already explored, but they are sounded with a clarion that will sound and sound again over the coming hundred and twenty years – the clarion of radical criticism and socialist-anarchism against which the prison system itself was increasingly wielded as a blunt suppressive machine.

It is particularly interesting that, in one of his various differentia-tions between himself and the common prisoners, Wilde reflects on the relative familiarity of imprisonment to working-class men. 'The poor are wiser, more charitable, more kind, more sensitive than we are. In their eyes prison is a tragedy in a man's life, a misfortune, a casualty, something that calls for sympathy in others. They speak of one who is in prison as of one who is "in trouble" simply. It is the phrase they always use, and the expression has the perfect wisdom of Love in it. With people of our rank it is different. With us prison makes a man a pariah' (98). One of the tasks of Wilde's letter, a covert and inexplicit one, is to accept his inevitable repositioning within the class system after he has internalised his status as a pariah. He must become more like the poor, for whom prison is just one of life's innumerable adversities, and take upon himself – devious

---

[10] It is a phrase echoed in his characterisation of Christ: 'For him there were no laws: there were exceptions merely' (126).

socialist that he is[11] – 'the sufferings of those whose name is Legion and whose dwelling is among the tombs, oppressed nationalities, factory children, thieves, people in prison, outcasts, those who are dumb under oppression and whose silence is heard only of God' (115). The most productive aspect of his adoption of the Christian-Stoic voice in *De Profundis* is this growth of his socialist-anarchist politics through identification with the wretched of the earth. It is an identification made inevitable, in that frequent adoption of the first-person plural pronoun, by his incarceration alongside common criminals for whom he now must learn to speak. The 'people in prison' whom he explicitly identifies as privileged objects of God's love are those who have taught Wilde the lesson that 'There is no prison in any world into which Love cannot force an entrance' (160).

So, even if it remains the case that 'The important thing, the thing that lies before me, the thing that I have to do, or be for the brief remainder of my days one maimed, marred, and incomplete, is to absorb into my nature all that has been done to me, to make it part of me, to accept it without complaint, fear, or reluctance' (104), it turns out that a crucial element of that absorption, that incorporation and acceptance, consists in the passage of the 'person of rank' that Oscar Wilde had been and still, in all his grotesque inappropriateness to circumstance, *was* in Reading Gaol, through the very ranks of the poor and the dispossessed – those for whom prison is simply a spell of 'trouble', and who must now become part of Wilde. In this wondrous crux is the point of origin of all the work to follow in this book. Wilde's shattering culmination of the Christian-Stoic tradition of prison writing is a gauntlet thrown down to the coming century, a challenge for imprisoned writers to transcend a merely moral and an ethical frame of reference in preference for a genre of political reckoning, a worldly judgement not of the 'Soul' but of the apparatus of state that would make of the individual a medium for its own political extension. As chapter after chapter will endeavour to show, while rudiments of the stoic voice remain a constant, this is precisely what happened over the coming century: jailed writers turned their critical judgements on the states that had thought to silence them through separation, guilt and incrimination. Oscar Wilde merely opened the door.

---

[11] Wilde was the author of *The Soul of Man under Socialism & Selected Critical Prose*, edited by Linda Dowling (London: Penguin, 2001).

Chapter 2

Defamiliarising the Dungeon: Alexander Berkman's *Prison Memoirs of an Anarchist*

The darkness of despondency gathers day by day; the hand of despair weighs heavier. At night the screeching of a crow across the river ominously voices the black raven keeping vigil in my heart. The windows in the hallway quake and tremble in the furious wind. Bleak and desolate wakes the day – another day, then another –

Weak and apathetic I lie on the bed. Ever further recedes the world of the living. Still day follows night, and life is in the making, but I have no part in the pain and travail. Like a spark from the glowing furnace, flashing through the gloom, and swallowed in the darkness, I have been cast upon the shores of the forgotten. No sound reaches me from the island prison where beats the fervent heart of the Girl, no ray of hope falls across the bars of desolation. But on the threshold of Nirvana life recoils; in the very bowels of torment it cries out to be! Persecution feeds the fires of defiance, and nerves my resolution. Were I an ordinary prisoner, I should not care to suffer all these agonies. To what purpose, with my impossible sentence? But my Anarchist ideals and traditions rise in revolt against the vampire gloating over its prey. No, I shall not disgrace the Cause, I shall not grieve my comrades by weak surrender! I will fight and struggle, and not be daunted by threat or torture.[1]

Alexander Berkman's prose, an energetic English beaten out of vigorous Russian timbres, prefers description to narration; or, more accurately, imparts much of its frustrated narrative momentum to the business of description. One of the reasons for that redistribution of force is simply the disappearance of incident relative to the infinite dilation and empty succession of prison time – sentenced

---

[1] Alexander Berkman, *Prison Memoirs of an Anarchist*, edited by Jessica Moran and Barry Pateman (Chico, CA: AK Press, 2016), 174.

to twenty-two years for the attempted assassination of Henry Clay Frick in 1892, and serving fourteen, Berkman exists in a space essentially out of time. In a situation where, for the most part, nothing happens, the effort to wrest experience from that blank expanse of unmarked temporality falls to a language in which absence thickens, assumes mythic dimensions, while speculative lines are drawn between the inert 'no part' being played by the imprisoned subject and distant 'life' itself.

Given to melodramatic Gothic tropes that subsequent literary history will swiftly invalidate as an adequate approach to such material, Berkman revels stylistically in the crushing weight of 'the hand of despair' and the 'screeching of a crow', working up to personifying his bloated enemy (capitalist persecution) as 'the vampire gloating over its prey'. This is all in service of a presiding conceit that separates his persona from 'the world of the living', casting him in a penumbral shadow of undeath and half-life, ever sinking into Tartarean oblivion out of 'the pain and travail' of human effort. Apathy and agony conspire to swallow his 'spark' of life in a pervading 'gloom', a 'darkness' that is as spiritual as it is literal.[2] Cast 'upon the shores of the forgotten' where a 'black raven . . . keeps vigil in my heart', Berkman metaphorises his despair and abandonment in figures fetched from Homer, Dante and Poe. The negativity extends to all senses: 'no sound' penetrates from without, 'no ray' warms the skin through 'the bars of desolation'. Moreover, the grammar confirms the alienation of the subject from all things lively, as verbal constructions trap the narrating 'I' in a tarpit of entropy: 'I lie', 'I have no part', 'I have been cast', nothing 'reaches me'. Outside the Gothic machinery, the accent falls on seriality: 'day by day', 'another day, then another', 'day follows night'.

Then, in a clear recourse to the stoic and Christian traditions of earlier prison writing – which discovered various ways of wresting spiritual growth and enlightenment out of the dungeons – Berkman engineers a rhetorical *volte-face*, replete with exclamation and dramatic reversal. 'But on the threshold of Nirvana life recoils; in the very bowels of torment it cries out to be!' This is not the first time in the *Memoirs* that the narrator has found the wherewithal to subdue thoughts of suicide and despair, but the turnaround is

---

[2] Fifty years earlier, a Philadelphia prisoner-poet known as 'Harry Hawser' depicted Pennsylvania's Eastern State Penitentiary as 'a living tomb'. See Harry Hawser, 'The Captive', in *Buds and Flowers, of Leisure Hours* (Philadelphia: Geo. Johnson, for the Author, 1844), 70.

rarely as emphatic as here. Personified abstractions stand in the van of this revolution: life, persecution, resolution and the Cause, all rallying round the passively constructed first person and goading it into animation. Now at last the subjunctive emerges, with its transformative optative mood, spilling out of a 'were I' construction in a torrent of defiant wish and desire, hardening in certainty from 'should' to 'shall' to the future tense of 'will': 'I should not', 'I shall not', 'I shall not', 'I will'. Setting himself apart from the 'ordinary' prisoner by virtue of his political convictions, he submits his individual case to the tribunal of the Cause (the anarchist's Big Other), where, multiplied by the number of comrades he can conjure before his imagination, he ceases to think of himself as cut adrift or isolated. A cell in a larger organism, he is no longer a lone spark in the gloom, but part of the living tissue of revolutionary activism. Life has flooded the prose, active clause after active clause, exclamation after exclamation, ranks of active participles and auxiliary verbs in tight formation; even as it has returned to the undead persona, full-blooded and assertive again, infused by his imperishable ideal.

This is not, to be sure, great prose writing. It is too formulaic, too predictable, to excite much admiration. But it is effective and, for all its generic trappings and obvious transitions, obviously sincere. The most electrifying of its qualities, which runs throughout the entire text, is the present-tense narration of what is essentially an 'iterative' narrative situation. This device transforms routine syntactical constructions built around the frequentative or habitual grammatical aspect into present-tense accounts rich with allegorical intensity; so the typical iterative 'gathers day by day' is sprung into dynamic shape by 'apathetic I lie on the bed'. The tense never changes, but the aspect shifts constantly, even in the space of a sentence: 'Bleak and desolate wakes the day – another day, then another – ' This rich grammatical resource drives the text through its more conventional patterns and movements, and, at its best, allows the narrator to put aside his self-pity and his sustaining rhetorical formulae in order to concentrate on the phenomenology of incarceration in a way that no writer has yet succeeded in doing:

> Total darkness. The blackness is massive, palpable, – I feel its hand upon my head, my face. I dare not move, lest a misstep thrust me into the abyss. I hold my hand close to my eyes – I feel the touch of my lashes upon it, but I cannot see its outline. Motionless I stand on one spot, devoid of all sense of direction. The silence is sinister; it

seems to me I can hear it. Only now and then the hasty scrambling of nimble feet suddenly rends the stillness, and the gnawing of invisible river rats haunts the fearful solitude.

Slowly the blackness pales. It ebbs and melts; out of the sombre gray, a wall looms above; the silhouette of a door rises dimly before me, sloping upward and growing compact and impenetrable.

The hours drag in unbroken sameness. Not a sound reaches me from the cell-house. In the maddening quiet and darkness I am bereft of all consciousness of time, save once a day when the heavy rattle of keys apprises me of the morning: the dungeon is unlocked, and the silent guards hand me a slice of bread and a cup of water. The double doors fall heavily to, the steps grow fainter and die in the distance, and all is dark again in the dungeon. (167)

Vestiges of the dominant style crop out in this prose – 'sinister' and 'maddening' seem redundant and tendentious – but there is a distinct new temper at work. Palpable darkness and audible silence are conventional enough as conceits, but they do not pad the prose here with inherited Gothicism. Rather, they lead the narrator towards specific sensory qualia: the eyelashes brushing against the unseen hand; the rats' faint gnawing and scuttling in the distance. Such efforts at the finer grain of description charge the prose with an ethic absent from the more doctrinaire apostrophes and asides, as defiance and rousing refusal make way for accuracy and exactitude.

Indeed, these *Prison Memoirs* are best understood as transitional in the history of prison writing: straddling a Victorian sensibility and a modern, disabused phenomenology, drawing deeply on both a traditional 'dungeon' tropology and an unprecedented fidelity to sense experience and affective mood. Hitherto, there has been no place in the prison memoir as a subgenre of autobiography for anything as granular as: 'Slowly the blackness pales. It ebbs and melts; out of the sombre gray, a wall looms above; the silhouette of a door rises dimly before me, sloping upward and growing compact and impenetrable.' Berkman's intuitive recourse to the realm of phenomena, sidestepping freighted adjectives in favour of verbs that resonate with mood – 'pales', 'ebbs', 'melts', 'looms', 'rises', along with the participles 'sloping' and 'growing' – allows the prose to assume a dynamism at the level of shifting impressions and mutable forms that the narrative situation disallows for the agent of these sensory registrations. The very emphasis on that fact in the subsequent paragraph – 'I am bereft of all consciousness of time' – retroactively charges the protean phenomenology with an energy necessary to the maintenance of interest in what, by definition, must be repetitive, inactive and devoid of narrative drama in an honest account of prison existence. So, when Lukács complains that description 'debases characters to the level of inanimate objects' in modern prose,[3] he negates the very process on display here: a character denied movement, become an object by state fiat, whose lively description of his own sense impressions imparts an animacy to objects themselves; who, in his own inertia and seriality, manages to find the pulse of existence in the shadow-play of walls, doors and barred grates.

The object world in *Prison Memoirs* is supercharged with significant animation. Out of the oppressive gloom, an instrument of suicide appears: 'I grope about the cell. The wall is damp, musty. The odors are nauseating. . . . I cannot live here. I must die. This very night. . . . Something white glimmers in the corner. Cautiously I bend over. It is a spoon' (74). Just outside, the world scratches at the senses: 'The distant puffing of fire engines, the shrieking of river sirens, accentuate my loneliness' (66); 'The full moon hangs above the river, bathing the waters in mellow light. The strains of a sweet lullaby wander through the woods, and the banks are merry with laughter' (158). At one point, in the middle of the night, what sounds like a riot: 'The cell-house is raging with uproar: crash after crash booms through the hall; it thunders against the walls of the cell, then rolls like some monstrous drum along the galleries, and abruptly ceases' (180). Aural phenomenology works overtime with whatever is available on the visible spectrum to render an account of the mystery.

> The heavy doors of the rotunda groan on their hinges. Shadowlike, giant figures glide past my cell. They walk inaudibly, felt-soled and portentous, the long riot clubs rigid at their sides. Behind them others, and then the Warden, a large revolver gleaming in his hand. With bated breath I listen, conscious of the presence of other men at the doors. Suddenly wailing and wild laughter pierce the night: there is the rattling of iron, violent scuffling, the sickening thud of a falling body, and all is quiet. Noiselessly the bread cart flits by, the huge shadows bending over the body stretched on the boards.
>
> The gong booms the rising hour. The morning sun glints a ray upon the bloody trail in the hall, and hides behind the gathering mist. (180–1)

The method here is sharply distanced from the nineteenth-century approach to narrative explanation and has adapted spontaneously to a new century's preference for raw data over amplification.

---

[3] Georg Lukács, *Writer and Critic*, translated by Arthur Kahn (London: Merlin, 1978), 133.

Hemingway, Hammett are already implicit in this refusal to step outside the flow of phenomena and offer an Archimedean vantage point. 'Show not tell' means this first of all: allow the things to tell the story, supply no unnecessary commentary. Left to themselves, and properly accounted for, things in prison show a prodigious appetency for agency. Consider how the grammatical status of subject shifts in the following passage, from the first-person singular pronoun to a range of concrete nouns which take the humble activity of the 'I' to new and higher levels:

> I ransack the cell-house for old papers and rags; with miserly hand I gather all odds and ends, broken tools, pieces of wood, a bucketful of sawdust. Trembling with fear of discovery, I empty the treasure into the sewer at the end of the hall, and tightly jam the elbow of the waste pipe. The smell of excrement fills the block, the cell privies overrun, and inundate the hall. The stench is overpowering; steadily the water rises, threatening to flood the cell-house. The place is in a turmoil: the solitaries shout and rattle on the bars, the guards rush about in confusion. (293)

A simple sequence of low-grade acts, available within the severely limited repertoire of moves open to the protagonist, leads to an ever-widening ripple effect as the 'actor-network' of the prison system (industrial waste, pipes, toilets, excrement, water, hall, cells, prisoners, guards) springs into automatic action and reaction. It is in the system itself, the integrated organism within which each element has its designated place, that agency is located: its routine operation entails continual graft, abuse and exploitation; but any blockage leads swiftly to turmoil and crisis. We note, in passing, the remarkable substitution of the prison complex as a whole for the abstract 'Cause' as the higher-level organism to which this imagination now submits itself; only, the prison not as an inflexible automaton, but a lively, responsive social network with its own politics and subversive potential. Berkman's prose is an effort to wrest revolutionary dynamism out of the most severe glaciation of eventfulness imaginable: fourteen years in Auburn-style isolation, silence, and prolonged stints in the 'basket'.[4] He has located in the despised act

---

[4] 'The Auburn model prescribed the individual cell during the night, work and meals in common, but under the rule of absolute silence, the convicts being allowed to speak to the warders, with their permission and in a low voice. It was a clear reference to the monastic model; a reference, too, to the discipline of the workshop.' Michel Foucault, *Discipline and Punish: The Birth of the Prison*, translated by Alan Sheridan (London: Penguin, 1991), 238.

of description a sacred principle of modernist political aesthetics: *defamiliarisation*. The closer and more searching the inspection of a thing, the less it comes to feel finished and *déjà-vu*, the more it feels available for remaking.

* * *

On a moral, thematic level, this is the same lesson that *Prison Memoirs* wants to draw from its account of the Bildungsromanesque development of its protagonist's soul while incarcerated at Western State Penitentiary (aka Riverside), just west of Pittsburgh on the banks of the Ohio River, between 1892 and 1906. For just as poetic *ostranenie* works against the intellectual reification of what Shkolvsky calls 'habitualization' – where objects, unseen because overly familiar, 'function as though by formula and do not even appear in cognition'[5] – by rendering the familiar unfamiliar in form, so too Berkman's prison Bildung begins with a youth's shop-worn conceptual habits of intellectual abstraction and, by exposing them to the conditions of a long term in the 'House of Death', gradually dismantles them in favour of the sensuous particulars of a narrow, close-range experience, amassed over a decade. And it is in the writing of particular characters that this effect is achieved, by allowing the peculiar physiognomy of the person to emerge – in speech, gesture and act – from beneath the crude sociological caricature behind which it had initially been obscured. As a result of allowing the honest writing of character to proceed according to its own laws and logic, the prose also enables its central observing Berkman-persona, 'Aleck', to overcome his own most spontaneous prejudices and even the selfish impulses of his own desire; so that by the end of the text, a blinkered, jejune anarchist autodidact has matured into one of the most open-minded, generous, searching, moving narrators in the history of prison literature.

The striking character studies of Berkman's fellow inmates, particularly those of 'Wingie', 'Boston Red', Doctor George, and the gentle young men, 'Felipe', Russell, and Harry, do the literary work of defamiliarising that most invidious of conceptual abstractions in circumstances of prolonged incarceration: *the criminal*. For this notion of 'the criminal' is most prejudicial and deleterious to

---

[5] Viktor Shkolvsky, 'Art as Technique', in Lee T. Lemon and Marion J. Reis, eds, *Russian Formalist Criticism: Four Essays*, 2nd ed. (Lincoln & London: University of Nebraska Press, 2012), 12 [3–24].

the perceptual and intellectual powers of the political prisoner who enters the penitentiary – not only as regards his fellow prisoners, but in relation to his own horizons as a political thinker. The narrative voice works according to conventional ironic protocols, presenting its twenty-two-year-old self as the prisoner of his own preconceptions. 'Wingie' is first introduced through the filters of a prevailing 'left' stereotypy: 'he is a bourgeois, "in business". He is not worth while. Besides, he confessed that it is his third offence. He is a common criminal, not an honest producer' (41). Seen as the simple sum of his presumptive abstractions, 'Wingie' is dismissed as a 'common criminal' despite the evident appeal of his discourse and sympathetic attentions to the despised anarchist. And this cavalier, instrumentalist attitude towards the other inmates is characteristic, too, of Berkman's own self-perception in these early sections. 'My own individuality is entirely in the background; aye, I am not conscious of any personality in matters pertaining to the Cause. I am simply a revolutionist, a terrorist by conviction, an instrument for furthering the cause of humanity; in short, a Rakhmetov' (10). The Cause is, in this sense, merely a series of literary prescriptions and convictions which dictate the 'distribution of the sensible' in Berkman's character space. As 'a Rakhmetov', the narrator is knowingly conscripting his naive younger avatar to the crowded novelistic camp of Madame Bovarys and Lord Jims, whose ability to engage with the external world is wholly mediated by tropes and figures inherited from the books they inveterately reread. Berkman's world is Chernishevsky's world; he proves unable for some time to perceive anything other than the categories and types that define the politico-literary space of Russian nihilism.

So, the early character studies are stymied by prejudice. Berkman is cast among types, allegorical abstractions: 'The flatterer, the back-biter, the spy, – these find here a rich soil' (119). The individuals do not attain to individuality. 'Why does [Billy] love life so, I wonder. Of what value is it without a high purpose, uninspired by revolutionary ideals? He is small and cowardly: he lies to save his neck' (59); while of Lightning Al, he remarks, 'I have never before come in personal contact with a professional thief, and I entertain the vaguest ideas concerning his class. But they are not producers; hence parasites who deliberately prey upon society, upon the poor, mostly. There can be nothing in common between me and this man' (154). That, *in nuce*, is the rub of this writer's dilemma: a lack of commonality between the writer-subject of these reflections and their objects, all of whom fail to live up to any notable ideal. They are 'criminals' while 'I' am a 'political prisoner'. Disgusted when a defence lawyer sent to consider his case falls asleep while hearing Berkman's deposition (more Flaubertian irony here), the narrator scoffs, 'Perhaps he considers me a criminal' (64). Pleased that he has not given the trial judge any opportunity 'to proclaim the Anarchists vulgar criminals', Berkman continues: 'Such things help to prejudice the People against us. We, criminals? We, who are ever ready to give our lives for liberty, criminals?' (75) This ontological distinction between 'us' and 'them', criminals and revolutionaries, means that the narrator feels his isolation redoubled in the social space of the prison; the general population recedes into a Dantesque abstraction of treacherous otherness (109).

The irony is that it is 'the Cause' itself that supplies the means to unthink 'the criminal' as such, and to think with and through the social misfits who inhabit Riverside penitentiary. For anarchism has as one of its founding principles the topsy-turvy proposition that Law itself is crime. Although often used as an exculpation for the political prisoner and agent of the *Attentat* – 'I don't believe in your laws, I don't acknowledge the authority of your courts. I am innocent, morally' (48) – this principle can, at a pinch, be extended to cover the entire prison population. 'The law is immoral: it is the conspiracy of rulers and priests against the workers, to continue their subjection' (56); 'Government, with its laws, is the common enemy. All weapons are justifiable in the noble struggle of the People against this terrible curse. The Law! It is the arch-crime of the centuries. The path of Man is soaked with the blood it has shed. Can this great criminal determine Right?' (56). It is just that, in the early sections of the *Prison Memoirs*, this truth cannot be admitted in anything other than a self-glorifying register. It awaits the characterological *ostranenie* we have been adumbrating to shift its reference from the ironised 'Rakhmetov' narrator to the general prison population of 'social scum', 'lumpens' and 'parasites'.

It is a Black inmate, Lancaster, who is the first fully to impress his character on the text, albeit in the mode of its absence; for Lancaster, having assaulted a shop officer and been chained to the wall of the dungeon for ten straight days, has lost his mind:

> The witless negro crawls on the floor, unwashed and unkempt, scratching with his nails fantastic shapes on the stone, and babbling stupidly, 'Going, Jesus going to Jerusalem. See, he rides the holy ass; he's going to his father's home. Going home, going home.' As I pass he looks up, perplexed wonder on his face; his brows meet in

a painful attempt to collect his wandering thoughts, and he drawls with pathetic sing-song, 'Going home, going home; Jesus going to father's home.' The guards raise their hands to their nostrils as they approach the cell: the poor imbecile evacuates on the table, the chair, and the floor. Twice a month he is taken to the bathroom, his clothes are stripped, and the hose is turned on the crazy negro. (212)

It is in this key that Berkman's memoir finds its true vocation. This devastating mini-portrait, which integrates verbal formulae ('going home'), a flurry of adjectives and adverbs (witless, unwashed, stupidly, pathetic, poor), a representative habitus (crawling, scratching, drawling, defecating), and the referred actions of the guards as they approach his cell, is at once a highly particularised, specific image of Prisoner 8523, and an apt allegorical image of an institutional tendency to bestialise and destroy the mental health of Riverside's less educated denizens. Berkman remarks 'how quickly the solitary drives certain classes of prisoners insane. Especially the more ignorant element, whose mental horizon is circumscribed by their personal troubles and pain, speedily fall victims. Think of men, who cannot even read, put *incommunicado* for months at a time, for years even!' (272) The portrait of Lancaster is pitched at the precise point where exemplarity and singularity converge in that much-maligned, misunderstood category of *the typical*. Prisoner 8523 is entirely typical of the long-term Black prison population in having collapsed around his own individuality, leaving signs only of the generic, the universal: religious aspiration, physical animality. His not-being-there is a vivid cipher of everything the prison dissimulates about its mission: 'The prison authorities desire to treat every prisoner in their charge with humanity and kindness' (213).

Other portraits are less typical and more ostentatiously eccentric, most remarkably in the case of 'Boston Red', an old-timer 'with benevolent white beard and stately carriage' (126) who becomes Berkman's assistant in the socking shop, whom the editors of the *Prison Memoirs* are inclined to believe is entirely fictionalised. It is Red's explicit narrative function to introduce Berkman to the happy eroticism of 'man-boy' relationships in prison; but that little explains the extraordinary oddity of his extensive verbal performances, which alternate between ornate college-educated English (strewn with classical and Shakespearean citations and pretentious polysyllabic diction) and exaggerated tramping slang. One moment he is all orotund periods and circumlocution – 'I brook no sceptical attitude regarding my undoubted and proven perspicacity of human nature', 'my settled estimate of the world's supercilious righteousness' – and the next he is neck-deep in period idioms: 'He was no punk, either, an' don't you forget it. True as steel, he was; stuck to me through my four-spot like th' bark to a tree'; 'you jest rattle me with your crazy talk. Why, you're bugs to say it's impossible. Man alive, the dump's chuckful of punks' (131–5). Red is the impossible sum of these irreconcilable verbal energies, his character an improvised literary routine in Mark Twain's back paddock: 'the face expressive of a deep-felt conviction of universal wisdom, the eyes of humorous cynicism, and the ludicrous manner of mixing tramp slang with "classic" English', all quite disarming and implausible. And that is entirely the point: a composite figure, patched together out of fourteen years' worth of human experience at Riverside, 'Boston Red' stands as a testament to everything the prison cannot break, though it is broken in every particular case. 'Daily I behold the machinery at work, grinding and pulverizing, brutalizing the officers, dehumanizing the inmates' (216). 'Boston Red' is a kind of characterological scrapbook, where Berkman could collect and collate all the unbroken shards of humanity among the inmates, sweepings from the floor of the machine-room, and make a patchwork man of them.

The portraiture of the *Prison Memoirs*, then, serves ends both typical and redemptive as regards its real-world material; but its truer purpose is to contribute something essential to Berkman's carceral Bildung. In these portraits, *through* them, the youth is allowed to watch the scales fall from his eyes, and to see men appear where before there were mere notions and abstractions. It all culminates in this remarkable passage:

> But the threads of comradeship have slowly been woven by common misery. The touch of sympathy has discovered the man beneath the criminal; the crust of sullen suspicion has melted at the breath of kindness, warming into view the palpitating human heart. Old Evans and Sammy and Bob, – what suffering and pain must have chilled their fiery souls with the winter of savage bitterness! And the resurrection trembles within! How terrible man's ignorance, that forever condemns itself to be scourged by its own blind fury! And these my friends, Davis and Russell, these innocently guilty, – what worse punishment could society inflict upon itself, than the loss of their latent nobility which it had killed? . . . Not entirely in vain are the years of suffering that have wakened my kinship with the humanity of *les misérables*, whom social stupidity has cast into the valley of death. (317–18)

Such literary *ostranenie* has something remarkably historical about it; Berkman's discovering the 'man beneath the criminal' is a product of a very specific conjuncture in social space-time. We are at the opposite extreme from a Dickensian cult of sympathy here, though 'sympathy' is the very emotional vibration at issue, and the residual Victorian rhetoric is securely in place; for whereas a Dickens will work by building up the protagonist prior to incarceration, and establishing the 'breath of kindness' in the very language of characterisation over and against a grim background of barely legible, barely human inmates, here, on the contrary, the anonymous 'criminal' backdrop is hauled by main force into view, manhandled and inspected at close quarters, only to find behind each and every type and sociological abstraction 'the palpitating human heart' we expect only from novelistic protagonists and their kind. The evocation of Hugo is earned and profoundly correct, as the anarchist-presumed-to-know has had the reductive epistemology of the prison turned on its head by his sustained immersion in 'years of suffering' alongside, and as one of, those sentenced to living death for a lack of compliance with the state. Here stands revealed that truth of anarchist doctrine which Berkman had parroted without understanding: that Law is Crime, that bourgeois society is prison writ large, and that solidarity without 'kinship with the humanity of *les misérables*' is politically vacuous. This is, in the history of prison writing, the equivalent of an endorsement of Rancière's 'aesthetic regime':[6] the moment at which a radical perspectival egalitarianism destroys the ontological distinction between 'us' and 'them', major and minor, 'political prisoner' and 'criminal', and we are all become one in the movement of the wretched of the earth against the monstrous powers feasting on human essence. This shift in the politics of perception aligns with the much later statement of Black Panther Zayd Shakur, to the effect that 'all of America is a prison where the people are being held captive by the real arch criminals', and indicates the true nature of Berkman's textual radicalism.[7]

* * *

[6] 'The aesthetic regime abolishes the hierarchical distribution of the sensible characteristic of the representative regime of art, including the privilege of speech over visibility as well as the hierarchy of the arts, their subject matter, and their genres. By promoting the equality of the represented subjects, the indifference of style with regard to content, and the immanence of meaning in things themselves, the aesthetic regime destroys the system of genres and isolates "art" in the singular.' See Gabriel Rockhill's full definition in Jacques Rancière, *The Politics of Aesthetics: The Distribution of the Sensible* (London: Continuum, 2004), 81.

[7] Zayd Shakur, 'America Is the Prison', in *Off the Pigs! The History and Literature of the Black Panther Party*, edited by G. Louis Heath (Metuchen, NJ: Scarecrow, 1976), 247–80.

The Prison Memoirs of an Anarchist is distinct in the tradition for this reason above all, that it profoundly modernises the conventional 'synecdochal' reading of the carceral institution and makes a case for its own status as a monument of social realism.[8] This wily generic inversion of the various expectations of sensationalism, exoticism, criminality, liminality and so on, which inevitably beset the 'prison memoir' form, is Berkman's greatest claim to literary genius, and it hinges on his knowing deployment of various figures of microcosmic allusion from within Riverside to the larger America of which it is a pure product. The reader's gradual realisation that, far from exploring some disreputable and extreme heterotopia, the text in her hands has transformed into something out of Hugo or Balzac – a sober realist indictment of an entire social order of things – is an astonishing achievement. It comes in small doses but builds relentlessly into crescendi of rhetorical ululation against the monotonous, eventless narrative walls in which time itself has, as it were, been incarcerated.

> Far removed from the strife and struggle of the larger world, I yet witness its miniature replica, more agonizing and merciless within the walls. A perfected model it is, this prison life, with its apparent uniformity and dull passivity. But beneath the torpid surface smolder the fires of being, now crackling faintly under a dun smothering smoke, now blazing forth with the ruthlessness of despair. Hidden by the veil of discipline rages the struggle of fiercely contending wills, and intricate meshes are woven in the quagmire of darkness and suppression. (216)

If, indeed, the prison is a 'perfected model' of the surrounding social formation, then this institutionalised perfection has not been able to extinguish those 'fires of being' that compromise all disciplinary social orders with their unruly insistence on expression, at the level both of group and of individual. Berkman's metaphors are at their most successful here, and the trope carries within it that earlier presentation of his own life-force, his inextinguishable *virtù*, as a 'spark' in the darkness: 'like a furnace spark belched forth amid fire and smoke into the blackness of night' (66). Only here, the image

---

[8] See Fludernik's discussion of the 'two related topoi of English literature from the late Middle Ages to the twentieth century: the topos of the prison as world and, inversely, that of the world as prison. Depending on the perspective, the world of the prison is, on the one hand, posited to be a mirror image of society at large; or, on the other hand, the prison is seen as emblematic of human existence and/or society.' Monika Fludernik, *Metaphors of Confinement: The Prison in Fact, Faction, and Fantasy* (Oxford: Oxford University Press, 2019), 60.

is extended in all directions, a latent 'smoldering', 'now crackling', 'now blazing forth': it is politics as such, flaring up along the lines of antagonism, the unquenchable life-force of the *zoon politikon* and of the subordinate classes. Foucault's 'veil of discipline', of which Western State Penitentiary was to have been such a sterling instance, is unable to dampen this fire indefinitely; 'fiercely contending wills' finally render impossible that 'omni-disciplinarity' through isolation, labour and correction so devoutly wished for by the authorities. Politics will out, thanks particularly to the central place of labour within the carceral regime itself, 'the very machinery that transforms the violent, agitated, unreflective convict into a part that plays its role with perfect regularity. [. . .] If, in the final analysis, the work of the prison has an economic effect, it is by producing individuals mechanized according to the general norms of an industrial society.'[9]

Berkman's proposition is that, to the very degree the prison models itself on a workhouse, an industrial factory, so too is it riven by class antagonism and 'fierce contention'. Most of the book's episodes of violent confrontation and brutal punishment take place on the prison's factory floors: the mat shop and the hosiery shop, the two prison industries in which Berkman was engaged as an unwaged (slave) labourer. The mat shop is a 'crank shop', used for exceptional punishment and explicitly designed to foreshorten life through pestilential dust-filled air; it is a place where the very extremity of the conditions breeds violent acts (99–100). Even here, where labour is a death sentence, in this darkest 'disciplinary shop, to which are generally assigned the "hard cases"', a place 'of special supervision and severest discipline', proto-political acts are commonplace (102).

In the hosiery department, where discipline is less exacting, Berkman becomes a veteran semi-skilled labourer over many years, and, quite contrary to Bérenger's recommendations,[10] experiences in the work a directionless freedom of thought:

> Practice lends me great dexterity in the work, but the hours of drudgery drag with heavy heel. I seek to hasten time by forcing myself to take an interest in the task. I count the stockings I turn, the motions required by each operation, and the amount accomplished within a

[9] Foucault, *Discipline and Punish*, 242.
[10] 'By occupying the convict, one gives him habits of order and obedience; [. . .] with time, he finds in the regular movement of the prison, in the manual labors to which he is subjected . . . a certain remedy against the wanderings of his imagination,' Bérenger, qtd in Foucault, *Discipline and Punish*, 242.

given time. But in spite of these efforts, my mind persistently reverts to unprofitable subjects: my friends and the propaganda; the terrible injustice of my excessive sentence; suicide and escape. (103)

The stocking shop is also the place where Johnny Davis, Berkman's premier love interest, goes through a brutal education in industrial relations. His youthful vigour makes him a highly productive stocking-turner, a fact noted by one Jack Bradford, who periodically steals piles of Johnny's socks to add to his own pile. Indignant, but refusing to squeal, Johnny is sent to the dungeon for striking his tormentor with a blow. This happens repeatedly. 'Poor Johnny is already the fourth day in the dreaded dungeon. His third time, too, and yet absolutely innocent. My blood boils at the thought of the damnable treatment and the officer's perfidy. It is my duty as a revolutionist to take the part of the persecuted' (122). A tall boy, on return to the shop Johnny requests the use of a 'high gear' machine to turn stockings, but is refused and, bent over double for eight hours at a time, he suffers a haemorrhage, collapses and refuses to work further; for which insolence he is again punished with the dungeon. The situation is Dantesque in its circular logic:

> But the boy has grown obdurate: he is determined not to go back to the shop whose officer caused him so much trouble. The prison discipline takes no cognizance of the situation. Regularly every Monday the torture is repeated: the youth is called before the Deputy, and assigned to the hosiery department; the unvarying refusal is followed by the dungeon, and then Johnny is placed in the solitary, to be cited again before the Warden the ensuing Monday. I chafe at my helplessness to aid the boy. His course is suicidal, but the least suggestion of yielding enrages him. 'I'll die before I give in,' he told me. (177)

Ultimately, returning again to the hosiery department, Johnny comes up against the predations and slander of 'Dutch' Adams, whom he attempts to murder in a fit of accumulated shop-floor rage; but is sent again to the dungeon where, finally avowing his love for Berkman in the book's most touching scene, he eventually succumbs. It all ends with 'my grief over Johnny Davis. My young friend had grown ill in the foul basket. He begged to be taken to the hospital; but his condition did not warrant it, the physician said. Moreover, he was "in punishment". Poor boy, how he must have suffered! They found him dead on the floor of his cell' (278). This savage interpersonal drama exposes the degree to which industrial labour breeds conflict, oppression, brutality and the consumption of life. Its setting in a prison only concentrates the broader form of the problem; 'life outside does not differ so very much from prison existence', as Berkman writes to Carl Nold (357–8).

In such wise, a putatively limited purview on a single instance of the 'penitentiary apparatus' broadens allegorically into that horizon of social totality reserved for the great practitioners of social realism: the Balzacs, the Zolas and the Upton Sinclairs, for whom the political question of reform, reaction or revolution is secondary to the fundamental epistemological task of illuminating the central mechanism of the whole social organism. After a brief respite of labour discipline during a change of Warden, the inevitable returns. Censured by prison inspectors 'because of the reduced profits from the industries', he is terrorised into reaction; 'the tasks have been increased, and even the sick and consumptives are forced to work. The labor bodies of the State have been protesting in vain. How miserably weak is the Giant of Toil, because unconscious of his strength!' (359). Social necessity stamps its miserable identity on every institution, reiterating the self-same division of labour, extraction of surplus value, and premature extinction of the 'latent nobility' it thrives on as fuel. Meanwhile, unconscious at the machine, but 'far from being mummified', the Giant of Toil stokes the weakened fires of its being in daydream and the restless idiom of wish.

Chapter 3

An Immense World of Delight: Rosa Luxemburg's Prison Writing

And oh, what a lovely recollection I have from Alexanderplatz! Do you know, Hänschen, what Alexanderplatz is? The month-and-a-half stay that I had there left gray hairs on my head and rent my nerves in such a way that I will never get over it. And yet I have a small recollection from there that pops up like a flower in my memory. Night began there as early as 5:30 – it was late autumn, October, and the cell had no lighting at all. There was nothing left for me to do in that eleven square meter space than to stretch out on the plank bed, which was stuck in between indescribably ugly pieces of furniture, and amidst the hellish music of the municipal transit trains continually thundering by, making the cell shake as bits of red light flashed on the vibrating window pane, I recited my Mörike in a low voice to myself. After 10 p.m. the diabolic concert of the city trains would grow somewhat softer, and soon after that the following little episode from the life of the streets would become audible. First you could hear dimly a hoarse male voice, which had something demanding and admonishing about it, then in reply, a young girl singing, probably around eight years old; she sang a children's ditty while hopping and jumping and at the same time letting go with silvery peals of laughter which had a bell-like purity of tone. The man's voice must have been that of a tired, bad-tempered janitor, who was calling his little daughter home to go to sleep. But the little rascal didn't want to obey, let the deep gruff voice of her father go in one ear and out the other, kept flitting around in the streets like a butterfly, and countered the oncoming strictures and threats with a merry children's rhyme. One could vividly picture the short skirt flapping and the thin legs flying in dance steps. In the hoppity-hop rhythm of a children's song, in the rippling laughter, there was so much carefree and triumphant joy of life that the whole dark and musty building of the central police headquarters was enveloped as though by a silver cloak of mist and in my foul-smelling prison cell the air was suddenly scented with the perfume of dark-red roses falling through the air ... Thus, everywhere, one picks up a bit of happiness from the street and is tempted over and over again to believe that life is rich and beautiful.[1]

This passage is unusual among Luxemburg's letters from prison in that it directly treats, in its brief reflections on the Alexanderplatz police cells, the damage done by her serial incarcerations. Her six weeks in these infamous interrogation cells (in July 1916) were, according to her biographer, 'the worst prison experience of Rosa's life'.[2] She told of a 'hell-hole', a 'cave', an 'eleven square metre cell, without light both mornings and evenings', and overrun by a 'pack of dogs'.[3] Yet very little of this manifests in her correspondence – none of which was dispatched from Alexanderplatz – and only ever in retrospect. For their rarity alone, then, the remarks on her greying hairs and torn nerves stand out as testimony to what she would generally prefer not to mention. That this is not the typical tone of her prison writing is abundantly evident from the remainder of the passage, which rounds on those 'rent nerves' and grey hairs with an exuberant exercise in redemptive reading, as if to negate them once and for all under a deluge of affirmation. It is a frequent rhetorical manoeuvre. Her avowedly 'small recollection', the anecdote of the dancing girl, is a mere 'bit' or 'little episode' in the unmentionable trauma of her time in the dungeons, but it strives to be, stylistically and allegorically, as momentous as anything in Proust. Its tonal and imagistic transfiguration of her 'hell-hole' in a swelling major key runs all the risks of mawkish sentiment and Panglossian eudaimonism, which it avoids thanks to its phenomenological precision, characterological wit, and novelistic negotiation of the play between narrative and iterative modes.

Her anecdote is above all acoustic in orientation – the last of three exquisite sound-scenes in this same letter – emphasising the penumbral darkness of the cell in order to fall back on strong aural sensations which begin infernally (the 'hellish' cacophony or 'diabolic concert' of the streetcars) and then modulate into the repeated

[1] Rosa Luxemburg, Letter to Hans Diefenbach, 29 June 1917, in *The Letters of Rosa Luxemburg*, edited by Georg Adler, Peter Hudis and Annelies Laschitza, translated by George Shriver (London: Verso, 2011), 424–5.

[2] J. P. Nettl, *Rosa Luxemburg: The Biography* (London: Verso, 2019), loc. 11574.

[3] Luxemburg, qtd in Nettl, *Rosa Luxemburg*, loc. 11574; Letter to Mathilde Wurm, 28 December 1916, and Letter to Clara Zetkin, 12 May 1916, *Letters*, 363, 360.

late-night scene she is at pains to recreate. It is important to note, I think, that the auditor's distance from 'the street' is not merely the physical fact of being walled off from it; rather, for all her revolutionary fervour and conscription to the cause of the masses, Luxemburg has no organic relationship with them. One of the features of her time in prison is the close quarters she is obliged to keep with proletarians, her unhappy discovery of 'such a mass of stupidity, such a base mentality' in even the most promising-looking convicts, crushed under 'the most profound human degradation', that she must always look away.[4] She routinely 'spares herself the sight' (430) of her fellow prisoners; intimacy is shared only with her educated correspondents. It is fitting, then, that sound should be the medium through which she now confabulates her solidarity with them, in the person of this young girl and her nightly defiance of the 'old janitor' her jailor-father. Their sounds are antiphonic and counterbalancing in timbre and pitch: below, a thoroughbass male voice, 'hoarse', 'tired, bad-tempered', 'deep gruff', full of 'something demanding and admonishing'; and trilling above it, the sprightly piccolo of 'a young girl singing . . . a merry children's rhyme' and 'letting go with silvery peals of laughter', liquid 'rippling laughter' with 'a bell-like purity of tone'. In this measured counterpoint Luxemburg detects the 'hoppity-hop' rhythm of the girl's feet, 'hopping and jumping', 'flitting around in the streets like a butterfly'; and this percussion emerging from the counterpoint of voices allows for a sudden transposition from the aural to the visual: 'One could vividly picture the short skirt flapping and the thin legs flying in dance steps.'

The visual is the home of the imaginary, and here we find the molten core of Luxemburg's political imagination: an organic body in ecstatic, self-pleasuring motion, immediately alive to its own limitless capacities. As she wrote of the mass strike emerging from the life of the people rather than a theorist's blueprint:

> Instead of the rigid and hollow scheme of an arid political action carried out by the decision of the highest committees and furnished with a plan and panorama, we see a bit of pulsating life of flesh and blood, which cannot be cut out of the large frame of the revolution but is connected with all parts of the revolution by a thousand veins.[5]

[4] Luxemburg, Letter to Sophie Liebknecht, 2 August 1917, *Letters*, 430.
[5] Luxemburg, 'The Mass Strike, the Political Party, and the Trade Unions', in *The Rosa Luxemburg Reader*, edited by Peter Hudis and Kevin B. Anderson (New York: Monthly Review Press, 2004), 191.

It is the same with the delightful figure of the girl. As she writes in her letter about the nocturnal sounds of prison, 'In the darkness of the night, mysterious links stretched out and connected people who never knew or saw one another' (424). Just so, the 'bit of pulsating life of flesh and blood' that the night sounds have conjured in Luxemburg's imaginary – the laughing girl dancing like a butterfly – *cannot be cut out* of the social totality, although it has never featured in any political theory; for Luxemburg, indeed, it is the key to how that totality moves, to its inner spark and life. Transfigurative spontaneity inheres in this figure as the very pulse of protopolitical action, nightly defying the paternal injunction. It conveys 'so much carefree and triumphant joy of life that the whole dark and musty building of the central police headquarters was enveloped as though by a silver cloak of mist and in my foul-smelling prison cell the air was suddenly scented with the perfume of dark-red roses falling through the air'.

This girl is Rosa Luxemburg, of course; she is imagining herself in a role she excessively cultivated, the lively little girl full of *joie de vivre* and devil-may-care defiance. But the girl is also the proletarian Other and the Other in general – including the 'poor victims on the rubber plantations of Putumayo, the Blacks in Africa with whose corpses the Europeans play catch' (376) – whom Luxemburg cannot see (or cannot look at) and must, as an isolated prisoner, hold tight in the political imaginary. The vivid phrase 'short skirt flapping and the thin legs flying' works hard to create a figure not unlike Yeats' 'dancer and the dance', in which the individual is dissolved into her activity, the humble particular raised into the sublime universal. Prison forced Luxemburg 'to see and hear from a distance those things that for me mean life and happiness' (426), and in that distance was the opportunity to 'use [her] eyes and ears, and thus to create an inner equilibrium and rise above everything petty and annoying' (431), into the 'ceaselessly moving . . . changing sea of phenomena' where social revolution rolls and tumbles.[6] Such imaginary operations obeyed a very specific and peculiar logic in her work, however, and that requires some further examination.

* * *

These are some of the things that happened to Rosa Luxemburg during the First World War. Apart from a five-month period of liberty in

---

[6] Luxemburg, 'The Mass Strike', 191.

early 1916, she served her time in solitary for antiwar propaganda in four different locations over the war's four devastating years: Barnim Street Women's Prison in Berlin (18 February 1915 – 18 February 1916; 21 July – 25 October 1916), Alexanderplatz police interrogation cells (10–20 July 1916), Wronke fortress, Poznan (26 October 1916 – 22 July 1917) and Breslau prison (23 July 1917 – 8 November 1918). Of all her comrades, she was the most incarcerated, the most feared. Leo Jogiches, an ex-lover, was arrested in Berlin in March 1918 and imprisoned in the Moabit investigations prison, where he was killed a year later. Her close comrade Karl Liebknecht was sentenced on 8 December 1916 to confinement at Luckau penitentiary, where he was held until October 1918. This imposed a severe mental and emotional strain on Luxemburg's close friend, Karl's wife, Sophie Liebknecht. Her friend Julian Marchlewski was held in the Havelberg internment camp from November 1916 until the last days of the war. The 1917 February Revolution in Russia, followed by the Bolshevik Revolution in October, created enormous repercussions for her political theories. The SPD, the party to which she had given the better part of her life, had persevered with its craven capitulation to the forces of chauvinism and imperialism, despite the lashings of her pen. Twenty million people were killed and twenty-one million wounded, in the war she was incarcerated for protesting, all much as she had predicted. And to cap it all, her beloved Hans Diefenbach – physician, writer, lover, soldier, recipient of the letter on the dancing girl – was killed at the Western Front, in France, in late October 1917.

It is impossible to read her prison letters without bearing this litany of horrors constantly in mind, alongside the tragic fact that she and Karl Liebknecht would both be tortured and murdered by the Freikorps then tossed into the Landwehr Canal a mere two months after her final release from prison, in the death-throes of the German Revolution. Few revolutionaries in history have had to endure as much loss – of life, of liberty, of loved ones, of the horizon of praxis itself – as Luxemburg did in these years as a result of her organising against the very reason for those losses: a cataclysmic world war. What she wrote in Barnim Street Women's Prison in her *Junius Pamphlet* (1915), the greatest document of this unconscionable mass slaughter, summarises the stakes for her and for the history of her cause: 'the war is not only a grandiose murder, but the suicide of the European working class. The soldiers of socialism, the workers of England, of France, of Germany, of Italy, of Belgium are murdering each other at the bidding of capitalism, are thrusting cold, murderous irons into each other's breasts, are tottering over their graves, grappling in each other's death-bringing arms.'[7]

That Rosa Luxemburg's prodigious 'pessimism of the intellect' was sharpened to a razor's edge on the grindstone of world history by the time she was thrown into prison is abundantly evinced by this extraordinary text. Undertaken as an 'unsparing self-criticism' (316) of German Social Democracy itself after its 'miserable collapse' (327) in the Reichstag, 4 August 1918, this lacerating pamphlet stares into the crater of the 'imperialist volcano' (316) without once blinking in the sulphurous steam. Disabused, bitter and unreconciled, Luxemburg excoriates the entire apparatus of state and capital, and its elected SPD stooges, for preparing the grim scene where 'millions of proletarians are falling on the field of dishonor, of fratricide, of self-destruction, the slave-song on their lips' (321). As 'the horror of endless massacre and bloodshed in all countries grew and grew, as its imperialistic hoof became more and more evident, as the exploitation by bloodthirsty speculators became more and more shameless' (331), Luxemburg's prison cell became Europe's documentary camera obscura, every forgotten moment of its recent past focused to a shocking definition of *civilisation as war*, a bloody shambles stretching in every nightmare direction:

> The 'civilized world' that has stood calmly by when this same imperialism doomed tens of thousands of Hereros to destruction; when the desert of Kalahari shuddered with the insane cry of the thirsty and the rattling breath of the dying; when in Putumayo, within ten years forty thousand human beings were tortured to death by a band of European industrial robber-barons, and the remnants of a whole people were beaten into cripples; when in China an ancient civilization was delivered into the hands of destruction and anarchy, with fire and slaughter, by the European soldiery; when Persia gasped in the noose of the foreign rule of force that closed inexorably about her throat; when in Tripoli the Arabs were mowed down, with fire and swords, under the yoke of capital while their civilization and their homes were razed to the ground. (339)

It is no wonder that, with this Boschian tide now engulfing Europe itself, Luxemburg was moved to revive Engels' canonical dilemma – 'either an advance to socialism or a reversion to barbarism'[8] – with

---

[7] Luxemburg, *The Junius Pamphlet: The Crisis in German Social Democracy*, in *The Rosa Luxemburg Reader*, 341.

[8] The editors of the *Luxemburg Reader* tell us that this phrase is located in Engels' 'Introduction to *The Class Struggles in France*' [1895], but it isn't. Nor is it exactly

a stark new twist: we are already in barbarism. '*This world war* means a reversion to barbarism' (321; emphasis in original): the war has exposed capitalism, here and now, 'shamed, dishonored, wading in blood and dripping with filth', as 'a roaring beast, as an orgy of anarchy, as a pestilential breath, devastating culture and humanity' (313). Socialism would appear to have been the great missed opportunity, the balance of forces between it and barbarism now irretrievably lost – 'imperialism has been victorious. Its brutal sword of murder has dashed the scales, with overbearing brutality, down into the abyss of shame and misery' (321). Without the SPD standing firm in its 'moral prestige' as a minority voice, lighting the way in the infernal dark, preserving 'the intelligent proletariat from delirium' (331), the chances for socialism that inhered in the very catastrophe itself, requiring intensive political and intellectual effort in working-class leadership, were squandered.

Of course, there are noises made in the contrary direction in *The Junius Pamphlet*; protestations of 'the hope of socialism' yet (340), that 'the workers . . . will wake up out of their drunken sleep' (341). But the emphasis is on a sober admission of defeat. Her summary statement is chilling:

> The international proletariat suffers, not from a dearth of postulates, programs, and slogans, but from a lack of deeds, of effective resistance, of the power to attack imperialism at the decisive moment, just in times of war. It has been unable to put its old slogan, war against war, into actual practice. (343)

It is something like this that Theodor Adorno meant when he wrote that the historical moment to 'realize philosophy' had been missed.[9] The SPD's defection from the one essential component of its cause 'at the decisive moment' spelled the ruin of socialism's chances in Europe for a hundred years and more.

How a prison cell in Berlin became the stifling space in which the thinker best equipped to snatch a socialist victory out of the jaws of a barbarous defeat instead bore witness to the global triumph of anarchy and mass murder, is one of the twentieth century's more emblematic ironies. By isolating her from her comrades,

---

to be found where Norman Geras tells us, in the *Anti-Dühring*, where we find the locution 'ruin or revolution'. Luxemburg, without her extensive library in prison, was obliged to access the library of her memory, where things often looked somewhat different.

[9] Theodor W. Adorno, *Negative Dialectics*, translated by E. B. Ashton (New York: Continuum, 2007), 3.

incarcerating her with a proletarian 'mass of stupidity' that she had never encountered at close quarters, forcing her 'to see and hear from a distance', the German authorities created the perfect conditions for an 'unsparing self-criticism' of the fatal direction of socialist leadership. The pessimism of the intellect has seldom produced a document as harrowing, overwhelming in its sense of doom. Not even the outbreak of the Russian Revolution could temper this grim negativity. Her 1918 prison writings on this topic, smuggled out but unpublished in what little remained of her life, acknowledged the Bolshevik coup as the 'mightiest event of the World War', precisely for its proof of the adjacency of socialism and barbarism, and gave it credit as 'the salvation of the honor of international socialism'.[10] But the revolution's dangerous alienation of the peasantry, its break-up of the country at Brest-Litovsk, its espousal of hollow nationalism, its use of terror, its suppression of democracy in the Constituent Assembly and support of dictatorship, all served as further evidence (to Luxemburg) of 'the bankruptcy of international socialism in the present world war' (309).

In her letters, she reflects repeatedly on Lenin's gamble. 'The events in Russia are of amazing grandeur and tragedy,' but 'Of course they won't be able to hold out in this Witches' Sabbath.'[11] Her sense of the overarching conditions of ruin and defeat imposed by the war was adamant. As an occasional salve, she avails herself in gaol of that oldest article of Marxist faith in the inevitability of success despite mountains of contrarian evidence, the 'dialectic of history': 'history itself always knows best what to do about things, even when the situation looks most desperate' (370); 'it is precisely when everything has the outward appearance of being terrible with absolutely no way out, just then a complete turnaround is being prepared' (371); 'I'm counting on the dialectic of history, which in the end must surely find a way out of all this confusion and come out onto a grand and open road' (459). But this, the weakest aspect of Marx's Hegelian inheritance, looks absurd in context, and has every appearance of a quasi-religious self-assurance, if not a self-delusion. Yet it is fundamental to Luxemburg's position, and even if it does not fully define the nature of her 'optimism of the will', to which we are about to turn in earnest, it does serve to underscore the imperishable quality of her hope for a transfigured world. Luxemburg's optimism

---

[10] Luxemburg, 'The Russian Revolution', in *The Luxemburg Reader*, 281, 290.
[11] Luxemburg, letters from Breslau prison to Clara Zetkin and Luise Kautsky, both 24 November 1917, *Letters*, 447, 452.

is always grounded in a thoroughgoing admission of everything her pessimism was able to lay bare. As she wrote, 'world history nowadays certainly reads like a bad book, a sensationalist novel in which glaring effects and bloody deeds pile up with gross exaggeration and in which one sees no real people but just wooden puppets in action. Unfortunately one cannot simply throw this bad book away, one has to grit one's teeth and go through it. Nevertheless – "it does move"' (459–60). It is only by 'going through' the contemporary 'abyss of shame and misery' that one can seize the rhythm of history's underlying movement. This, Luxemburg's version of Brecht's 'Don't start from the good old things but the bad new ones,'[12] gave her political reflections their uniquely unsentimental tone and tempered her faith with the acid corrective of a full and unexpurgated account of where we stand. But being obliged to 'go through the sensationalist novel' of historical fact could not, in fact, extirpate the deeper wellsprings of Luxemburg's ardent socialism in romanticism and poetry, on the one hand, and scientific naturalism, on the other. The most moving achievement of her prison letters is how she managed to bring together these obscured anchors of her political imagination in an entirely new discursive register which, as we are about to see, furnished vivid and moving Aesopian allegories of her optimism without sinking her to the level of an anodyne Pollyanna.

* * *

Rosa Luxemburg's ability to transcend the ostensibly paralysing lucidity of her intellect's pessimism hinges on a scalar tipping point. As she was fond of pointing out, there comes a moment when the staggering immensity of bad news, the sheer preponderant enormity of the ongoing disaster, makes holding on to mere *feelings* about it an unaffordable luxury. Dispensing with worry, anxiety, stress, guilt, shame, then becomes a function of acknowledging the degree to which everything has gone wrong; and this leads back to her inalienable emotional ground-note, cheerfulness. It was, again, in prison that she was able to articulate this peculiar contentment that follows from naming 'the worst', this dialectic of the disaster:

> The catastrophe has taken on such huge dimensions that ordinary ways of measuring human guilt and human pain no longer apply;

---

[12] Brecht's maxim is quoted in Walter Benjamin, *Understanding Brecht*, translated by Anna Bostock (London: Verso, 1998), 121.

the elemental devastation indeed has something calming about it precisely because of its immensity and blindness.[13]

Don't you understand that the overall disaster is much **too great** to be moaned and groaned about? I can grieve or feel bad if Mimi is sick, or if you are not well. But when the whole world is out of joint, then I merely seek to **understand** what is going on and why, and then I have done my duty, I am calm and in good spirits from then on.[14]

This sanguine equanimity – which has nothing in common with the thundering rhetoric she would let fall on those responsible for the shambles – is then explicitly related to the habitus of a natural scientist.

The more the general bankruptcy takes on gigantic dimensions and steadily persists, the more it will become obvious in an elementary way that appropriate measures must be taken against it. It is ridiculous to become indignant against humanity as a whole, one must study and observe things with the calmness of a research scientist.[15]

Here it becomes possible to ascertain a certain proclivity specific to Luxemburg's intellectual and political character: to pull away from the dangerous temptations of sentimental empathy around the individual case ('if Mimi is sick') and assume a disinterested scientific view of the whole. 'I am', she writes from Breslau, 'always buried in books, preferably of the kind that take me away from the present and from the species Homo sapiens. I'm referring to scientific works' (443). Science, with its famous 'Archimedean position', precludes what Marx called 'an extraordinarily cheap kind of sentimentality' and what Richard Wright would label the 'consolation of tears'.[16] Not having to wring one's hands left them free to play.

By setting aside the human scale – *Homo sapiens* and its lamentable condition – this outlook permits the critic to treat the totality with a calm and purposeful detachment, attentive to any signs of life in the slumbering future. Luxemburg discovered in prison that this steely and necessary resolve to remain disinterested does not

---

[13] Letter to Franz Mehring from Barnim Street Women's Prison, 31 August 1915, *Letters*, 353.

[14] Letter to Luise Kautsky from Wronke, 28 December 1916, *Letters*, 366. Emphases in original.

[15] Letter to Clara Zetkin from Breslau prison, 24 November 1917, *Letters*, 447.

[16] Karl Marx, *Capital*, vol. 1, translated by Ben Fowkes (London: Penguin, 1990), 277; Richard Wright, 'How Bigger Was Born', http://xroads.virginia.edu/~MA01/White/anthology/bigger.html.

disable the wellsprings of her socialist humanism in pity, empathy, care and love for the oppressed; rather, it displaces the sphere of influence of these *tendresses*, shifts them onto other species and genera. Luxemburg can no more vault over her prodigious love for living things than she can reconcile herself to the imbecility of her former comrades in the Reichstag, but what the scientific bracketing of 'humanity as a whole' entails is an enrichment of the animal and vegetable kingdoms as sources of wonder and rapture. The entire animate universe – including clouds that scud, stars that twinkle and wind that shakes the barley – takes the place of human beings, which the 'gigantic dimensions' of 'the overall disaster', the mass suicide of the European working class and imperial genocide have made too dangerous to admit; her heart, we feel, was literally capable of exploding with grief. And in this substitution, whose proximate cause was prison's separation of her from her kind, Luxemburg's optimism of the will was vouchsafed; indeed, it was burnished and transformed into art.

In her earliest letters from prison, in Zwickau in 1904, she holds that life is 'not inside me, not here where I am, but somewhere far off'.[17] By the time of her four-year incarceration during the war, this has ceased to be true; only life, it turns out, was not human. 'I am doing botany again here!' she writes to Kostya Zetkin upon detainment at Barnim Street in 1915; working in 'the lovely green infirmary garden', she delves deep into botanical science with a relish and freedom she is unable to give to her political work.[18] The social world being both denied her view and impossible to contemplate with equanimity, 'there still remains everything else that makes me happy: music and painting and clouds and doing botany in the spring', she writes to Luise Kautsky (366). In prison she realises the immense importance of this latter work:

> I suddenly plunged into the study of botany the way I do everything, immediately, with all my fire and passion, with my entire being, so that the world, the party, and my work faded away from me and only one passion filled me up filled me up day and night. . . . As a result I am now at home in the realm of greenery. I have conquered it – by storm – and what you take on with fire and passion becomes firmly rooted inside you.[19]

[17] Letter to Luise Kautsky from Zwickau, September 1904, *Letters*, 176.
[18] Letter to Kostya Zetkin from Barnim Street prison, 10 April 1915; letter to Sophie Liebknecht from Breslau, 2 August 1917, *Letters*, 349, 430.
[19] Letter to Hans Diefenbach from Wronke, 30 March 1917, *Letters*, 386.

That 'taking root' has consequences more than intellectual. The vegetable kingdom's colonising of Luxemburg's imagination, its vehiculation of her passion, leads us deep into her political unconscious, where the annual regeneration of plant life cannot be separated from her faith in a socialist reawakening after the holocaust of war. She writes, against her own political prognosis, 'as happened last year, a revitalization will come of its own accord, especially since spring will soon be on its way'.[20] She runs through the 'magnificent blossoming' of species at Wronke fortress, in whose garden she was free to wander every day: sycamore, poplar, acacia, chestnut, cherry, currant, privet, hazel, lilac and more, declaring, 'These bushes will bloom one after another beautifully, and I'm waiting for that without impatience, because the buds alone give me great joy.'[21] Springtime manifests itself in her prose as a confluence of scientific taxonomy and romantic moods, an interanimation of dispassionate classification and passionate Wordsworthian intensities.

Luxemburg's propensity for romantic personification runs riot with the avian life that throngs in this great blossoming.

> The great titmice are in loyal attendance in front of my window, they already know my voice exactly, and it seems that they like it when I sing. Recently I sang the Countess's aria from *Figaro*, about six of them were perched there on a bush in front of the window and listened without moving all the way to the end; it was a very funny sight to see. Then there are also two blackbirds that come at my call every day, I've never seen such tame ones.[22]

The sheer incongruity of the scourge of Bernstein cast as a Disney princess amplifies the ebullience; Red Rosa's cameos as Snow White avoid mawkishness by virtue of their determination to concede nothing to 'the catastrophe', and at all costs to spare Nature her pitiless wrath. With her birds, Luxemburg's language can suspend its furious will to dominate; indeed, they put her to school in a new speech, a new poetics. 'Only two syllables will be allowed to appear on my gravestone: "Tsvee-tsvee". That is the call made by the large blue titmouse, which I can imitate so well that they all immediately come running.'[23] This erasure of the linguistic gap between human and non-human is a leitmotif. The return of her favourite blue titmouse after the end of winter sparks a remarkable disquisition on avian language, as its

[20] Letter to Hans Diefenbach from Wronke, 5 March 1917, *Letters*, 378.
[21] Letter to Clara Zetkin from Wronke, 13 April 1917, *Letters*, 390.
[22] Letter to Louise Kautsky from Wronke, 26 January 1917, *Letters*, 368–9.
[23] Letter to Mathilde Jacob from Wronke, 7 February 1917, *Letters*, 373.

'funny little song, *tsee-tsee-bay*' of the autumn is now augmented by a reverberant trebling: 'three times in brief succession, *tsee-tsee-bay*, *tsee-tsee-bay*, *tsee-tsee-bay*'. Spinning a veritable georgic out of this rhapsody, in which she hears the bucolic work ethic of a young mother ('I've no time to spare – oh yes, it was lovely – but spring is quickly over'), Luxemburg then speculates about her incipient Dr Doolittlism:

> I myself am like King Solomon: I too understand the language of the birds, and of all animals. Not, of course, as if they were using human words, but I understand the most varied shades of meaning and of feeling conveyed by their tones. Only to the rude ear of one who is quite indifferent does the song of a bird seems always the same. If one has a love of animals, and a sympathetic understanding of them, one finds great diversity of expression, an entire 'language'.[24]

This extraordinary aural sensitivity, quickened by the visual depletion of prison existence, leads her to this simile for a duck's quack – 'like some worldly-wise pronouncement, which by being repeated regularly every night was declaring something irrevocable, something that has held true since the beginning of the world, since time immemorial, like some Coptic precept' – and this account of the cascading affective returns of a robin's 'tremulous tone of infinite sweetness':

> it sounds quite misty and affects a person like a memory lost in a dream. My heart contracts with both joy and sorrow when I hear this song, and I immediately see my life and the whole world in a new light, as though clouds had parted and a bright ray of sun had struck the earth. Today from this delicate little song, sung on the wall, everything in my heart has become so soft and tender. At once I regretted everything angry that I had ever inflicted on anyone, all harsh thoughts and feelings, and I decided once again to be kind, simply to be kind at all costs.[25]

Birds are portals to the infinite for Luxemburg, where that 'infinitely gentle/Infinitely suffering thing' resides with which she craved total union. There is a late summer afternoon at Wronke fortress made perfect by the apparition of a murmuration of swallows who 'with their sharp pointy wings snipped the blue silk of space into little bits, shot back and forth, overtaking one another with shrill cries, and disappearing into the dizzying heights. I stood with my little watering can dripping in my hand with my head tilted back and

---

[24] Letter to Sophie Liebknecht from Wronke, 23 May 1917, *Letters*, 412.
[25] Letters to Hans Diefenbach from Wronke, 29 & 23 June 1917, *Letters*, 422, 418.

felt a tremendous yearning to dive up into that damp, shimmering blueness, to bathe in it, to splash around, to let myself dissolve completely in that dew, and disappear.'[26]

Bird life's ability to 'snip the blue silk of space' is genetically related to Blake's question: 'How do you know but ev'ry Bird that cuts the airy way/Is an immense World of Delight, clos'd by your senses five?'; offering unique succour to alienated, imprisoned Man, having 'closed himself up till he sees all things thro' narrow chinks of his cavern'.[27] Luxemburg's prison romanticism is properly Blakean and participates in a rather different logic of scale and proportion from that governing her intellectual pessimism: here, it is precisely the humility, the tiny insignificance of the organic creature (wasp, ladybug, mouse, robin, titmouse, duck, swallow) that guarantees its access to the immense 'resplendence and glory' that circumvolves our struggles.[28] The underlying reason for this is a nigh Buddhist sense of the insignificance of the ego itself in relation to the obscure little things it can properly attend to only in prison, withheld from the struggle in order that it might dissolve itself in 'the process': 'on the whole I feel that I am no more important than the ladybug and I am inexpressibly happy with this sense of my insignificance'.[29] As her vision enlarged, her sense of self contracted; and 'her vision [was] never more far-reaching than when she was in a prison cell'.[30] This is a precise correlative of her sanguine relationship to 'the disaster' – in each, being calm and buoyant depends upon a surrendering of individuality to an integrated immensity its own agency cannot affect.

> The prison yard was empty and, as always, I was alone, a stranger to everything around me. From the open windows of the prison came the thumping and knocking sounds of Saturday's scrubbing and scouring, and now and then a loud reprimanding voice could be heard; meanwhile the chaffinch, way up high in the poplar tree, kept repeating its birdcall over and over, and the trunk of the poplar tree, which is still quite bare and leafless, gave off a silvery gleam in the slanted rays of the departing sun. Everything breathed of such peace, and my gaze was fixed on the softly smiling cloud formation far off there in the sky. – I stood there as though enchanted, and I thought

[26] Letter to Hans Diefenbach from Wronke, 29 June 1917, *Letters*, 425.

[27] William Blake, *The Marriage of Heaven and Hell*, edited by Michael Phillips (Oxford: Bodleian Library, 2011), 66, 73.

[28] Letter to Hans Diefenbach from Wronke, 29 June 1917, *Letters*, 429.

[29] Letter to Luise Kautsky from Wronke, 15 April 1917, *Letters*, 393.

[30] Jacqueline Rose, *Women in Dark Times* (London: Verso, 2014), 43.

to myself, and to all of you: Do you not see how beautiful the world
is? Do you not have eyes as I do and a heart like I do to rejoice in it
all? (394)

In the topsy-turvy world of the catastrophe, it is the prisoner who
must offer solace to the freewoman, the incarcerated who must teach
the liberated how to be free. In letter after letter from Wronke and
Breslau prison, Luxemburg reaches out to despairing comrades who,
taught in part by her own lucid appraisals of the present conjuncture,
can see no path forward, no cause for anything other than shattering
grief and suicidal pain. Knowing full well how deeply the fields of
Western Europe are saturated in the blood of the soldiers of socialism, how total the living hell is through which the survivors must now
travail, Luxemburg recalls us to the deepest reasons for struggling in
the first place. It is not power communism wants, not the state, the
economy, the means of production and distribution, for these are
mere means; it is, rather, the freedom to stand under the canopy of
heaven and feel inalienably at one with everything and everyone else,
because, at last, your substance is not being stolen from you. *Rien
faire, comme une bête.* What Luxemburg's letters from prison work
towards is an aesthetic of redemption offered in defiance of the catastrophe. They say: 'you and I have done everything in our power to
prevent hell on earth, but hell has arrived; millions are dying and will
continue to die to whose service we have committed our own lives.
We are not responsible, though we are accountable, and our account
is being written. Meanwhile, I have considered the birds, the bugs,
the flowers of the field. I have watched the clouds dancing in the sky,
the trees reaching up from an imponderable past into an unknowable
future. The world asks only to be seen, to be heard, to be held, that
is all it wants from us. My acute sensitivity to it proves that I am a
part of it. Imperialist war is grinding it into dust and ashes, but I will
do the only thing I can having been cast into prison for objecting to
it: I will take the world just as it asks to be taken, as the medium of
my being. For I am nothing and you are nothing. And war is nothing.
But ev'ry Bird that cuts the airy way is an immense World of Delight,
and if you want me, that is where you will find me.'

None of this contradicts the titanic achievements of Luxemburg's
intellectual labour. The astonishing analyses of *The Accumulation
of Capital*, extending Marx's *Capital*, vol. 2, into the imperialist
present and culminating in a harrowing depiction of the 'struggle
against peasant economies' around the world; the pioneering cri-
tiques of dogmatic party leadership in the name of the mass strike;

the infectious theories of spontaneity and revolution; her courageous affirmations of contradiction and 'thinking differently'; and finally, the devastating portraits of socialist party policy around the Great War – what are these but immortal testaments to the incomparable contributions made by this great Marxist to the central tradition of the communist international? It is fatuous for anyone to suggest that the Luxemburg of the letters is an 'alternative' figure, more attractive and user-friendly to a contemporary readership, from whom we can detach the meticulous economic and political theorist. Yet it is just as short-sighted, I think, to decide the 'confusion' of her letters' 'reason and passion, ideology and emotion' in favour of the former, by 'bringing out the political element' hidden under the romantic naturalism.[31] The challenge is, as Benita Parry insists, to read the *Letters* 'together with her theoretical writing'.[32] Our own more limited proposition is that *The Junius Pamphlet* is the necessary companion to any tour through the prison letters, but the underlying point is critical: each gains strength from the other, while remaining mutually irreducible. Of course, there are times when the Aesopian imaginary tilts decisively in the direction of allegory, as with the well-known episode of the water-buffalo. These captured Romanian beasts, 'accustomed to their freedom', and not yet resigned to the weight of the yoke, are pressed into service carting wagons around Breslau, where Luxemburg first sees one having difficulty clearing the threshold to the prison courtyard. Beaten and beaten, until its skin is broken and bleeding, unable to get away from the fury of his keeper, the beast assumes the expression 'of an abused child'.

> I stood before it, and the beast looked at me; tears were running down my face – they were **his** tears. No one can flinch more painfully on behalf of a beloved brother than I flinched in my helplessness over this mute suffering. How far away, how irretrievably lost were the beautiful, free, tender-green fields of Romania! How differently the sun used to shine and the wind blow there, how different was the lovely song of the birds that could be heard there, or the melodious call of the herdsman. And here – this strange, ugly city, the gloomy stall, the nauseating, stale hay, mixed with rotten straw, and the strange, frightening humans – the beating, the blood running from the fresh wound. . . . Oh, my poor buffalo, my poor, beloved brother! We both stand here so powerless and mute, and are as one in our

---

[31] Sobhanal Datta Gupta, *Marxism in Dark Times: Selected Essays for the New Century* (London: Anthem Press, 2012), 106.

[32] Benita Parry, 'Perspectives on Rosa Luxemburg 2', *new formations: a journal of culture/theory/politics* 94 (2018): 50 [49–60], muse.jhu.edu/article/707051.

pain, impotence, and yearning. – . . . And the entire marvelous pano-
rama of the war passed before our eyes. (458)

But what is most magnificent about this passage is not the 'dry
final sentence [which] acquits the letter of mawkishness', though
it is powerful indeed.[33] Rather, it is the way the 'beloved brother'
expands in its mute impotence before human violence to become
a figure of the catastrophe itself; absorbing every monstrous crime
perpetrated on a peasant economy in the name of profits; a figure of
every aboriginal inhabitant of a different sun, a different wind, torn
from his *pays natal* and cast adrift to eke its stunted living in 'the
ugly city'. What leaves the deepest impression is this simple empathic
recollection: '[H]ow different was the lovely song of the birds that
could be heard there, or the melodious call of the herdsman.' To
all the lost worlds brought under the rod by capitalism's merciless
predations, Luxemburg took her exquisite ear; in the mute depths of
a brutalised beast of burden she heard resounding the immemorial
songs of primitive communism. As, on another day, she could hear
the dancing girl of history starting up all over again, rousing herself
from the ruins of time, and proving 'that life is rich and beautiful'
because its ceaseless regeneration points always in the direction of
redemption.

---

[33] Christopher Hitchens, 'Red Rosa', *The Atlantic* (June 2011), https://www.theatlantic.
com/magazine/archive/2011/06/red-rosa/308500/.

Chapter 4

Uncle Ez Do the Polis in Different Voices: *The Pisan Cantos* as Prison Writing

There is a passage midway through Ezra Pound's seventy-fourth canto (**74.314–62**), the first of a new sequence composed during his incarceration at Pisa in 1945, that is representatively dizzying in its rotating frames of reference and associational logic.[1] Its basic proposition, however, is relatively straightforward: as opposed to the philistine 'they' who have defaced London's old Adelphi Theatre with a new Art Deco façade (in 1930, sight unseen by Pound), and who thus stand in for the circumvolving chaos of Circe's pigsty, there are readily available signs and portents, gestures and acts, rules and principles, by which we may yet learn to live a worthy life together. This canto is the first to be offered under the sign of Paradise, albeit a *paradiso* compromised and imperilled in its essence by the catastrophic course of contemporary history; its embattled defence of the necessary elements of a just renewal is therefore issued in the inevitable key of irony. Pound sits in a US Army Disciplinary Training Center, as a trainee, planning what he will say to Stalin, to Truman, to Hirohito, to negotiate a just peace, and concretising his wisdom in poetic form; while all around him fascism, the 'enormous tragedy of the dream' (74.1), collapses under the Allied campaign and the US government prefers charges of treason against him. And yet, notwithstanding the hateful deployment of a racist epithet in the second

---

[1] For reasons having to do with copyright protection of poetry, we will not quote the passage in full. Readers are referred to Ezra Pound, *The Pisan Cantos*, edited by Richard Sieburth (New York: New Directions, 2003), 12–13; or *The Cantos of Ezra Pound*, fourteenth printing (New York: New Directions, 1998), 454–5. Further line references are indicated in text in the format above: 74 [Canto number].314–62 [line numbers]. Extended passages that readers are asked to read in full are indicated in bold: **74.314–62**.

line, there is rather more here than defiance, and considerably less than repentance. Rather, what the poet seeks to achieve is something like a metamorphic poesis of the lost cause, its prosodic transposition into broken cadences, fallen metres, gemlike verbal remains, seeds of a better day to fertilise the ruins. And prison, where Pound took his eucalyptus seedpod and text of *The Unwobbling Pivot*, is the ideal situation to arrange for such a metamorphosis; as, behind the barbed wire and the guard towers, with no radio over which to bark, no library with which to commune, there is only the work of form – finally, after years of avoiding the Muse, a locked door, a notebook and a pen.

What is so striking about this passage is the specific evidence it gives that the idealised cities of Zion, Dioce (Ecbatana, with its seven concentric walls of different colours) and of the Fasa (Wagadu, thrice destroyed, thrice rebuilt, the last time indestructibly) are not distant, unattainable exemplars of the mythic past, but incarnate in the life of the DTC itself. The prison is a city of 4,000 souls, and, despite the injustice on which it is founded, now and then a just one. It is just because its inmates – most of them Black, charged with AWOL, desertion, murder, theft, rape, all the usual crimes of the city and the army – are capable of treating one another, under the punitive eye of military authority, with care, consideration, respect and sympathy. In this passage, Henry Hudson Edwards, a Black GI 'trainee' about whom we know little other than that, while imprisoned for an unspecified crime, he crafted a makeshift writing desk out of a medical supply chest for a crazy old white poet for no reward, requests that Pound tell no one of his kindness. Ecbatana and Wagadu can have had no sounder civic foundation than this simple act. '[A]nd the greatest is charity,' the poet remembers Corinthians 13:13. Faith and hope may abide, but they are redeemed (or, as per Pound, ruined) by their fruits. Only charity is perfected and accomplished in the instant as in the hereafter. The poet remarks, like Wilde before him, that charity is to be found almost exclusively among those who have nothing to give; the 'poor are wiser, more charitable, more kind, more sensitive than we are. [. . .] If I got nothing at the house of the rich, I would get something at the house of the poor. Those who have much are often greedy. Those who have little always share.'[2] And one who has nothing at all shall furnish the material conditions for one of the greater poems of the twentieth century. Is it a problem

---

[2] Oscar Wilde, *De Profundis and Other Prison Writings*, edited by Colm Tóibín (London: Penguin, 2013), 98, 102.

that Pound has had to violate the terms of the agreement in order to clinch the proposition that 'with justice [Zion] shall be redeemed' (Isaiah 1:27)? The 'no one' in 'doan you tell no one' presumably extends to us, the poem's readers, who are caught in this inevitable ethical bind where breaking a promise is the best chance of a glimpse of the good life.

In one of his notorious wartime broadcasts for Radio Rome, on 6 November 1941, Pound addressed the agonising topic of the 'war on youth – on a generation'. Like any great conflict, the war for and against fascism was such a war, leaving seventy-five million dead, twenty million of them soldiers of fighting age; this pitiless consumption of young lives, Pound reflected, struck at the very heart of Europe's and America's future. Observing that the young generation currently being sacrificed to the profit motive was itself a 'revolution . . . moving toward what the decent Reds [of the Bolshevik revolution] wanted', the poet goes on to argue that the counter-revolutionary alternative, American individualism, is not a viable social solution. The solution must involve an acceptance and advocacy of 'COHABITATION with other men. POLIS, a city, politics, right way for people to live together in a city. Greek cities very small. Aristotle bothering about a system for 5,000 citizens, etc. Five million, 130 million, bit more of a job; better regulations needed.'[3] There have been few poets as committed to the nourishing of the hungry *Zoon politikon* [ζῷον πολιτικόν] that Aristotle knew we were, always hectoring and goading, guiding and illuminating us, away from depoliticised ideas of our species, from that '"Tribeless, lawless, heartless one", whom Homer denounces', that isolated 'lover of war',[4] and towards what our speech, our cultures, our traditions vouchsafe in us – our sacred sociality, our a priori participation in the polis. It is one of the chief beauties of this part of Canto LXXIV that in their illicit compact Edwards and Pound spontaneously enact this microcosmic political participation, this understated realisation of 'the process', in a manner defined by 'filial, fraternal affection' – 'the root of humaneness/the root of the process' (74.440–1). Having nothing in common apart from imprisonment,

---

[3] Ezra Pound, broadcast for Radio Rome, 6 November 1941, in *'Ezra Pound Speaking': Radio Speeches of World War II*, edited by Leonard W. Doob (Westport, CT: Greenwood Press, 1978), https://archive.org/details/EzraPoundSpeaking-Radio SpeechesOfWorldWarIi/page/n15/mode/2up.

[4] Aristotle, *Politics*, Book I: 1253a1, 4–5. In *The Complete Works of Aristotle*, revised Oxford translation, vol. 2, edited by Jonathan Barnes, translated by B. Jowett (Princeton, NJ: Princeton University Press, 1984), 1988.

they meet in the carceral depths of 'the bottom' (74.452) to affirm what is best in us. The camp yokes together the old poet with the young GI in the mutual condemnation of a criminality that has stripped them of every worldly possession other than their hands, their speech and their 'humaneness'. In this they discover a nucleus of the state, a 'right way for people to live together in a city', 'a black delicate hand/a white's hand like a ham' (74.532–3).

Such a small gesture, however, is a far cry from that 'bit more of a job' that Europe, fallen, now requires. The germ (the euca-lypt pod) is not its fulfilment, though it may be the pattern for it. What follows springs from this misalignment of scale. It is all too easy to fall back on that bloated pentameter that sustains the poet in his egregious commitments: 'I surrender neither the empire nor the temples/plural/nor the constitution nor yet the city of Dioce'. Edwards's 'jacent benignity' has not supplanted the dreams ruined by defeat; his charity recedes before a precedent faith. Prison, walling out the greater world, keeps it simmering in the Ideal. A philistine 'tack hammer' imperilling '300 years of culture' is no match for the secure cadence of a higher masonry, aiming at 3,000: 'till the shrine be again white with marble/till the stone eyes look again seaward'. Imperial fantasies die hard, carved by prosody into friezes propae-deutic of an eroticised Eternal City. Aeneas, en route to Rome by way of the Libyan shore, recognises the deity of his mother: '"Oh, a goddess, without a doubt!" [. . .]/and her stride alone revealed her as a goddess./He knew her at once – his mother – '.[5] In Pound's mind Terracina, which Aeneas passes between Gaeta and the Tiber (and which is described by Virgil as 'Circe's land' [VII, 10]), serves as the site of Venus's birth and of a future shrine to be erected in her honour.[6] Rome will rise from its ashes, unsurrendered to the Allies, Duce still resonating in Dioce, fertilised by divine love – Botticelli's great vision transposed into the political by main force.

And in a movement that typifies the *Pisan Cantos*, this sudden magnification in scale and ardour next recedes like the backwash of a wave, leaving only the minor world, the phenomenological

[5] 'O, dea certe – [. . .]/et vera incessu patuit dea. Ille ubi matrem/adgnovit'. Virgil, *AENEIDOS LIBER PRIMVS*, ll. 328, 405–6; translation by Robert Fagles, *The Aeneid* (London: Penguin, 2006), 58, 61.

[6] Recent archaeological findings have confirmed Pound's intuition here: the great temple to Jupiter Anxur seems to have been dedicated, under Sulla, to Venus – a derivation from the cult of Feronia, and a powerful reorientation towards Rome. See 'Il Tempio di Giove Anxur a Terracina', https://web.archive.org/web/20120304035917/http://www.italiadascoprire.net/turismo-italia/177/il-tempio-di-giove-anxur-a-terracina.html.

and entomological, in stark relief against the poem's shithouse 'literariness'.[7] The little coda on the 'herbs menthe thyme and basilicum' and the injured 'new green katydid' is as serene and tender as the preceding attempt at *paradiso* had been forced and – dread word – *artificiel*. Just as it had magnified the absent social world of wars and constitutions in the poet's imagination, so prison could cancel it at a stroke with the penetrating odour of mint 'under the tent flaps' (74.120) and the sudden appearance of a young *Tettigoniidae*. The human, reduced to mere flashes and fragments by the DTC's ban on interaction, is unable to enter the prisoner's tent; but the minor world flourishes, attracts sensory attention, attains to a sort of characterology. *Chthonia gea, Mêter*, not Venus, now manifests herself in the living shrine of this heaven-sent creature and the censer-swung scents of nearby herbs. The poet is of a sudden depersonalised, shot through with Messianic chips of 'now-time' that has no reference to his or any past: 'from whom and to whom,/will never be more now than at present'. And in a perfectly self-contained movement, we have followed his epic verse from an anecdote of intimate protopoliticality, into grandiose dreams of an unrelinquished State, and finally out into the absolute, unmitigated 'now' of phenomenological immanence, where the gods still dwell. The retreat from politics is rendered inevitable by the drive to which political ideation is still submitted in *The Cantos*. The question remains whether the non-renounced fascist commitment indelibly contaminates these other, smaller, more plausible fidelities; or whether, in some as yet undetermined way, these latter might temper and qualify the larger ways in which 'COHABITATION with other men' is imagined in Pound's epic form. And what, for that matter, incarceration has to do with the answers to these questions.

* * *

It is one of the signal virtues of the *Pisan Cantos* that in them not only is nigh sixty years' experience compressed into an abbreviated *Tottel's Miscellany* of idiosyncratic lyric touchstones, but a working image is offered of the very genre to which the group itself is knowingly contributing, namely prison writing as such. For scattered

---

[7] Charles Olson had remarked that, when writing the goddess in these cantos, Pound 'goes literary'; and that the better parts of the Pisans are the mundane and empirical. See Charles Olson and Robert Creeley, *The Complete Correspondence*, vol. 1, edited by George F. Butterick (Santa Barbara: Black Sparrow Press, 1980), 92.

across its eleven *canti* are shorthand references and more extended homages to a number of important precedents for this work, written under terrible strain and in captivity while its author was detained awaiting trial for treason. Ron Bush has shown how deeply Richard Lovelace's 'To Althea, from Prison' (1642), anthologised in the camp's 'jo-house' copy of Professor Speare's *Pocket Book of Verse* (1940), managed to penetrate Pound's imaginative faculty at this time.[8] Meanwhile, Wilde's 'The Ballad of Reading Gaol', also printed in Speare's collection, makes a minor contribution to Canto LXXXI, along with reminiscences of the poet Wilfred Scawen Blunt, imprisoned for anti-British activism; while e. e. cummings' *The Enormous Room* (1922 – about his period of confinement for conscientious objection to the First World War) is gestured at obliquely through multiple memories of the poet, as is Basil Bunting, who did time for the same offence. Another feature of this suite of cantos is how it obliges the overarching structural debts to Homer, Virgil and above all Dante to assume new pertinence and piquancy, given the poet's sudden detention in a kind of inferno; the very nature of the *nekuia* and *katabasis* as structural requirements for the epic poem takes on unexpected gravity thanks to the unavoidable parallelism between imprisonment, the underworld and divine punishment. But the most remarkable and sustained act of sympathetic affinity with the tradition of prison writing comes in the form of the *Pisan Cantos'* active patterning in conformity with the style and manner of Villon's poetry, particularly his *Testament* (1461), a work to which Pound was close for a number of reasons, not least his composition of an opera based upon it some twenty-five years previously.

It has often been remarked how rich and sustained the esteem was in which Pound held the medieval French poet. Two of the most emblematic contributions to *Personae* (1909) were 'Villonauds'; in them, the characteristic Villonesque blend of personal observation and reflection with a detached (because highly formalised) style set a precedent for a significant modernist tradition of mordant, if not morbid, satire. Indeed, Villon's 'Ballade des pendus: epitaphe', written for his hanged comrades while detained and awaiting execution himself, provided a critical touchstone for Pound throughout his life – particularly while he, too, was expecting to be executed by his own government. This haunting ballad, written in the posthumous plural (choral) voice of a half-dozen hanged men swinging on

---

[8] Ronald Bush, 'Poetic Metamorphosis: Ezra Pound's *Pisan Cantos* and Prison Poetry', *Rivista di Letterature d'America* XXIX.126–7 (2009): 37–60.

the gallows, details the physical decomposition of the dead – their decayed flesh, crumbling sun-bleached bones, and, most distressingly, how *Pies, corbeaux nous ont les yeux cavés* – while yet hoping (in the refrain of each stanza) for divine absolution, that they will not sink into hell. Pound first freely translated it as 'A Villonaud: Ballad of the Gibbet' in *Personae*; then worked it into anti-war Canto XIV before, at Pisa, using it again to leaven his sudden sympathies with the Black prisoners being executed all around him (**74.95–107**). The 'infantile synthesis' of the figure of Barabbas permits the verse at this moment to conflate, around the doomed persona of the poet, two older companions of the Paris years, and two younger inmates at the DTC. The epithets associated with Thomas Wilson and Mr K (presumably Kernes) are almost Homeric, and the second of these, 'said nothing foolish', both exemplifies a key Confucian moral doctrine and extends the Hemingway aesthetic into everyday life. The sage counsel of humble accountability ('if we weren't dumb we wouldn't be here') is absorbed by the 'infantile synthesis' and refers everything back to the scene at Golgotha and the high pathos of the supreme sacrifice. Even if the point of the epic simile here is to raise Pound's suffering (like Wilde's before him) to that of Christ, the dramatic accent lies with the thieves, the '*comes miseriae*' (74.396) alongside whom he has been crucified, the reviled and the damned. Surreptitiously, the anti-militarist invective of Canto XIV uses the cover of Villon to re-enter the Pisan section as an elegy for the 'black that die in captivity' (74.242), begging for absolution. The 'six potences' of Villon's poem rhymes 'phanopoeically' with the 'ideogram of the guard roosts', melding medieval gibbets with the army gallows overhanging these avatars of Villon's 'pendus' – their 'voiceless' voice sounding through the hubbub of 'bumm drum and banners' thanks to Pound's supersensitive ear and eye for correspondences, in the minor key of insect herb and sparrow.

Later, Villon provides the adequate frame for another expression of solidarity with the Black '*comes miseriae*' whose helpless situation in the 'a.h.' of the army our poet now traces back to the Middle Passage. He embraces them as 'Comites', but the literary reference has shifted from the sympathetic comrades of the gibbet towards the ironic speaker of the 'Ballade Pour Prier Nostre Dame', whose desire for redemption hinges on his terror of the painted hell at his local church 'où damnés sont boullus', and attraction to the 'Paradis peint, où sont harpes et luths' on the same premises (**74.389–410**). The Villon provides a mock-devout scaffolding around the realisation that, with or without the 'painted paradise' of an orthodox

Christian reward, Pound and his fellow prisoners are, here and now, already in that unpainted, non-artificial hell where the souls are being burned: in the imperialist pigsty, the filthy *harum* of a great spiritual darkness, between the three-foot-high decks of a slaver, prone and bound, on a Golgotha abandoned by a faithless Father. Moreover, the mediation of this section through Villon casts a sceptical eye on Pound's own 'literary' applications to the benevolent goddess, since Villon's speaker's wily appeals to 'Notre Dame', made under duress, tip the moral scales of the ballad's refrain in syntactical favour of the final word: 'En cette foi je veuil vivre et mourir.' A vulgar chorus of the damned, evoking Dante, is quoted to give dramatic salience to the life of the *harum*, and donate a makeshift music to the terror of this permanent sacrificibility of Black lives.[9] The song 'The First Thing Ev'ry Morning (And the Last Thing Ev'ry Night)', penned by Gaby Fish during the Depression, has its puerile romanticism turned inside out by the new setting, where 'the things I say and do' will do nothing to alter the course of execution. Finally, the roll is called, and name after name confronts the reader with the luminous fact that the inhabitants of Circe's swine-sty bear the names of the founding fathers grown fat on African slavery, having raped their chattel and reaped this wretched reward.

There is, of course, something extremely distasteful about this appropriation of the history of the Atlantic slave trade and the poet's casting of his lot, metaphorically, with these descendants of that multimillion-pound economy in human flesh. A later gesture in this same direction ('in limbo no victories, there, are no victories –/that is limbo; between decks of the slaver', 77.174–5) dispenses with the dramatis personae altogether, in order to cement the association with the purgatorial DTC itself and the poet's entrapment amidships. Mutual imprisonment justifies to a certain extent Pound's intermittent sense of solidarity with his Black inmates; but casually dropped epithets such as 'little coon' and 'the big black' are more than period markers or authentic reportage. Rather, they immunise the poetic voice against the culture of the damned, just where it dissembles maximal identification. Marking the limits of Villon's habits of mocking belittlement and acerbic epithets in the contemporary discursive space, such tags drive an ontological wedge between the subject and the objects of this insider's view of 'the slaver as seen between decks'. Given this distinction, the earlier humility ('if we

[9] 'Sergeant XL thought that excess population/demanded slaughter at intervals,' Canto LXXVI, ll. 167–8.

weren't dumb, we wouldn't be here') is not-so-subtly disengaged from any sense of self-recrimination. Neither does Villon sanction any of this queasy detour through the rhetoric of race and nation; his empathy with the hanged and the damned, however qualified, springs from a genuine camaraderie based in class and culture, whereas Pound's persona claims privileges and distinctions while simultaneously banking on an opportunist and appropriative metaphor to claim (as the founding fathers did in their rhetorical war against King George) that he, too, is a slave bound to the wheel.

This is, among other things, a war of position against Roosevelt and usury, where anything goes in the effort to highlight the undeniable fact that 'America' is not one, and that its historical violations of its own principles stretch back centuries, such that the sacred 'early American names' borne by 'descendants of slaves who took the names of their masters' are being crucified alongside their greatest poet in a gruesome theatre of American bad faith.[10] The 'slaver' that symbolises America's original sin is deployed to emblematise its current dependency on a fiscal policy that, amongst other things, emboldened the Allied pirates to sack Rome and cast into prison a sexagenarian prophet, enslaving freedoms for profits. The DTC *is* a slaver seen between decks; the striking lines 'Put down the slave trade, made the desert to yield/and menaced the loan swine' (78.91–2) come as a direct corrective to the American 'root stench' (78.165) of usury and slavery, and are of course a list of Mussolini's notable achievements in Abyssinia and at home. Fascism, in these *Cantos*, is not the cause of slavery, but its cessation. To be in army prison in Pisa, 'amid the slaves learning slavery' (74.222), is to be granted exceptional insight into the American state's great wrong turn, from which vantage point Mussolini's social experiment comes to look liberatory. So the early affinity with Henry Edwards, a precious germ of charitable cohabitation, gives way to a crass and unforgivable exploitation of his ancestry in order to score points off a common enemy (America the slave-driver) in favour of something worse. It is true that his act is reprised in Canto LXXXI: 'What counts is the cultural level,/thank Benin for this table ex packing box/"doan you tell no one I made it"/from a mask as fine as any in Frankfurt/"It'll get you off'n the groun"' (81.66–70); but already the incident has become a museum piece, not a living act of friendship, the man himself an artefact on display. Memory itself has shifted ground as,

[10] Pound, *Ezra Pound and Dorothy Pound, Letters in Captivity 1945–1946*, edited by Omar Pound and Robert Spoo (New York: Oxford University Press, 1999), 177.

'amid the slaves', the poet has taken what he needed and, table at hand, rewritten its origins into some anecdote about 'cultural levels'.

Perhaps this explains why the *Pisan Cantos*' most conventional appeal to Villon's prison poetry, that poet's variation on *ubi sunt* in 'La Ballade des dames du temps jadis' – *où sont les neiges d'antan?* – steers Pound away from the environs of the DTC entirely, towards his own crowded memories of the dead and lost. 'Où sont', the poet asks of fellow traitor Pétain (79.27) in relation to Carl Goedel and Giorgio Paresce. This Villonesque device enables the sequence to build towards its moral climax – 'What thou lovest well remains' (81.134) – by spreading out a billowing canvas of 'traces carved in the mind', and catching the winds blown by Clio, Terpsichore ('The Muses are daughters of memory', 74.719) to the very place where memory lives. The dogged inclusion of Pétain, Laval, Quisling and other disgraced lackeys of the fascist cause in the sacred company of Joyce, Yeats, Eliot, Ford and cummings, comes at the expense of the Black *comes miseriae* who, though named and quoted with care, never quite attain to this elect status. Traces carved in the poem, but not, one feels, the mind, Mssrs Edwards, Kernes, Green, Wilson and company belong to a more nebulous category of temporary and enforced affiliation, alongside whom the poet learns to suffer and to appreciate passing acts of kindness, but from whom, ultimately, he is happy to extrapolate a chiaroscuro aesthetic: 'I like a certain number of shades in my landscape' (79.31). Or, at its most benevolent, the poetic gaze prefers the green on the prisoners' uniforms to their skin colour: 'and those negroes by the clothes-line are extraordinarily like the/figures del Cossa/Their green does not swear at the landscape' (78.15–17). It is true that, when the swelling climax comes, it brings with it a distant echo of Villon:

> Pull down thy vanity
> Thou art a beaten dog beneath the hail,
> A swollen magpie in a fitful sun,
> Half black half white
> Now knowst'ou wing from tail
> Pull down thy vanity
> (81.154–9)

Villon's magpie is working to clinch a larger aesthetic judgement on the piebald, not pecking the eyes out of hanged men; now it, rather than the 'pendus', is dead under the sun, and what matters about it is its Zoroastrian colour-scheme, 'Half black half white'. It has become a harlequin symbol of Vanity, alienated from 'the green world' (81.148) by this monochrome patterning, wing indistinguishable from tail: one of Circe's people. Whereas, before, Pound was able to glimpse a germ of the good life in 'a black delicate hand/a white's hand like a ham' (74.532–3), and later playfully reworks Burns into 'ye spotted lambe/that is both blacke and white/is yeven to us for the eyes' delight' (84.15–17), now the piebald is stamped with infamy, forced to make way for 'the green casque' (81.152) of paradise, or Erigena's light of all lights, 'all of a whiteness' (79.2), 'snow on the marble/snow-white/against snow white' (84.43–5). The chequerboard culminates in violence; 'The chess board too lucid/the squares are too even . . . theatre of war . . .' (78.11–12). It is true that this magpie falsity is characterised as 'niggard in charity' (81.163), and that the grotesque pun in that phrase resurrects the memory of H. H. Edwards – 'the greatest is charity' – but the man himself, like all his fellow inmates, is not, finally, 'part of thy true heritage' and has thus been 'reft from thee' (81.137–8) by the 'new suavity of eyes' that announce this climactic lyric (81.118). In the end, not the descendants of slaves, but 'The ant's a centaur in his dragon world' (81.144).

* * *

> Thus saith Kabir: 'Politically' said Rabindranath
> 'they are inactive. They think, but then there is
> climate, they think but it is warm or there are flies or
> some insects'
> (77.287–90)

Prison, while it may concentrate the political thought of a captive, and surcharge political metaphors and metamorphoses (such as, for instance, Ezra Pound as a slave, a martyr, a 'pendu'), nevertheless tends to keep the isolate 'inactive'. This enforced passivity before 'the process' is a humbling corrective to the rhetorical volcano who would advise Truman, correct Stalin and negotiate peace with Hirohito. As Olga Rudge remarked, 'I felt it the best thing they could have done for the *Cantos*, to shut you up for a while.'[11] The critics have tended to agree with her, but Tagore's disdainful account of the 'inactive' rebounds on the poetic of its rencounter here: Pound's wrestling over the polis is, identically, subject to the vagaries of the weather and the advent of an insect.

---

[11] Olga Rudge, qtd in Massimo Bacigalupo, *Ezra Pound, Italy, and the Cantos* (Liverpool: Liverpool University Press, 2020), 330.

So it is with a good deal of prison literature. As we have seen with Berkman and Luxemburg, and will continue to observe, the smaller creatures of the earth, unhindered by bars or wire, play a disproportionate role in prison experience. Rats, mice, sparrows, flies: these are the prototypical fauna of detention writing; and if Pound's 'gorilla cage' and tent flaps permitted a more various bestiary, it was because of the open-aired nature of the facility itself, the Pisan setting and the summer-to-winter period of his incarceration. In the passage treating Edwards, Venus and the katydid, we learned that these creatures tend to emerge in the poem as a sort of convenient alibi, a short-circuiting of the impossible ideological contradictions the verse wants to navigate in periplum: the quest for good government, and the squalid defence of an ignoble lost cause. The katydid conveniently shunts the poem in the direction of the aesthetic, leaving in suspension its larger political ambitions. As David Trotter has observed, the 'ant's forefoot' (83.145) of the Pisans was deployed to save the larger *Cantos* 'at once from too much Fascism and from too little poetry'.[12] Natives of the precious 'green world', bugs are where the poetry tends to gather in conspicuous displays of virtuosity, as witness:

> nor is it for nothing that the chrysalids mate in the air
> > color di luce
> green splendour and as the sun thru pale fingers (74.264)

In the first line here, two grand primus paeons (tetrasyllables) modulate at 'chrysalids' into two galloping dactyls, punctuated by a single stress on 'air'. The short Italian line trills its iambs gracefully; while the third line, reaching far out beyond any metre, is stretched across two framing spondees, Pound's quintessential foot. Poetic virtuosity is matched to these apparitions of the green world, as chrysalids mate to reaffirm what the *maestri di color* have always known: that the aesthetic is grounded in natural forms and eternal renewals. The verse is obliged to return to basics, rounding on its own fundamental resources, its feet, to stabilise the legitimacy of its vision. The ant's forefoot, housed in a remarkable description of Brother Wasp's labours, is at (**83.127–50**).

The initial long verse paragraph in *vers libre*, chatty, almost colloquial, gravitates towards a closing approximation of tetrameter and trimeter, as the heart of the experience is then committed to two

---

[12] David Trotter, 'Saved by the Ant's Fore-Foot', *London Review of Books* 27.13 (7 July 2005).

shorter stanzas, one in unrhymed quatrain, the next, more exquisite still, in blank tercet. Metrically, something is afoot. The line 'mint springs up again' opens with a molussus, segueing to a run of iambs over the next line and into the third, enlivened by an anapest, while the fourth line shifts to what will be the critical metric of this episode: the double iamb. This foot – already familiar from similar 'green' moments in *The Cantos* – carries the day, dominating the tercet and stamping its authority on the entire lyric passage. The next verse paragraph, longer than my quotation, returns to *vers libre* liberties, as it traces the infant wasp's journey into the underworld, its *nekuia*, to reaffirm the principle that aesthetic form is latent in phenomena, and that the gods abide with us. This proposition would be impossible to sustain without the detour through 'poetry' as such, and particularly the poem's ability to alight on certain strong feet – spondees, double iambs – where epic and lyric are profoundly intermingled. The strong, double-stressed feet work to establish the underlying matrix of regenerative life in lyric episodes that aspire to epic grandeur, at the risk of coming off 'mock-epic'.

What Rosa Luxemburg called the 'insignificance' of a ladybug in her prison letters was the guarantee of her own nascent sense of insignificance; but it is otherwise for Pound. For his poem, the 'insignificant' animal is imbued with significance by its participation in 'the process', the movement of things towards their perfection. Critically, that includes politics. The *katabasis* of the infant wasp, 'to carry our news . . ./to them that dwell under the earth' (83.151–2), rehearses that of the *Cantos*' epic hero, whose most urgent task is to 'have speech with Tiresias, Thebae' (83.155) and so recapture the art of significant life, the good polis. To date, nothing has worked:

> in short/the descent
> has not been of advantage either
>   to the Senate or to 'society'
>   or to the people
>   The States have passed thru a
>   dam'd supercilious era
> (83.228–33)

In order for 'the descent' to bear fruit in social and moral rebirth, it requires mythic overtones and grace notes. These the smaller creatures supply. There are rules about their performance: 'Be welcome, O cricket my grillo, but you must not/sing after taps' (78.107–8). In the case of the camp birdlife, this music is both literal and figural, played out over arcane numerological distributions on the camp's electric wires across Canto LXXIX. The notation comes thick and fast: '4 birds on 3 wires, one bird on one' (79.66), '5 of 'em now on 2;/on 3; 7 on 4/thus what's his name/and the change in writing the song books/5 on 3' (79.74–8), '2 on 2/what's the name of that bastard? D'Arezzo, Gui d'Arezzo/notation/3 on 3/chiacchierona the yellow bird' (79.104–8), 'with 6 on 3, swallow-tails' (79.115) – before attaining its climax in Canto LXXXII:

> Be glad poor beaste, love follows after thee
> Till the cricket hops
>   but does not chirrp in the drill field
>   8ᵗʰ day of September
>   f f
>
>   d
>
>   g
>   write the birds in their treble scale
>
> Terreus!   Terreus!
> (82.73–81)

Swallow or nightingale? On this mystic treble scale, such differences dissolve. Another pastiche of Burns brings together cricket rasp, birdsong and the 'unsung melodies', sweeter still, of the music Pound has seen forming and unforming above him, opening up a direct channel to the gods and their metamorphoses. This transcription, and the earlier one in Canto LXXV (Jannequin's 'Le Chant des Oiseaux'), rhyme in ways that defy easy listening.

Lovelace is an irresistible reference here, and Pound is good enough to make good on the connection. Ronald Bush has linked Pound's recourse to Lovelace's 'To Althea, From Prison' to an ethic of resistance to civil tyranny, and to reaffirming an unrelinquished Cause.[13] But it is the birds that seem to matter most. All but one of the extant manuscript copies read (along with Speare's anthology):

> WHEN Love with unconfinèd wings
>   Hovers within my gates;
> And my divine Althea brings
>   To whisper at the grates;
> When I lie tangled in her hair
>   And fettered to her eye,
> The birds that wanton in the air
>   Know no such liberty.

---

[13] Bush, 'Poetic Metamorphosis', 48.

But the original printing alters 'birds' in the seventh line to 'Gods', which 'must be accepted as the correct reading as that which was finally approved by the poet'.[14] It is this very interchangeability between gods and birds that admits them so conspicuously into the inner workings of the *Pisan Cantos*. Tracking the origins of poetry back to the ritual uses of song, and thence to birdsong and Natura's generative murmuring, Pound allies his prison poem with a principle before which 'Stone walls do not a prison make/Nor iron bars a cage.' If there be 'at my grates no Althea' (81.96), yet there are birds, gods, whose 'unconfinèd wings' spring his fettered spirit from the confines of the DTC into some version of paradise. 'When the equities are gathered together/as birds alighting/it springeth up vital' (83.98–100).

> if calm be after tempest
> that the ants seem to wobble
> as the morning sun catches their shadows (80.677–9)

> as the young lizard extends his leopard spots
> along the grass-blade seeking the green midge half an ant-size
> (80.768–9)

> And now the ants seem to stagger
> as the dawn sun has trapped their shadows (83.87–8)

Ants are paradigmatically social creatures, as are wasps and bees: the polis lurks in these insects as it does in the camp population of the DTC, regulated by similarly rigid codes and rituals. What the *Pisan Cantos* achieved for Pound, under the shadow of the gallows, was to galvanise and somewhat reorient his political imaginary, away from the fascism that had captivated it for a decade and towards a more satisfactory image of 'COHABITATION with other men. POLIS, a city, politics, right way for people to live together in a city.' Not that this latter had yet displaced or defused the former, but its lineaments, hatched in the forced cohabitation of his carceral compound and nurtured under the aegis of brother wasp and comrade sparrow, were now clearer.

---

[14] *The Poems of Richard Lovelace*, edited by C. H. Wilkinson (Oxford: Oxford University Press, at the Clarendon Press, 1930), 284.

Chapter 5

Seeing the Gorgon: Primo Levi's
If This Is a Man

To sink is the easiest of matters; it is enough to carry out all the orders one receives, to eat only the ration, to observe the discipline of the work and the camp. Experience showed that only exceptionally could one survive more than three months in this way. All the musselmans who finished in the gas chambers have the same story, or more exactly, have no story; they followed the slope down to the bottom, like streams that run down to the sea. On their entry into the camp, through basic incapacity, or by misfortune, or through some banal incident, they are overcome before they can adapt themselves; they are beaten by time, they do not begin to learn German, to disentangle the infernal knot of laws and prohibitions until their body is already in decay, and nothing can save them from selections or from death by exhaustion. Their life is short, but their number is endless; they, the *Muselmänner*, the drowned, form the backbone of the camp, an anonymous mass, continually renewed and always identical, of non-men who march and labour in silence, the divine spark dead within them, already too empty to really suffer. One hesitates to call them living: one hesitates to call their death death, in the face of which they have no fear, as they are too tired to understand.

They crowd my memory with their faceless presences, and if I could enclose all the evil of our time in one image, I would choose this image which is familiar to me: an emaciated man, with head dropped and shoulders curved, on whose face and in whose eyes not a trace of a thought is to be seen.[1]

Primo Levi's prose, characteristically so spare and dry, sometimes hits upon themes and materials over which it is obliged to pause and

[1] Primo Levi, *If This Is A Man/The Truce*, translated by Stuart Woolf (London: Abacus, 2013), 101.

pass judgement. Judgement is not generally his *metier*; this he prefers, on balance, to leave to his reader.[2] And so, his sentences tend to move ahead with the crisp and spartan dutifulness of evidentiary reportage, over which there periodically arises a broader canopy of dull irony and sour humour. From time to time, however, approaching the greatest outrages, room must be made for serious reflections and protracted asides, as the survivor's numbed chronicle of day-to-day incidents collapses into the enormity of the situation. It is, in almost every case, a question of the relationship between ground and figure. What occupies the foreground of this text are mute but legible signs of the banal, rendered significant by their power to carry the narrator through the day: a bowl, a spoon, a shoe, a crust, a needle, a piece of string. With these items, a semblance of culture can be preserved against the general ruin, an economy can prosper, a futurity can be hallucinated. But all of it is a survivor's fiction told against the backdrop of general annihilation; and, as a dream rapidly evaporates in morning light, this fiction of luminous figures and functions must fatally dissolve into the dark ground against which it distinguishes itself.

It is at these moments that the chronicle forces itself to attend to what should never have had to be written, and the prose develops new densities and complications. Here, the matter at hand is, if we can put it this way, the ground of the human itself in the general prison population of 'non-men', that unspeakable because unspeaking 'anonymous mass' of 'faceless presences', 'endless' in number and enclosed in a silence so total, so absolute, as to have blotted out, 'drowned', the 'divine spark' of *zoon politikon* itself. Humanity made silent, emptied of its innermost capacity for speech, reason and sociality, is humanity unmade, unfounded. To look this in the face is to experience the last wreckage of one's own kind, and to find that ruin in oneself, a lurking abyss, an emptiness against which all presence is called radically into doubt. Confronted with this, the great truth of the Lager, the narrator has unexpected recourse to what can only be described as literature: figures (metaphor, symbol, paradox, hyperbole, synecdoche) and obvious intertextual resonance (Dante's *Inferno* above all, as we shall see).

And this, in *If This Is a Man*, is exceptional because *If This Is a Man* does not want to be mistaken for literature. It is crucial that it

---

[2] 'I thought that my word would be more credible and useful the more objective it appeared and the less impassioned it sounded; only in that way does the witness in court fulfil his function, which is to prepare the ground for the judge. It is you who are the judges.' Levi, *If This Is A Man/The Truce*, Postscript, 422.

not be mistaken for literature, that its author not be mistaken for a writer, because those classifications would amount to a category error with serious ethical and epistemological consequences.[3] 'I had one precise idea in mind, and it was certainly not to write a work of literature. It was rather to bear witness, and a witness is all the more credible the less he exaggerates.'[4] 'I prefer the role of witness to that of judge,' Levi remarked (435), 'I have limited myself strictly to reporting facts of which I had direct experience.' The role of witness seems to have been sufficient for him, uncomfortable as he was with the role of 'writer': 'if I had not lived the Auschwitz experience, I probably would never have written anything. I would not have had the motivation, the incentive, to write' (444–5). Agamben is adamant on this point: 'Levi does not consider himself a writer; he becomes a writer so that he can bear witness. In a sense he never became a writer. In 1963, after publishing two novels and many short stories, he responds unhesitatingly to the question of whether he considers himself a writer or a chemist: "A chemist of course let there be no mistake".'[5] Levi remarks of his writing that 'problems of style seemed ridiculous to me' (444). Literature is not just secondary to the ethical imperative of bearing witness; it is a positive impediment.[6] One of the key episodes, as we shall see, concerns the annihilation of literature by the camp, and if Adorno's infamous quip about poetry after Auschwitz being barbarous has any meaning, it is this: the *Muselmänner* have no literature, their vacant gaze is where it went to die.

Yet, at the very moment when Levi's text turns to confront this unholy place where literature died, to bear witness to it with the plain-spoken reportage of the factory chemist, there again literature re-emerges, as if in guilty admission that *what cannot be written* can

[3] 'My model was that of the weekly reports, a normal practice in factories: they must be concise, precise and written in a language accessible to all levels of the firm's hierarchy,' Levi qtd in Translator's Afterword to *If This Is a Man*, in *The Complete Works of Primo Levi, Vol. I*, edited by Ann Goldstein (New York: Liveright, 2015), 199.

[4] Primo Levi, interviewed in Marco Belpoliti and Robert Gordon, eds, *The Voice of Memory: Primo Levi – Interviews, 1961–1987*, translated by Robert Gordon (New York: New Press, 2001), 250.

[5] Giorgio Agamben, *Remnants of Auschwitz: Homo Sacer III*, translated by Daniel Heller-Roazen (New York: Zone Books, 1999), 16.

[6] 'This has led to an underestimation of the literary quality of Levi's first work, since he insisted through most of his life that its episodes were merely written versions of the oral testimonies that had preceded them.' Lawrence Langer, 'The Survivor as Author: Primo Levi's Literary Vision of Auschwitz', in Risa Sodi and Millicent Marcus, eds, *New Reflections on Primo Levi: Before and After Auschwitz* (London & New York: Palgrave, 2011), 134 [133–47].

only be written as literature. That which demands the highest degree of objectivity and honesty, the most unflinching eye and utmost sincerity, has already, in its very existence, invalidated the pose of sincerity itself, exploded the forensic dream of objectivity; and in this impossible situation, only literature will answer. And answer, let it be said, in the negative. There is a 'slope' to 'the bottom' and it is all too easy to follow its decline 'like streams that run down to the sea', pulled by gravity and inevitability into the zero-degree. The simile itself seems reassuring in its naturalism, but the referent deforms it from within: the Lager is the sea into which we sink out of ourselves, from form into formlessness. Another image presents the camp as an 'infernal knot of laws and prohibitions', and our inability to 'disentangle' it is a remand to the sea-level of being. But it is the next sentence that shoulders the burden of this paragraph, and it is fretted with incomposable figures: 'Their life is short, but their number is endless; they, the *Muselmänner*, the drowned, form the backbone of the camp, an anonymous mass, continually renewed and always identical, of non-men who march and labour in silence, the divine spark dead within them, already too empty to really suffer.' The endlessness of number is the first figure assigned to this group persona, and it establishes a hazy ground of infinite iterability, swallowing up every individual in its numerical sublime. Next, a mixed metaphor, as if to underline the instability and lack of focus pertaining to this persona: drowned, but also a backbone. But this opens up the syntax of apposition, as phrase after phrase hazards a new effort to nominate what is incapable of nomination. It is a question of style, of course, keeping the pulse of the period alive despite the inadequacy of each appositive modifier to clinch the matter; their flurried sequence signalling a crisis of description in its very excess. And amidst all this, there is that ungainly, vulgar noun, italicised and Germanised by Stuart Woolf, but left in standard Italian by Levi, *musulmano*, in order to establish the bland continuity of it with the narrative voice itself.

If we can continue to speak of the performativity of literary figuration, then Primo Levi's text seems perversely committed to the thankless task of exposing that performativity to an immitigable failure. Tropes swarm to the void in language opened up by the *musulmano* – its non-representativity – and there perform their incapacity to do more than flail and perish in the vicinity of the zero-degree. Raised gamely into the fittest synecdoche for 'all the evil of our time', the Musselman seems to impair the very category of synecdoche itself, making a mockery of the movement from particular to general, from part to whole. Indeed, in the closing image, that disturbing noun dissolves into the general anonymity of an indefinite article: 'an emaciated man, with head dropped and shoulders curved, on whose face and in whose eyes not a trace of a thought is to be seen'. The rhetorical logic of the passage requires us to identify this image with the Musselman, but it is now stripped of figuration; restored to the indicative, the descriptive language has reneged from literature, but only manages to secure its powerful affective sting on the basis of the recently deployed literary language that it negates.

'Not a trace of thought is to be seen' in the eyes of this Beckettian persona; and with this clue we can begin to trace a genealogy of the figure, from Dante's damned through Berkman's insane to Heidegger and the category of 'das Man' (the '*they*') – that grey, anonymous horde of others against which the signal projects of Dasein flare out in salience, if they are not absorbed in advance. 'Everyone is the other, and no one is himself. The "*they*" [. . .] is the "*nobody*" to whom every Dasein has already surrendered itself in Being-among-one-another.'[7] Where the properly human, the living, deciding Man is not, there *they* are: the blank, the generic, the serial, the witless and exhausted. The '*they*' presents, most importantly, as a zoological substance into which the genuine individual is constantly threatening to be resolved by the technosocial subsumptions of institutional existence. For the writer, it is a question of characterology as much as anything else: how to present what cannot be presented, what does not allow of a subject position or individual will? Nameless, generic and deprived in advance of any distinguishing characteristic or trait, such personae resist being drawn into definition, and so baffle the very coordinates of literary writing; which is why Dante's damned are all named, equipped with sins and characters, and allowed to speak. Far harder to tarry with the damned in their blank and nameless identity with one another:

> engulfed and swept along without rest by the innumerable crowd of those similar to them, they suffer and drag themselves along in an opaque intimate solitude, and in solitude they die or disappear, without leaving a trace in anyone's memory.[8]

Because they all 'have the same story, or more exactly have no story', to inscribe them at all is to threaten to surrender to statistical

---

[7] Martin Heidegger, *Being and Time*, I.4.27, 129, translated by John Macquarie and Edward Robinson (Oxford: Basil Blackwell, 1962), 165–6.
[8] Levi, *If This Is a Man*, 99.

reportage; just like statistics (they all have numbers tattooed on their forearms), they leave no trace in the memory other than through the force of their sheer numeric enormity. They are the 'six million', of course, and if the pulverising force of Levi's account is that *they have no story*, the challenge is simply what, as a writer, to do with them.

Even in Levi's slim volume, it is the narrator and his named allies – Alberto, Schlome, Steinlauf, Jean the Pikolo – who attract most attention, because they *do* things, have *purpose*, share and commiserate, and in their own ways strive to resist the descent to the 'bottom'. But here, too, Levi is careful to interpolate a cautionary tale about the named character in this inauspicious place: Kraus, the honest, clumsy boy who cannot adapt readily enough to circumstance and rapidly becomes the generic 'Null Achtzehn':

> everyone was aware that only a man is worthy of a name, and that Null Achtzehn is no longer a man. I think that even he has forgotten his name, certainly he acts as if this was so. When he speaks, when he looks around, he gives the impression of being empty inside, nothing more than an involucre, like the slough of certain insects which one finds on the banks of swamps, held by a thread to the stones and shaken by the wind. (46–7)

Epic simile comes to the service of this effort to capture what it is, precisely, that tells a named human being from a numbered Musselman; which turns out to be, again, a figure of emptiness: insect husks rattling in the wind. In this book, the named – even if (like Alberto) they eventually perish – are the *survivors*; they can be written, fleshed out, given acts to perform, in a plausible textual space. What they survive is their own anonymisation, their drift into numeral indifference; the book vouchsafes them a foothold in Being, by virtue of their commitment to an *ethos*. But the book is, finally, not written for them; it does not stand testimony to their survival. Rather it stands precisely for what cannot be written, for what cannot survive: for the anonymous multitude of the *musulmano*.

This is the true challenge of Levi's book, that its deepest commitment is not to those who stood fast by their names and, through chance and determination, never truly reached bottom, but to those who did. Its presentation consists in admitting this impossibility of giving a 'local habitation and a name' to what has lost them, and yet persevering with the moral responsibility of assuming their place:

> we, the survivors, are not the true witnesses. [...] We survivors are an anomalous and negligible minority. We are the ones who,

because of our transgressions, ability, or luck, did not touch bottom. The ones who did, who saw the Gorgon, did not come back to tell, or they came back mute. But it is they, the 'Muselmänner', the drowned, the witness to everything – they are the ones whose testimony would have a comprehensive meaning. They are the rule, we are the exception. [. . .] Even if they had possessed pen and paper, the drowned could not have borne witness, because their death had already begun before the body perished. [. . .] We speak in their stead, by proxy.[9]

In Auschwitz, any lingering pretence of the reformatory, penitentiary qualities of the prison is abandoned. The Lager is not a place for the redemption of wayward souls or the improvement of their work ethic. Rather, the point of the labour camp is emblazoned explicitly over the entrance: *Arbeit Macht Frei*. Work will free you, quite so; but from what? Well, the answer is now clear: from humanity. In Auschwitz the prison is concentrated into a space where the latent promise of all prisons is finally made explicit: here, if all goes according to plan, you will cease to be a human being thanks to the work you will do for the State; you will 'die before your body does' and then you will be gassed and cremated en masse. It is a form of freedom, to be sure. Freedom from scruples, from morals, from stories, from names, from individual features, from thought and introspection, and quickly enough from the exhaustion of life itself. Work, that of which your body is capable without the involvement of your preference, will liberate you from these oppressive shibboleths of the human, and so of humanism and of life. The camp is a site of exemplary anti-humanism, and all of the *Häftlinge* are potential exemplars. And this is because the camp is explicitly designed to *make* this freedom out of labour and prison discipline: 'To sink is the easiest of matters; it is enough to carry out all the orders one receives, to eat only the ration, to observe the discipline of the work and the camp.' Behaving as an exemplary subject of the Lager is submitting to the Inhuman and becoming it.

In this way, the Lager is not an exception or a limit-case of the prison as a modern disciplinary institution, but simply its ideal incarnation. Doubtless this will be misunderstood, but I mean it quite literally when I say that this explicit function of Auschwitz – to free prisoners from their humanity, to drown their 'divine spark' in a sea

---

[9] Levi, *The Drowned and the Saved*, translated by Michael F. Moore, in *The Complete Works of Primo Levi, Vol. III*, edited by Ann Goldstein (New York: Liveright, 2015), 2468–9.

of meaningless toil, to render them undead – is a latent function of the prison as such and has always been so recognised by those who have committed their prison experience to writing. What is distinct about Levi's work is his drawing of the lesson out from the obscure background of every prison text, and his explicit formulation of the Musselman as the purest product of a global industry in the business of making docile bodies out of recalcitrant social subjects, through an inflexible disciplinary and labour regime. (It goes without saying that neither Levi nor any writer can give first-hand evidence of the gas chambers themselves; it is as a prison system that he arraigns Auschwitz.) It is the exquisite ethical torsion of every act of prison writing that 'the ones whose deposition would have a general significance' are not the ones wielding the pens; and yet it is only those wielding the pens who make that horizon of 'general significance' visible in the first place. 'Literature' is the working solution to this problem of how to speak, by proxy, for the mute and the drowned, of how to assume responsibility for their Gorgon-stricken, unspeakable witness; but it is a solution that must fail, because tropes and intertextuality, adducing nothing but a generalised *différance*, steer the particular out into the general, and surrender the singular to the resonance of the iterative. And yet, it is only there, on the open seas of literary allusiveness, that one can now and then make out the dismal sites of 'shipwreck driven by tempestuous wind./No fertile isle, no spar on which to cling . . ./But oh, my heart, listen to the sailors sing!'[10]

* * *

We will want to return to these sailors and their doomed songs shortly, but not before a detour through the specifically proletarian qualities of Levi's text. For it is in relation to *Arbeit* as such that these *Häftlinge* are disposed as 'standing reserve'. 'This camp is a work-camp, in German one says *Arbeitslager*; all the prisoners (there are about ten thousand) work in a factory which produces a type of rubber called Buna, so that the camp itself is called Buna' (26–7). Note that in this grammatical construction it is the *factory* that produces the rubber; the factory that was built and run by IG Farben and its

---

[10] '. . . qu'un vent penche sur les naufrages/Perdus, sans mats, sans mats, ni fertile îlots . . ./Mais, ô mon coeur, entends le chant des matelots!' Stéphane Mallarmé, 'Sea Breeze/Brise Marine', *Collected Poems*, translated by Henry Weinfield (Berkeley: University of California Press, 1994), 21.

auxiliary companies, just as the camp itself, Auschwitz III, was built and paid for by the same corporate entity to house its slave labour prior to eventual extermination. If the factory is the responsible productive agent of nitrile butadiene rubber (for use in automotive transmission belts, hoses, O-rings, seals and other essential applications during wartime), then that is because Buna (Auschwitz III) does not supply productive labour as such. Rather, it supplies an endless quantity of unskilled labour power, which the factory somehow manages to consume without any production whatsoever. The camps, as 'bottomless pools of ever-replenished slave labor', existed above all to *be* such pools, to arrest the damned in a holding pattern of 'standing-reserve' prior to the inevitable immolations.[11]

On the one hand, this is regarded as a positive benefit by the narrator, who begins with the observation that he should have nothing to narrate, and not exist to narrate at all, but for the regime's alarms over a 'scarcity of labour':

> It was my good fortune to be deported to Auschwitz only in 1944, that is, after the German Government had decided, owing to the growing scarcity of labour, to lengthen the average lifespan of the prisoners destined for elimination; it conceded noticeable improvements in the camp routine and temporarily suspended killings at the whim of individuals.

At the critical moment when, confronting the suicidal economic illogicality of its extermination campaign, the Reich decided to 'suspend killings', it thereby privileged labour power over death, and appeared engaged in a notorious episode of what Marx called the quest for 'absolute surplus-value'. As distinct from 'relative surplus-value', which concerns intensification, acceleration and technological fixes to productivity, absolute surplus-value means simply extending the working day to its natural limits.[12] In Buna, as in any slave camp, due to prevailing security concerns those limits are fixed by the rising and setting of the sun, for the entirety of which period, in all seasons, every able body is put to work beyond the bearable limits of organic elasticity.

But doing what? Well, anything but productive labour. The desultory scenes of work that Levi chooses to depict are notable above all

---

[11] Levi, *Drowned and the Saved*, 2413. On 'standing-reserve', see Martin Heidegger, 'The Question Concerning Technology', in *The Question Concerning Technology and Other Essays*, translated by William Lovitt (New York: Garland, 1977), ff. 16–20.

[12] See Karl Marx, *Capital*, vol. 1, translated by Ben Fowkes (London: Penguin, 1990), 280–667.

for their struggles with inertia and against collapse. As he put it later, the labour lessons of Buna were simple: 'how to hold tools, move your arms and torso correctly, restrain your exertions and withstand pain, and know how to stop at the brink of exhaustion, even if that meant being slapped and kicked'.[13] In an open yard, massive, bulky iron levers are supplied to the *Häftlinge*; a cast-iron cylinder weighing several tonnes must be unloaded. Sleepers will have to be laid to allow the trucking of the cylinder to its destination in the plant.

> Now the cylinder lies on the ground and Meister Nogalla says: '*Bohlen holen.*'
> Our hearts sink. It means 'carry the sleepers' in order to build the path in the soft mud on which the cylinder will be pushed by lever into the factory. But the wooden sleepers are mortized in the ground and weigh about 175 pounds; they are more or less at the limits of our strength. The more robust of us, working in pairs, are able to carry sleepers for a few hours; for me it is a torture, the load maims my shoulder-bone. After the first journey I am deaf and almost blind from the effort, and I would stoop to any baseness to avoid the second journey. (74)

The point of such work is not to achieve any real productive goal. It is purely to extort from the (starved, ruined) body its absolute physical maximum of effort; to convoke, in the name of capital and state, a scenography of the purest exploitation among 'the almost costless workforce provided by the camps'.[14] Levi is clear about this: the point is never what the prisoners do at work, but *how* they do it; namely, at the threshold of what is bodily tolerable. The reduction to labour power in its purest state is a kind of out-of-body experience:

> When we reach the cylinder we unload the sleeper on the ground and I remain stiff, with empty eyes, open mouth and hanging arms, sunk in the ephemeral and negative ecstasy of the cessation of pain. In a twilight of exhaustion I wait for the push which will force me to begin work again, and I try to take advantage of every second of waiting to recuperate some energy. (75)

In this cruel theatre of energetics, the individual worker experiences his depletion of vital force as a component part of a larger draining, a catatonic subsidence into 'our anonymous and concord tiredness and hunger' (77). The extraction of absolute surplus-value operates

[13] Levi, *Drowned and the Saved*, 2508.
[14] Levi, *Drowned and the Saved*, 2415.

at this corporal limit for the entirety of the working day; only the value in question is never the value of a given commodity. It is, rather, the value of a purely political propaganda – that the Jew, confined to his 'twilight of exhaustion', is simply *available*, 'revealed as standing-reserve',[15] disclosed as a mere quantum of energy for the state's productive forces, without a shadow of moral consequence, in the vanishing instant before his death.

To be sure, slaves are variable capital of a sort: '[The] German chemical trust . . . paid four to eight marks a day as salary for our work. Paid, but not to us: just as you don't pay a horse or an ox, so this money was handed to our masters, that is, to the SS ruling the camp.'[16] But the function of this exchange is not to accumulate capital, but to make a spectacle of bestialisation, for guards and inmates alike.

> He has not even the rudimentary astuteness of a draught-horse, which stops pulling a little before it reaches exhaustion: he pulls or carries or pushes as long as his strength allows him, then he gives way at once, without a word of warning, without lifting his sad, opaque eyes from the ground. He made me think of the sledge-dogs in London's books, who slave until the last breath and die on the track.[17]

It is precisely this *spectacularisation of the limit* that underwrites the significant investment made by IG Farben and other corporations in this otherwise supremely unproductive workforce. Private capital pays exorbitantly for the fixed productive forces (factory and environs), the maintenance of the slave army (Buna itself) and the right to exploit it (hired from the State), not for the valorisation of rubber-based commodities, but to delineate the limit at which a worker becomes a corpse.

It is for these reasons that, when Levi turns to describe the workplace as any proletarian writer must, he does so as a Gothic travesty of Marx's chapter on the productive forces:

> Buna is desperately and essentially opaque and grey. This huge entanglement of iron, concrete, mud and smoke is the negation of beauty. Its roads and buildings are named like us, by numbers or letters, not by weird and sinister names. Within its bounds not a blade of grass

---

[15] Heidegger, 'Question Concerning Technology', 18.

[16] Levi, quoted in Judith Woolf, 'From *If This Is a Man* to *The Drowned and the Saved*', in *The Cambridge Companion to Primo Levi*, edited by Robert S. C. Gordon (Cambridge: Cambridge University Press, 2007), 36.

[17] Levi, *If This Is A Man*, 43. Levi maintained a lifelong interest in Jack London's dogs. See his short, late essay, 'Buck of the Wolves', in *Complete Works of Primo Levi*, Vol. III, 2748–51.

grows, and the soil is impregnated with the poisonous saps of coal and petroleum, and the only things alive are machines and slaves – and the former are more alive than the latter. (80–1)

A rustbelt ruin *à l'avance*, a monument to its own moral oblivion, Buna presents as the sepulchre of industrial society and the negation of natural productivity. *Ex nihilo nihil fit.* It is the Beckettian place par excellence, where 'nothing happens and nothing continues to happen' (23). Small wonder, then, that 'the Buna factory, on which the Germans were busy for four years and for which countless of us suffered and died, never produced a pound of synthetic rubber' (81). A factory only of death, its workforce was deployed to convince a dying regime of the legitimacy of its cause – by participating, at gunpoint, in the associated labour of its own mutual annihilation. Any 'race' capable of working itself to death for nothing at all, must never have been worth the business of keeping alive.

* * *

I have said that, overall, Levi prefers in his first book not to judge, but only to present. The evidence he calls upon from his memory is, in its unaccommodated submission, sufficient to prompt learned processes of analysis and evaluation that make commentary redundant. And I have said that *If This Is a Man* is at some pains to avoid, in its style and form, any misidentification as literature. These two negative ambitions – not to judge, and not to 'literarise' – are aspects of the same basic urge to bear witness: to deliver the unadorned, unadjudicated truth. And yet, as David Rothman writes, 'At the core of his book, at the place where he claims to judge all men, *Levi calls on us to read Dante.*'[18] That is to say, it is not only that Levi should after all reveal his place on the bench, sitting in judgement of the entire apparatus of state power and human complicity that spawned Auschwitz and all the other camps, the war and the fifty million dead, but that he should do so precisely by the quintessential literary gesture of affiliating his text to the peerless Italian imaginative masterpiece of moral judgement. Forensics and affidavits give way, ultimately, to a deeper need to stand in the thick of a written tradition and survey the ruins of the twentieth century from the vantage of the fourteenth – because there is simply no extant court, no constituted

---

[18] David J. Rothman, 'Primo Levi, Dante, and the Meaning of Reading', *Sewanee Review* 124.3 (Summer 2016), 504 [498–505]. Emphasis in original.

civil authority, capable of trying this evidence. Its process belongs, in an ontological sense, not to criminology but to literature.

The passage Rothman is referring to is a curious one at the end of the tenth chapter on the chemical examination that finally saves Levi from hard labour and the inevitable exhaustion and death it entails. It concerns an anti-intellectual *Reichsdeutscher* Kapo, Alex, who escorts our astonished narrator from his life-saving interview and gets his hands covered with thick black grease.

> Without hatred and without sneering, Alex wipes his hand on my shoulder, both the palm and the back of the hand, to clean it; he would be amazed, the poor brute Alex, if someone told him that today, on the basis of this action, I judge him and Pannwitz and the innumerable others like him, big and small, in Auschwitz and everywhere. (120)

This thoughtless, automatic gesture – so small in the litany of camp horrors – is the trigger for Levi's stepping so far outside his more comfortable role of invisible witness as to condemn the 'innumerable others everywhere' who treat human beings as things. This extraordinary exception can only be explained, Rothman argues, via the now generalised referral of Buna material to the *Inferno* itself. Alex himself has already been characterised 'as light on his feet as the devils of Malabolge' (120), and this reference to the smearing of black grease evokes those barrators of the Fifth *bolgia* in the Eighth Circle, plunged into *'una pegola spessa'* [a thick pitch] by Malebranche and his demonic cronies.[19] As Dante recoils in horror from the 'boiling birdlime' (21.124; 325), so Levi feels the touch of damnation in this intimate act of wiping; a damnation associated solely with its agent, not its recipient.

The Inferno vouchsafes to the narrator of *If This Is a Man* the right to judge. He infers from its pages that acts like the wiping of a filthy hand on a fellow inmate, or the look from one (free) chemist to another (imprisoned one) that implicitly says, 'This something in front of me belongs to a species which it is obviously opportune to suppress. In this particular case, one has to first make sure that it does not contain some utilizable element' (118) – that such acts may not be criminal, but they are manifestations of an unforgivable evil that has lapsed into banality. Just as Dante settles his historical grievances against particular Ghibellines by condemning them to

---

[19] Dante, *Inferno*, Canto XXI, l. 17, *Divine Comedy*, vol. 1, edited by Robert M. Durling (Oxford: Oxford University Press, 1996), 318.

his cosmological prison-house, so Levi (more discretely) will record every small act of the Kapos and Germans in Auschwitz III that reflects their policy of dehumanisation back on their own faces. *If This Is a Man* aspires, on occasion, to the status of a 'new Bible' (73), or at least seeks to prepare the way for such a sacred text, where 'my stories' are immediately 'everyone's' by virtue of an *allegoresis* built into the impossible responsibility of speaking by proxy for the mute and the drowned.[20] It is precisely the magnification of minor, merely personal gripes through the ground glass of the six million – the multiplication of every single grotesquely debasing gesture and act by however many times each of the dead had to endure them before going under – that raises the cosmological stakes of Dante's text all over again, on a still grander scale. Legal process is wholly inadequate to this scale; only epic literature is fit for the true enormity and fashions a scaffolding ready for its ascent.

At the very outset of his *Pisan Cantos*, written virtually simultaneously with Levi's prison experiences, Pound included this brief passage alluding to the Canto of Ulysses in the *Inferno*:

> 'the great periplum brings in the stars to our shore'
> You who have passed the pillars and outward from Herakles
> when Lucifer fell in N. Carolina[21]

Canto XXVI of the *Inferno*, of course, tells this story in a less abbreviated, less ornery fashion: the story of Ulysses' final voyage – not the one we read in *The Odyssey*, which Dante nor Virgil never knew, but one he imagined himself for this 'counsellor of fraud in war', damned with Diomedes to the endless flames of the Eight *bolgia* of the Eighth Circle in Hell. This Ulysses, the 'Odysseus of *The Iliad* is the trickster, the cold-blooded murderer of Dolon, the Trojan spy he and Diomedes catch and to whom they promise no harm will come – just before his head is removed.'[22] Without *The Odyssey* to leaven this picture of the Ithacan king, his place in a Christian Hell is fully justified; and yet his portrait by Dante flickers with admiration and pity. Ulysses, asked by Virgil on behalf of the poet to tell '*dove per lui perduto a morir gissi*' (26.84) [where, lost, he went to die], recounts his last trip from Circe near Gaeta out beyond the pillars of Hercules into '*del mondo sanza gente*', driven by 'the ardor that I had to gain

[20] Levi, *The Voice of Memory*, 151–2.
[21] Ezra Pound, Canto LXXIV, ll. 19–21, *The Pisan Cantos*, edited by Richard Sieburth (New York: New Directions, 2003), 3.
[22] Uri Cohen, 'Consider If This Is a Man: Primo Levi and the Figure of Ulysses', *Jewish Social Studies: History, Culture, Society* 18.2 (Winter 2012): 49 [40–69].

experience of the world' (26.97–8; 405) unto the foothills of Mount Purgatory (where, as Pound tells us, Lucifer fell to earth).[23]

To young Jean, the camp Pikolo, who speaks not a word of Italian, Levi strives to relate in *primo canto* Dante's exquisite rendering of this doomed voyage. As fading traces 'forg'd in the mind' by schoolboy study and subsequent literary devotion, the twenty-sixth Canto is haltingly forced into broken speech, one doomed inmate to another, in the flames of a modern damnation. The penultimate *terzina* is lost to memory, but the final one, with its additional hendecasyllable for the end of the Canto, can be imparted:

> *Tre volte il fé girar con tutte l'acque,*
> *a la quarta levar la poppa in suso*
> *e la prora ire in giù, com' altrui paicque,*
> *infin che l'l mar fu sovran oi richiuso.* (26.139–42)

[Three times it (a whirlwind) made the ship to turn about with all the waters, at the fourth to raise its stern aloft and the prow to go down, as it pleased another, until the sea had closed over us. (405)]

Levi intuits something in these lines that holds an elusive key:

> I keep Pikolo back, it is vitally necessary and urgent that he listen, that he understand this 'as pleased Another' before it is too late; tomorrow he or I might be dead, or we might never see each other again, I must tell him, I must explain to him about the Middle Ages, about the so human and so necessary and yet unexpected anachronism, but still more, something gigantic that I myself have only just seen, in a flash of intuition, perhaps the reason for our fate, for our being here today . . . (128)

But 'among the sordid, ragged crowd of soup-carriers' (128) and their encroaching Babel, the thread is lost. All that remains is the final line: 'And over our heads the hollow seas closed up.'

It is at this very instant, then, as the precious literary cargo of a doomed epic voyage is pointlessly handed from one galley slave to another, uncomprehending one – for 'tomorrow he or I might be dead' – that Levi can fully experience the genocidal tragedy,

---

[23] 'The first line is clearly an allusion to the disastrous last voyage of Dante's Ulysses, who [. . .] sails beyond "the pillars of Hercules (Straits of Gibraltar) . . . only to meet death by drowning upon approaching the mount of Purgatory". But the mount of Purgatory, antipodal to Jerusalem in Dante's mythic geography, stands over the site where Lucifer had plunged into the earth, as Virgil explains to Dante in *Inferno* 34.121–126.' Peter D'Epiro, 'Canto 74: New Light on Lucifer', *Paideuma* 10.2 (Fall 1981): 298 [297–301].

and assume the imaginary status of 'the drowned', those in whose nameless names he had hoped to offer his testimony. Going down, touching bottom in the futility of a moment's literary ardour, watching the *'mar fu sovra noi richiuso'*, Levi finally realises the 'reason for our fate, for our being here today' – to become contemporary types of Mallarmé's drowned sailors. Yes, it is to bear witness, but only to 'shipwrecks,/Lost, without masts, without masts, no fertile islands . . .'. The terrible end met by Ulysses and his crew – that anonymous and unsung fate in 'the world without people' (26.117; 405) – is the fruit of a quest forged in nobility, in a progressive humanism and enlightenment:

Considerate la vostra semenza:
fatti non foste a viver come bruti,
ma per seguir virtute e canoscenza. (26.118–20)

[Consider your sowing: you were not made to live like brutes, but to follow virtue and knowledge. (405)]

If neither Levi nor Jean was 'made to live like brutes', and if the delicate transference of the ancient story that says so is noble evidence of what it means 'to follow virtue and knowledge' in the darkest adversity; still, and the more wretchedly for their failed endeavour, they must go down. The 'they' here is not for these two specific *Häftlinge*, but for all the drowned *Muselmänner* who statistically engulf them and, in this exact instance, claim them as their own. To watch the sea closing over you, to become one with the six million and the doomed epic of a warrior-king wrapped in hellfire, is then also immediately to avow the literary reflux, 'something gigantic that I myself have only just seen', or heard: *But, o my heart, listen to the sailor's chant!*

Chapter 6

The Gulag Work Ethic: Aleksandr Solzhenitsyn's *One Day in the Life of Ivan Denisovich*

When it was a bit warmer, they all talked on the march, however much they were yelled at. But today they kept their heads down, every man trying to shelter behind the man in front, thinking his own thoughts.

A convict's thoughts are no freer than he is: they come back to the same place, worry over the same thing continually. Will they poke around in my mattress and find my bread ration? Can I get off work if I report sick tonight? Will the captain be put in the hole, or won't he? How did Tsezar get his hands on his warm vest? Must have greased somebody's palm in the storeroom, what else?

Because he had eaten only cold food, and gone without his bread ration at breakfast, Shukhov felt emptier than usual. To stop his belly whining and begging for something to eat, he put the camp out of his mind and started thinking about the letter he was shortly going to write home.

The column went past a woodworking plant (built by zeks), past a housing estate (zeks again had assembled these huts, but free workers lived in them), past the new recreation center (all their own work, from the foundations to the murals – but it was the free workers who watched films there), and out onto the open steppe, walking into the wind and the reddening sunrise. Not so much as a sapling to be seen out on the steppe, nothing but bare white snow to the left or right.[1]

The artless artfulness of Solzhenitsyn's prose strikes a balance between an emphasis on objective, contextual determinism (how the weather, the guards, the immediate physical circumstances oblige his characters to behave) and the surly subjectivism of his protagonist's

---

[1] Aleksandr Solzhenitsyn, *One Day in the Life of Ivan Denisovich*, translated by H. T. Willetts (New York: Farrar, Strauss and Giroux, 2005), 40.

free indirect discourse. In the sparks thrown off by the friction between these two registers the narrator finds opportunities either to make general statements and (much rarer) moral judgements, or to render them implicitly. The first site of tension in a narrative explicitly organised around a single winter's day is between the generally iterative (the abstract repetitiousness of prison narration familiar from Berkman and Pound) and the seasonally adjusted temporal continuum of a largely outdoor Gulag existence. We see this in our passage's contrast between the 'when it was warmer' of a now distant month's relative sociability, and 'today's' unforgiving -27°C temperature – which justifies the subsequent foreclosure of conversation and dialogue and the shift into snatches of directly recorded internal discourse. Yet the transitional phrase here – 'a convict's thoughts are no freer than he is' – is iterative in the stronger sense, and stands as a higher-order vindication of the narrative method that sets the liberty of subjectivism within inexorable objective limits. It is Solzhenitsyn's purpose to show how closely the domain of thought hews to the unfree, routinised demands of camp life; and in the brief litany of first-person questions to which we are privy, we see how all reflexivity and rumination is reduced to the either/or of a binary problem. Yes or no? Will he, won't he? Even the one 'how' question is immediately reframed as an either/or. Intellection has become computation.

Hunger, one of the great constants of prison writing, then re-emerges as a further vindication of Shukhov's determination to 'put the camp out of his mind'. Hunger fosters a paradoxical abstraction of the human being: although it calls consciousness inexorably back to the body (the 'whining and begging' of the stomach), it simultaneously *spiritualises* the entire mind-body complex, in the sense that the ongoing absence of nourishment steadily frays the ties that bind them.[2] So, the further retreat into 'each his own thoughts' – into letter writing, reverie and so on – which will permit the dramatic switch into backstory and historical context immediately following our chosen passage, is a function of the very starvation rations that (in another part of his brain) has the prisoner meticulously calculating every crumb and morsel of food that he can scavenge in a day. The mental 'liberty' that hunger and isolation on a forced march to labour permit the inmate proceeds from a repressive disavowal which Solzhenitsyn catches in the pattern of his syntax, and which

---

[2] We will see much more along these lines in the extraordinary prison writing of Bobby Sands in Chapter 9.

is the regime's authority over prison life displaced into the interior domain of consciousness itself.

And before we are carried back on the tides of memory to Shukhov's fictional home village of Temgenyovo [Темгеневе], our narrator interpolates a remarkable descriptive passage about the built environment through which the prisoners are marched out to the unforgiving Kazakh steppe. There, in brief parenthetic glosses on the various landmarks being passed – wood-processing factory, worker's settlement, recreation centre – we learn that the *zeks* [camp inmates] have been responsible for bringing it all into existence in the first place. The forced march of labour to the places of construction in the novella – the new *Sotsgorodok* [Socialist Settlement], the unfinished power station – is made before a daily reminder of the vast Promethean power of their collective labour to conjure an entire socialist way of life out of the frozen earth. Here indeed we find ourselves at an antipode from Levi's chilly ironic descriptions of the Auschwitz Lager where *nothing happens, and nothing continues to happen*; for in Solzhenitsyn's camp and its environs, the very world itself is daily created, fashioned by the indefatigable productivity of the Soviet prison camp, beyond which there is only 'the steppe, nothing but bare white snow to the left or right'. And as I will argue, although there is an insuperable irony in the fact that the Soviet utopia is being erected by prison slaves, nevertheless we are given to understand, even in the clipped semaphore of this brief passage, that the chasms between free and unfree labour in Stalin's USSR are political chasms, not class ones. 'Built by zeks' means something different from what 'built by proletarians' means in the West, and it is the clear intent of Solzhenitsyn's prose that this political distinction can and should be overcome by the stroke of a pen. The alienation of the prison labour that provides Soviet citizens with housing, entertainment and work, is preserved only through the Gulag system itself and the political will to maintain it, which will evaporate within months of, and in no small part due to, this text's 1962 publication on the pages of *Novyi mir*.

* * *

We can see more directly the principle at work in the passage on Gang 104's advent at the unfinished power station:

For two months the Power Station had stood abandoned, a gray skeleton out in the snow. But now Gang 104 had arrived. What kept body and soul together in these men was a mystery. Canvas belts were drawn tight around empty bellies. The frost was crackling merrily. Not a warm spot, not a spark of fire anywhere. All the same – Gang 104 had arrived, and life was beginning all over again. (59–60)

Sartre's 'practico-inert' is encountered here in the shape of the half-built power station, a concrete skeleton in the snow, left untouched since the autumn. In Marx's language, 'Living labour must seize on these things, awaken them from the dead, change them from merely possible into real and effective use-values. Bathed in the fire of labour, appropriated as part of its organism, and infused with vital energy,' the practico-inert surrenders its merely ontic givenness to a process of radical transformation into uses and possibilities.[3] So, in Solzhenitsyn's prose, the prison work gang brings the heat of labour, the spark of life, that will transform a lifeless skeleton into a generator of power for an entire district. Heat begets heat.

Shukhov and the other layers had stopped feeling the cold. Once they got their stride, that first glow passed over them – the glow that makes you wet under jacket, jerkin, overshirt, and undershirt. But they didn't let up for a single moment, they went on laying faster and faster, and an hour later the second glow hit them, the one that dries the sweat. The frost wasn't getting at their feet, that was the main thing, nothing else, not even that thin, nagging wind could take their minds off their work. (100–1)[4]

It is part of the Soviet ideology of collective labour, from which this text has not distanced itself an iota, that work is both an end in itself (keeping a company warm in the freezing cold, pumping blood through the veins, fomenting solidarity and group ethics) and a means to greater and yet greater social ends which the prison context itself cannot vitiate. This marks out the text of *Ivan Denisovich* as unique in the annals of prison literature in this sense above all: that it delineates an extreme situation of alienated prison labour with non-alienated labour as its nucleus.

The form of that nucleus is the work gang. Bound up in it, the first-person singular modulates irresistibly into a plural which feels its distinction from the anonymous others, the many hundreds of *zeks*, in a logic that is initially portrayed with copious cynicism.

[3] Karl Marx, *Capital*, vol. 1, translated by Ben Fowkes (London: Penguin, 1990), 289–90.
[4] Gillon Aitken translates жарок (here 'glow') as 'warmth', and Ralph Parker as 'heat'. See Solzhenitsyn, *One Day in the Life of Ivan Denisovich*, translated by Gillon Aitken (London: Sphere, 2005), 88; and Solzhenitsyn, *One Day in the Life of Ivan Denisovich*, translated by Ralph Parker (London: Penguin, 1963), 82.

Why, you may wonder, will a zek put up with ten years of back-breaking work in a camp? Why not say no and dawdle through the day? The night's his own.

It can't be done, though. The work gang was invented to take care of that. It isn't like a work gang outside, where Ivan Ivanovich and Pyotr Petrovich each gets a wage of his own. In the camps things are arranged so that the zek is kept up to the mark not by his bosses but by the others in his gang. Either everybody gets a bonus or else they all die together. Am I supposed to starve because a louse like you won't work? Come on, you rotten bastard, put your back into it! (61)

This constant lateral pressure in an economy of scarcity is presented as the raison d'être of the remarkable productivity of the teams, set in competition with one another to win advantages, through the tireless advocacy of the foremen or team leaders, in the form of additional servings of food. It is not, however, the kind of competition familiar to us from Levi's account of the Nazi labour camps, where the SS is constantly looking for reasons to liquidate more human capital; rather it is a quest for the Soviet equivalent of relative surplus value through competitive incentivisation.

However, this is hardly where the text's account of the Gulag work gang rests, and the wonder of the novella's climax in the scene of late-afternoon bricklaying is that the prisoners (most particularly Shukhov himself) are subsumed by a force – both ideological and industrial – latent in cooperative labour itself. It is here that the protagonist morphs from a sullen, disaffected inmate into a titanic figure of Stakhanovite [Стахановец] myth. Placed into a two-man unit with his reliable comrade Kildigs, and urged on by the benevolent figure of their foreman Tyurin, Shukhov is inscripted into a scene straight out of late-1930s socialist realism:

Kildigs was hurrying him up.
'Hey you, Stakhanovite! Hurry up with that plumb line.'
Shukhov jeered back at him.
'Look at all the ice on your wall! Think you'll get it chipped off before dark? Needn't have bothered bringing your trowel.' (96)

The irony here is half-hearted at best. In the pages that follow, the surly peasant is transformed into a Promethean demi-urge, setting out plumb lines, laying perfect rows of blocks in the severe sub-zero temperatures, applying the mortar with precise strokes, levelling, trowelling off, goading his fellow toilers, and generating enough internal heat to keep the glaciation of the practico-inert at bay.

Every now and then the foreman yelled 'Mortar', and Shukhov echoed him. Set a brisk pace and you become a sort of foreman yourself. Shukhov wasn't going to fall behind the other two: to hurry the mortar up that ramp, he'd have run the legs off his own brother. (101)

The spirit of the team is internalised, and the collective ethic suffuses the weary muscles and sinews of the alienated monad: competition has red-shifted into Stakhanovite pride. As the other work teams down tools and begin the long journey back to camp, Shukhov's is gripped by a power far greater than protective individualism.

> It was going like a house on fire. They were on the fifth course. They'd had to do the first doubled up, but the wall was breast-high now, or nearly. [. . .] Yes, the sun was going down. A reddish sun in a sort of grayish mist. We're really getting somewhere now. Couldn't be better. On the fifth course now, so we'll just finish it off. Then level it all up. (108)

The pronoun shifts from 'they' to 'we'; the 'I' is transcended. Shukhov brings the company with him: 'Don't give up yet, boys!' (109). The Stakhanovite logic compels a redoubled effort as the day ends. 'More haste, less speed. Now that the others were out to break records, Shukhov stopped forcing the pace and took a good look at the wall.' And the foreman with him.

> The foreman walked around checking what they'd done. Seemed pleased.
> 'Good bit of bricklaying, eh? For half a day's work. Without a hoist, or any other effing thing.'
> [Shukhov said:]
> 'Listen, men, go ahead and take your trowels to Gopchik, mine isn't counted, and I don't have to hand it in, so I can finish the job.'
> The foreman laughed. 'They'd be crazy to let you out! Any jail would be lost without you!'
> Shukhov laughed back at him. And went on laying. (111)

There is nothing like this sequence in the assorted annals of prison literature the world over: this intensely good-humoured, work-proud sensation of achievement and success is unimaginable in any situation other than the Soviet one in which *One Day in the Life of Ivan Denisovich* was first published. If Solzhenitsyn's early work strives to depict a 'society vitiated by the debilitating effects of Stalinist ideology and interpenetrated and controlled at every level by the coercive apparatus', it is impossible not to distinguish that vital ambition from the garden-variety anti-communism of other turncoats and renegades, and his own later work.[5] *Ivan Denisovich* enters literary history as a blow struck for the numberless victims of that repressive apparatus, given their most generic form, the zek. But the zek is, of course, as communist as the free workers who surround him; and greatly more so than the prison guards who, page after page, demonstrate their ignorance of Soviet law and communist principle. In a particularly significant exchange, the disgraced ship's captain Buynovsky (who will spend the next few nights being broken once and for all in a freezing punishment cell for this crime) reprimands the wolfish guard Volkovoy for stripping the inmates of their undershirts.

> Buynovsky shouted at the top of his voice – he'd been used to torpedo-boats, and had spent less than three months in the camp. 'You have no right to make people undress in freezing cold! You don't know Article 9 of the Criminal Code!'
> But they did have. They did know. It's you, brother, who don't know anything yet!
> The captain kept blazing away at them: 'You aren't real Soviet people!' ['Вы не советские люди!']
> Volkovoy didn't mind Article 9, but at this he looked as black as a thundercloud.
> 'Ten days' strict regime!' he shouted.' (35)[6]

For all the cynicism of the clipped paragraph in Shukhov's free indirect discourse, there is too much pathos in the dialogue to be discounted as irony. 'You are not true Soviet people!' – for a zek to speak these words to an armed officer of the Gulag indicates an extraordinary historical moment and underlines a major ideological foundation of Sozhenitsyn's novella.[7] For in *Ivan Denisovich*, the true Soviet people [Советские люди] are the ones under the lash.

It is just this sense of solidarity with the abiding principles of the Bolshevik revolution, his loyalty to the cause 'betrayed' by the Stalinist bloc, that is progressively toned down and finally removed from Solzhenitsyn's later Gulag texts, until it becomes a slobbering reactionary Christianity.[8] The abortive Khrushchev

---

[5] Francis Barker, *Solzhenitsyn: Politics and Form* (London: Macmillan, 1977), 5.

[6] Aitken translates the key phrase: '"You're not true Soviets! ... You're not Communists!",' 34. Parker goes with: '"You're not behaving like Soviet people.... You're not behaving like communists",' 32.

[7] In Georg Lukács' words, the novella's central purpose was 'to come to terms critically with the Stalin era', an end it shared with Khrushchev himself. Lukács, *Solzhenitsyn*, translated by William David Graff (Cambridge, MA: MIT Press, 1971), 10.

[8] The concept of 'betrayal' is Trotsky's, of course; Solzhenitsyn doesn't explicitly use it, though it is at least powerfully implicit in *Ivan Denisovich*. See Leon Trotsky, *The*

'thaw', its premature crushing by the Brezhnev coup in 1964, consolidated Solzhenitsyn's keen sense of disappointment and betrayal, and doubtless led him down a path more acceptable to his Western acolytes. By the time of his epic three-part 'literary investigation', *The Gulag Archipelago* (1958–68; 1973), the Gulag has already transformed into a vast shadow continent cut adrift from the main lines of force in the Soviet state, 'an almost invisible, almost imperceptible country inhabited by the zek people', as though they were yet another national minority set apart from 'communist man'.[9] As he was pushed further and further from the heartland of his youthful convictions and support for the revolution, his ethical compass snapped; and the Gulag hardened into his catch-all symbol of the Soviet system as a whole.

The inevitable allegorical reading of the early Solzhenitsyn is fraught with political difficulties. The standard anti-communist line developed most extensively by Stephen Carter has at least the benefit of clarity, and crystallises a metaphor already developed by Berkman: 'in such a situation, one can make no distinction between those in prison and the rest of society. Hence, prison and normal society seem in this sense to have no dividing lines between them.'[10] To be sure, the value of the novella form is to promote this open allegorical slippage between the fine-grained material particularity of 'one day' in a work camp and the generic dimension of life under Stalin:

> The concentration camp is a symbol of everyday Stalinist life and Solzhenitsyn's achievement is to make the representation of camp life itself a mere episode in the universality in which everything of significance for individual and social praxis in the present will be represented as the indispensable prelude to that present.[11]

And yet, as Lukács is at great pains to point out, Solzhenitsyn's carceral metaphor applies not to the Soviet experiment per se, but to its deformation and degeneration under a specific authoritarian state form. Like D. A. Lazurkina, a victim of the purges invited by Khrushchev to address the Twenty-Second Part Congress in 1961 (a year before the publication of *Ivan Denisovich*), the novella in its

Revolution Betrayed: What Is the Soviet Union and Where Is It Going? (New York: Pathfinder, 1972).

[9] Solzhenitsyn, *The Gulag Archipelago: 1918–1956, Parts I & II*, translated by Thomas P. Whitney (New York: Harper & Row, 1974), x.

[10] Stephen Carter, *The Politics of Solzhenitsyn* (London: Macmillan, 1977), 16.

[11] Lukács, *Solzhenitsyn*, 16.

very negativity preserves the spark of the revolution betrayed: 'Her ordeals, she maintained, had only served to confirm her faith in the communist creed.'[12] As we have seen, there is, even under the most excruciating, punitive conditions depicted by the novella, an ardent affirmation of the inextinguishable ethic of the workers' state in the zeks' comportment towards labour. There is even an implicit sense that the Gulag may be the last place in the Stalinist Soviet Union where the true Stakhanovite spirit still endures, indulged disinterestedly for its own sake at one moment, and as a strategy of sheer survivalism the next. Too often, the winter setting of *Ivan Denisovich* has been spared its place in the allegorical schema.

* * *

At any rate, perhaps the most important key to Solzhenitsyn's dramatic success with this slender manuscript was its central character, the eponymous protagonist Ivan Denisovich Shukhov. Khrushchev himself is said to have particularly admired this prototypical Soviet peasant, his doggedness and cunning under great duress, along with his profound averageness and representativeness: 'a striking new kind of Everyman, a Russian Sancho Panza or Good Soldier Schweik or a "shrewd Jack-of-all-trades" whose sly resourcefulness embodied the plight of the Russian people'.[13] In good part this generic, plebeian quality proceeds directly from the linguistic material out of which he is constituted.

> Large stretches of the text take the form of free indirect speech, with Shukhov's idiolect as its controlling function, a beautifully realized mixture of folksy language, camp slang, as well as a few politically tinged locutions that he has picked up over the years. At the same time, the diction is clipped, even 'ascetic'. This laconic, idiolectal style forms a contrast to the tale's meta-referent, [Dostoevsky's] *The House of the Dead*, and its wordy, discursive flow. Yet the 'fulcrum and neutral background' for the hero's distinctive speech patterns is standard literary Russian.[14]

It would be illegitimate for a non-specialist to opine at any length on this matter, but even in translation the third person as a mask for the

---

[12] Miriam Dobson, 'Contesting the Paradigms of De-Stalinization: Readers' Responses to *One Day in the Life of Ivan Denisovich*', *Slavic Review* 64.3 (Autumn 2005): 584.

[13] Michael Scammell, 'Solzhenitsyn the Stylist', *New York Times Sunday Book Review* (29 August 2008).

[14] Richard Tempest, *Overwriting Chaos: Aleksandr Solzhenitsyn's Fictive Worlds* (Boston: Academic Studies Press, 2019), 70.

clearly autobiographical content of much of *Ivan Denisovich* goes further and achieves more useful formal ends than mere authorial self-protection. For, in adopting the persona of a village everyman whose speech is saturated in *kolkhoz* and street slang, Solzhenitsyn not only appeals to the approved characterology of Soviet ideology of socialist realism – adumbrated in the Writers' Congress of 1934 under the direction of Radek, Zhdanov and Gorky[15] – but neatly displaces the glaring matter of his own status as a petty intellectual (he was working as a schoolteacher at the time of publication) and his frustrated literary ambitions.[16] Unlike any other author examined so far in this volume, then, Solzhenitsyn saw the pragmatic value of suppressing his identity as an intellectual and masquerading as exactly the type of character most likely to endear him to the authorities. 'Shukhov' is that linguistic mask, and there are ample pleasures in the grumbling anti-intellectualism of his posture towards those fellow inmates, like Solzhenitsyn himself, who are writers of one sort or another outside the grace of the Party apparatus.

The various half-glimpsed vignettes in which other characters furtively discuss intellectual and aesthetic matters, or covertly compose verse on camp time, are defamiliarised by their perception through the eyes of a thoroughgoing anti-intellectual. There is, in fact, no other reason for Shukhov to visit the sick bay in the morning (his supposed temperature and muscle pains disappear quickly and are clearly only a motivation of the device) than to watch the young orderly Kolya Vdovushkin writing at his desk:

> Shukhov took off his cap as though to a superior officer. He had the old lag's habit of letting his eyes wander where they shouldn't, and he noticed that Kolya was writing lines of exactly the same length, leaving a margin and starting each one with a capital letter exactly below the beginning of the last. He knew right off, of course, that this wasn't work but something on the side. (20)

The *ostranenie* of our protagonist's point of view renders poetic production an outlandish, obscure activity; yet its institutional association with illness, rest and escape from hard labour surrounds it with a halo of mysterious exemption. The depiction resonates with the author's own experiences in the Special Camp for political prisoners,

---

[15] See 'Soviet Writers' Congress 1934: The Debate on Socialist Realism and Modernism', https://www.marxists.org/subject/art/lit_crit/sovietwritercongress/index.htm.

[16] Ivan Denisovich 'resides in the realm of prehistory, stubbornly holding onto an identity and a way of seeing the world that is tribal and magical rather than national and secular'. Tempest, *Overwriting Chaos*, 21.

where he 'wrote' the lengthy narrative poem 'The Trail' and twenty-eight other significant works in verse;[17] but he doesn't quite trust the reader to make the inference.

> Meanwhile, Vdovushkin went on with his writing. It was, in fact, 'something on the side', but nothing that Shukhov would have comprehended. He was copying out his long new poem. He had put the finishing touches to it the night before and had promised to show it to the new doctor, Stepan Grigorich, that morning.
>
> It was the sort of thing that happens only in camp: Stepan Grigorich had advised Vdovushkin to call himself a medical orderly and had given him the job. Vdovushkin was [. . .] a former student of literature, arrested in his second year of university. Stepan Grigorich wanted him to write in prison what he hadn't had a chance to write outside. (23)

Just as the work camp can mysteriously preserve the truth content of Soviet society in an inverted image of slave labour, so too a prison sick bay can preserve and develop a promising literary career cut short by war and persecution. The brusque 'nothing that Shukhov would have comprehended' marks out the strong border between narrative voice and Shukhov's mental space, no matter how frequently it colonises the former, and renders literary praxis exceptional in camp life, something about which there is conjured a secretive, protective aura.

We need to remember here that Varlam Shalamov, who toiled fourteen years in the infamous Kolyma labour camps, spent the final five years of that sentence as a medical orderly, having reached the unspeakable limit of the *dokhodyaga* in 1946 – a point directly comparable to the *Muselmänner* of Auschwitz.[18] It was a merciful doctor-inmate, A. I. Pantyukhov, who risked his own life to secure for the gifted iconoclast an assistant position in the sick bay, which

---

[17] At the Ekibastuz Special Camp that served as the basis of his fictionalization in *Ivan Denisovich*, Solzhenitsyn wrote out numberless lines of verse on scraps of paper, which he burned as soon as he had memorised the words. 'If his thoughts were discovered on paper, he would certainly receive a further sentence of imprisonment, and he was determined not to make the same naive mistakes that had led to his initial arrest more than seven years earlier.' Joseph Pearce, *Solzhenitsyn: A Soul in Exile*, revised ed. (New York: HarperCollins, 1999), 119. 'In the interval between two barrowloads of mortar I would put my bit of paper on the bricks and (without letting my neighbours see what I was doing) write down with a pencil stub the verses which had rushed into my head while I was slapping on the last hodful. I lived in a dream, sat in the mess hall over the ritual gruel [. . .] deaf to those around me – feeling my way about my verses and trimming them to fit like bricks in a wall.' Solzhenitsyn, *The Gulag Archipelago: 1918–1956*, V–VII, translated by Harry Willetts (New York: Harper & Row, 1977), 104.

[18] The word means, literally, 'walking towards death'.

saved Shalamov's life and enabled him to write poetry on camp time, ultimately making possible the unimpeachable masterpiece of the *Kolyma Tales*. It is just such a scene we witness, as it were out of the corner of the narratorial eye, in *Ivan Denisovich*. Of Shalamov, Solzhenitsyn wrote that he read him in samizdat in 1956 and hailed him as 'a long-lost brother.'

> He, too, wrote in a camp. Keeping his secret from all around, like me expecting no answer to his lonely cry in the dark:
>
> A long, long row of lonely graves
> Are all I remember now.
> And I should have laid myself there,
> Laid my bare body down there,
> Had I not taken a vow:
> To sing and to weep to the very end
> And never to heed the pain,
> As though in the heart of a dead man
> Life yet could begin again.
>
> How many of us were there? Many more, I think, than have come to the surface in the intervening years. Not all of them were to survive. Some buried manuscripts in bottles, without telling anyone where.[19]

The Vdovushkin vignette conjures this terrible rollcall of the dead poets and intellectuals sacrificed to Stalin's paranoia but does so in a manner that equivocates between comedy and mystery and offers only oblique praise to the nameless doctor who made it possible. Solzhenitsyn uses Shukhov as a convenient mask behind which his deeper motives are masqueraded as indifference and cynicism. It is the same when he overhears snatches of debate between the filmmaker-inmate Tsezar and others on the aesthetic merits and political compromises of Sergei Eisenstein's career, with the added advantage here that explicit condemnation of Stalin can be expressed:

> Opposite him sat Kh-123, a wiry old man doing twenty years' hard. He was eating gruel.
> 'You're wrong, old man,' Tsezar was saying, good-naturedly. 'Objectively, you will have to admit that Eisenstein is a genius. Surely you can't deny that *Ivan the Terrible* is a work of genius? The dance of the masked oprichniki! The scene in the cathedral!'
> Kh-123's spoon stopped short of his mouth.

[19] Solzhenitsyn, *The Gulag Archipelago: V–VII*, 105.

'Bogus,' he said angrily. 'So much art in it that it ceases to be art. Pepper and poppy seed instead of good honest bread. And the political motive behind it is utterly loathsome – an attempt to justify a tyrannical individual. An insult to the memory of three generations of the Russian intelligentsia!' (He was eating his gruel without savoring it. It wouldn't do him any good.)

'But would it have got past the censor if he'd handled it differently?'

'Oh well, if that's what matters . . . Only don't call him a genius – call him a toady, a dog carrying out his master's orders. A genius doesn't adjust his treatment of a theme to a tyrant's taste.'

'Ahem!' Shukhov cleared his throat. He felt awkward, interrupting this educated conversation, but he couldn't just go on standing there. (85)

This is how the protagonist functions in the text: as the interrupter of furtive intellectual debate, and the pivot back to pragmatics and materiality. The phrase 'educated conversation' is laced with suspicion and no little fear, and his awkwardness is performative; Shukhov is the prison ethic incarnate – anxiety in the mode of dismissal, terror masked as cynicism. Rearranging his prison experiences for publication in 1962, Solzhenitsyn used a focaliser forged in the aesthetic ideology of socialist realism to serve as a narratorial alibi to exculpate the author from any charge of outright sedition; and worked his melancholy dirge to the fate of the Russian intelligentsia into the periphery of his vision.

* * *

If he is placed in the lineage of approved socialist realist types, however, Shukhov is so in a peculiarly mutated sense – a sense sniffed out by some dissatisfied early readers who wrote in disgust to the editor of *Novyi mir*: the 'hero' is 'supposed to be seen as a good person, but in actual fact he is shown to be a petty crook/ odd-jobber [*mel'kiiz hulik/masterok*] who swindles two extra bowls of soup from hungry comrades, a glutton, a toady (in his relations towards Tsezar), who doesn't have a single friend or a single honest thought. Is this really a "hero", is this realism? This is in fact an alien [*chuzhak*]!'[20] Even in the terms available from the reigning aesthetic ideology, the protagonist is apparently unstable and hybrid. It is one of the distinctive marks of literary development in this period that the

---

[20] Dobson, 'Contesting the Paradigms of De-Stalinization', 587.

protagonist of a Soviet prison saga could, at one and the same time, emanate signals of a socialist realist pedigree and seem to hail from a West Coast American hard-boiled crime novel. And it is perhaps the prison *topos* that informs this generic discontinuity in the central figure: Stakhanovite heroism and seedy, low-rent anti-heroism – Promethean collectivism and mercenary individualism – overlapping in the situation of mid-century incarceration itself, which elicits now the protagonist's titanic fortitude, and now his weaselly cunning. This other, 'alien' aspect of the text, which surely explains its immense success overseas as much as its anti-Stalinist pitch, suggests an extraterritorial dimension to the prison as such in a new international formation of geopolitical dynamics where the two 'superpowers' can begin to feel subterranean affinities in their increasingly mutual approach to structural dissidence. What Ruth Wilson Gilmore calls California's 'Golden Gulag', the immense build-out of prison infrastructure capable of housing millions of (largely Black) inmates, began serious construction only a decade or so after Solzhenitsyn's little book hit the presses, and just as the *Gulag Archipelago* sequence was being translated and the Gulag itself was decommissioned.[21]

But possibly the most important function of Shukhov is neither his linguistic energy, his service as anti-intellectual mask, nor his generic hybridity and contamination, but the far less evident fact that his very conspicuousness and noisy presence tends to conceal a host of almost subliminal mini-narratives secreted, as it were, in the side-view mirror of his voice. It is his very qualities as a long-term, canny and resilient zek that make him a repository of stories other than his own, since in order to survive the camp as a peasant with no active family connections on the outside, it is supremely important to know who among his fellow inmates has money and influence 'back home', and can be counted upon to receive packages laden with nourishing, fatty foods; who should be distrusted and avoided; and what the backgrounds are of everybody in his extended circle, to wheedle, manipulate and exploit as required. So it is that Shukhov himself dissolves into the 'mosaic' of information that constitutes his survival, which is itself a cross-section of Soviet life under Stalin.

> *Ivan Denisovich* offers up a mosaic of individual life stories, fictive
> dossiers of the major and minor characters, which are situated

---

[21] See Ruth Wilson Gilmore, *The Golden Gulag: Prisons, Surplus, Crisis, and Opposition in Globalizing California* (Berkeley: University of California Press, 2007). We will begin to connect these dots in earnest over the next couple of chapters.

within the tragic contexts of twentieth-century Russian history. These biographical chronicles are always centered round the political sins of commission or omission, of thought or deed, of parentage or association that led to the incarceration of the prisoner in question. Information about a zek's background is presented discontinuously, in snippets of fact scattered here and there in the text, which are sometimes delivered in the character's own distinct accents.[22]

Thus, in ways not impossibly distant from the schema of Joyce's *Ulysses* (another 'one-day-in-the-life' novel), this representation of a single day in a single camp, seen through the eyes of a single zek, becomes a moving collage of narratives half-told, glimpsed only in fragments, from which a plausible image of the Stalinist totality might emerge – a totality made of broken parts, lives half-lived, communists betrayed and buried alive. Shukhov is a screen on which we discover projected the distorted histories of Tsezar the filmmaker, Pavlo the likeable deputy team leader, Alyoshka the well-washed Baptist, Kildigs the plump red-faced Latvian, Buynovsky the former ship's captain (second rank), Fetyukov the 'shit-bag' scavenger and former office boss, the two inseparable Estonians (one a Baltic fisherman, the other a former exile in Sweden), Gopchik the teenager, Senka Klevshin the deaf Nazi concentration camp survivor who has made the fatal mistake of being liberated by the Americans, and of course the admirable team captain Tyurin himself, permitted the longest and most elaborated backstory within Shukhov's self-centred narration. Little of this wealth of peripheral narrative material is entrusted directly to Shukhov himself, who is rather an eavesdropper and intruder, an omnipresent ear into which pours the biographical lifeblood of the camp, for him to use or ignore as needed.

> 'How do you come to know so much about life in the British Navy?' somebody in the next rank was asking.
> 'Well, it's like this, I spent nearly a month on a British cruiser, had my own cabin. I was liaison officer with one of their convoys.'
> 'That explains everything. Quite enough for them to pin twenty-five on you.'
> 'Sorry, I don't go along with all that destructive liberal criticism. I think better of our legal system.'
> Bull, Shukhov said to himself (he didn't want to get involved). Senka Klevshin had been with the Americans for two days and he got nailed for twenty-five. You were sitting pretty on that ship of theirs for a month – how long does that entitle you to?

22 Tempest, *Overwriting Chaos*, 76.

'Only, after the war the British admiral took it into his blasted head to send me a souvenir, a token of gratitude, he called it. What a nasty surprise, and how I cursed him for it!'

It was strange when you came to think of it. The bare steppe, the deserted site, the snow sparkling in the moonlight. The guards spaced out ten paces from each other, guns at the ready. The black herd of zeks. One of them, in the same sort of jacket as the rest, Shch-311, had never known life without golden epaulettes, had been pals with a British admiral, and here he was hauling a handbarrow with Fetyukov.

You can turn a man upside down, inside out, any way you like. (126–7)

This is how the camp registers its complexity and irony through the character zone of its wily survivor. The task of extracting information is left to 'somebody in the next rank', who elicits a dangerously exposing confessional anecdote from the target (in this case Buynovsky), which in turn elicits a curt and dismissive private comment from Shukhov, who overhears everything but typically 'didn't want to get involved'. But in the end the anecdote precipitates a general sense of narratorial irony and relativity, rather than poignant pity or terror, which is precisely the emotional mood best suited to camp survival. The good captain's unflagging faith in the Soviet legal system is measured against Shukhov's cynical aside and found wanting: naive, self-destructive, stupid. And yet, despite this fixed narrative balance of powers according to which our focaliser always has the self-serving final word, the overarching impression of the novella is of a steady admixture of polyphonic accents and positions that turn the irony around upon the arch ironist in whose hands we find ourselves. For Solzhenitsyn, the Gulag is a concentrated image of the Soviet nation itself, with all its internal variety, its tapestry of national minorities and occupations, bureaucratic ranks and character types, all of whom find themselves converted into numbered zeks – proletarianised *in extremis*, under the eyes of the armed guards – without yet surrendering their voices. At this stage in his career, they are still proud Soviet men, preserving the best of the Soviet spirit and dream under duress; while beneath them the Gulag archipelago shudders in seismic seizures of the carceral state and breaks them from their faith, splintering the communist utopia into isolated ice-sheets and rogue glaciers, propelled into a new international imaginary where, broken, reified, reduced to biopolitical pawns, they can begin to reflect us all.

Chapter 7

Decorous Perceptions at the Cracking Point: Ruth First's *117 Days*

I was to spend the hour in the bricked-in quadrangle of the women's section of the brick and bar monster that is Marshall Square. Part of the building goes back to pre-Boer War days. The plumbing pipes are all external and they lace the walls of the quadrangles like a corset of iron trellis. Water and sewage pipes gurgle and splutter and flush up and down the two storeys and this little exercise yard is an excellent point from which to plot an ablutions graph for the white prisoners' cells. The few steps out of the cell were like a hurtle through space on a funfair figure of eight, and my stomach leapt as my legs moved across the concrete threshold. But the exercise yard was too like a cell. The sky was trapped by brick walls extending upwards and, like the warders regulating my stay in the courtyard, the brick walls officiously limited the shine of the sun. There was nothing for it but to walk round and round the courtyard.

On chill days I loped but tried to put out of my mind the thought of generations of prisoners doing the same. On sunny days I basked in the patch of sun, moving with it, if I could stay long enough, as it inched westwards across the courtyard and then out of reach.

There was another exercise yard for the women but it was used for men detainees until the women wardresses reasserted their, or our, claim. This was a sandy yard, four times the size of the women's quadrangle, deep in the bowels of the station and closed in by fourteen-feet-high brick walls, with mesh on top. To see what lay beyond the walls I stood in the pit of the quadrangle with my head thrown back. Then like a victim in the gladiators' den I could see and be seen by the elevated spectators, in this case the skyscrapers of Johannesburg's mining and finance houses. Marshall Square lies in the heart of the multimillionaire concerns mining South Africa's gold and diamonds: The new Chamber of Mines building is a stone's throw away. Anglo-American's twin giants, number 44 and number

45 Main Street, are paces away. The Stock Exchange is on the next block. The windows looking down on me were those of panelled board rooms and offices housing smooth desktops.[1]

In her vivid retrospective account of one hundred and seventeen days spent as a solitary detainee (without charge) in Johannesburg and Pretoria in late 1963, Ruth First compensates for the lack of pen or pencil during her detention by recreating – in London, a year later – as carefully as possible the physical and psychological facts of her incarceration. Fifteen years of professional toil as a journalist for the radical Johannesburg *Guardian* newspaper and the *New Age* and *Fighting Talk* journals (shut down by the state in November 1962) served her well when turning to her own experience as a story with comparable significance for the struggle against capitalist apartheid as the miners' strike or disappearances of comrades. An eye for detail and the telling juxtaposition directs her prose at every turn in the above passage, with its effortless shifts between objective and subjective data, its precise parataxis, and its deft deployment of the first-person voice, fully justified by the topic. Indeed, not the least interesting feature of this passage is the elimination of other people from the first-person accounts of time spent in the two yards – the way the references to 'women', the 'women's section', the 'women's quadrangle', shift inevitably to a radically estranged 'I' when the experiences are recounted, because as a political prisoner in solitary confinement, First is strictly prohibited from enjoying any company. Where other writers' accounts of yard time are almost always social scenes (think of Berkman and Pound, Levi and Solzhenitsyn), First, like Luxemburg, endures her prison time, outdoors and in, alone. She takes the air as a monad, a social atom, and that fact of separation is written into the style of the excerpt, with its sense of detached contemplation, comparison and analysis; everything rendered into an occasion for intellectual reflection, rather than drawn in lightly as the background of a scene. So, thanks to the precise acoustic indexing of water use through Marshall Square station's external piping system, 'this little exercise yard is an excellent point from which to plot an ablutions graph for the white prisoners' cells'. The journalist's acute perceptiveness strains to compensate for the absence of any human intercourse, by reading it through the plumbing; but the bathos of the observation only heightens the pathos of the situation.

---

[1] Ruth First, *117 Days: An Account of Confinement and Interrogation under the South African 90-Day Detention Law* (London: Virago, 2010), 41–2.

Her husband, Joe Slovo, had already become 'somewhat of a prison ethnographer' during his six-month detention in 1960, but First stakes out her own ironic territory here.[2]

As a radical writer, First is drawn to emphatic metaphor and simile. Marshall Square central police station is a 'monster' whose 'bowels' are where the arrested inmates exercise, the pipes that hug its walls are 'like a corset of iron trellis', and the yard itself is either a 'gladiator's den' or too much 'like a cell' to afford any sense of release. Following the strong line of these metaphoric conceits, we arrive naturally enough at a conception of some vast, tentacular entity spawned in 'pre-Boer War days', rooted at Marshall Square, and spreading out to ensnare and envelop the entire world around it: a concrete carceral cancer trapping the sky and 'officiously limit[ing] the shine of the sun' itself. Indeed, it is one of the primary purposes of First's book to persuade the reader that, under the Ninety-Day detention order – according to which any persons could be held for three months without charge and subject to limitless interrogation (and then, when released, be re-arrested) – the National Party's new South Africa was already a carceral regime. Metaphor and simile are as important to this task as a concentrated history of policy shifts and policing tactics. One of the key successes of this passage is the idea that leaving a cell is always stepping into another one. Even if the phenomenology of taking those first steps outside of solitary confinement is gut-churning – 'a hurtle through space on a funfair figure of eight' – the result is an iterative recapitulation of the conditions left behind. 'There was nothing for it but to walk round and round the courtyard,' just as there is nothing to do but pace the cell. The logic of contagious metonymy speaks figurally to the abiding idea of the Ninety-Day law itself: 'The Ninety-Day law recognized no demarcation of its territory, no delimiting of its power. All were within its grasp' (43).

But the greatest achievement of these three paragraphs is surely the transition the third one makes, thanks to its rarer setting in the male exercise yard, to what surrounds the Marshall Square station. The prose makes a critical fold between the archaic carceral monster (whose belly the 'I' engorges) and that new, glittering complex of high-rise edifices whose upper storeys are visible from the centre of the yard; a juxtaposition that testifies to the complicity of international capital with South Africa's racist state. Later, one

---

[2] Alan Wieder, *Ruth First and Joe Slovo in the War against Apartheid* (New York: Monthly Review Press, 2013), 115.

of First's interrogators will croon with pride how 'Investors abroad were showing confidence in the Nationalist Party Government even if I was not; a great multimillion pound hotel was going up on an old brewery site' (145), but here already the point is made in a brilliant figural collage. 'Johannesburg's mining and finance houses' rise from the solemn and enforceable promises of apartheid's carceral system as regards labour discipline and a two-tier wage structure. The critical geography of this paragraph, opening out from the 'gladiator's den' at its centre, draws a jagged line connecting the architectural gigantism of 'the multimillionaire concerns mining South Africa's gold and diamonds', the Chamber of Mines, the finance sector's Stock Exchange, and the beating carceral heart of the whole system. The panopticism implicit in the skyscrapers' 'elevated spectators' with their 'panelled board rooms and offices housing smooth desktops' is strategically reversed: their optical indifference ('Did they know what they were looking at? Did they care?' 43) is inverted into this razor-sharp urban physiognomy of the mutual dependency of capital investment and apartheid's racial barbarism.

As with most other writers considered in this book, the personal is immediately political here, because the status of the political prisoner is such as to saturate every stray datum of time served in solitary with the palpable interests of the state. The better part of First's incarceration taking place in a working central police station, her sense experience there serves as a critical optic on the violent machinery of law.

> My ears knocked with the noise of a police station in operation. The cell was abandoned in isolation, yet suspended in a cacophony of noise. I lay in the midst of clamour but could see nothing. Accelerators raced, exhaust pipes roared, car doors banged, there were clipped shouted commands of authority. And the silence only of prisoners in intimidated subservience. It was Friday night, police-raid night. Pickup vans and *kwela-kwelas* ['get on board' police vans], policemen in uniform, detectives in plain clothes were combing locations and hostels, backyards and shebeens to clean the city of 'crime', and the doors of Marshall Square stood wide open to receive the haul of the dragnet. (9)

The deluge of auditory phenomena, overwhelming the narrow range of visual experience by an order of magnitude, is broken down by the analytic intelligence into its component tracks; cacophony resolves into an audio-image of Power sweeping the demographic litter of the streets into its detention. It is, indeed, precisely the 'suspension' of the 'I'/eye that permits the image to appear, too complex and multi-faceted to allow of any single form or aspect. 'I could dispense with my eyes. Ears were more useful in isolation' (26). Prison, depriving the subject of visual stimuli, trains the cortex to parse the incessant clamour for signs of systemic significance; and equips the ear with political radar, capable of new ranges of journalistic perception. Over and against which, human beings are perceptible principally through the void they make in audible space. 'And the silence only of prisoners in intimidated subservience.' Sound is, however, the medium in which the artificial separation between 'criminals' and 'politicals' is transcended, and, suggestively at least, where the abolition of apartheid itself is rehearsed.

> The Ninety-Dayers were locked away from this mainstream of police station life, but the sounds and some of the sights washed us nevertheless. Washed and were welcome in a series of endless days when time was determined only by the scratches on the wall and the visits of Security Branch interrogators. The politicals were in separate cells, segregated from the other prisoners, but sounds filtered through the thick walls, especially at night. (29)

Community may be negated by the state's enforcement of segregation, and its prison apparatus of division and distinction (whites apart from Blacks, political from criminals, men from women), but 'sounds filter through' the walls to create, if not the actuality, then at least the promissory note of a community to come.

Inevitably, the Dantesque analogue is triggered by the noise.

> Friday nights were inferno-like, especially at month-end when pensions were paid and the disabled-turned-drunks spilled from the benches in the parks into the vans. On the pavement outside Marshall Square the pickup van doors clanged open and shut and roared off for another swoop. Africans were herded into the charge office to shouts of '*Kom aan, kom aan*' [Come on, get a move on] and the sherry-gangers howled and swore through the night, till the shouts turned into gravel-sounding alcoholic snores and it was time to eat the dry bread and hard-boiled egg and join the queue to court. (33)

Hyphenated compound words do much of the stylistic work of bridging the existential gaps between inside and outside, sound and image, particular and general; and Dante supplies the inevitable reference point for an image of the social in terminal, sinking crisis. Note that First never seeks to demonise the damned, who 'howl and swear' only at the talon-pricks and torments of their infernal captors. Indeed, the analogy is sharpest around the impress of prison labour, when the howls belong to the wardresses, not their charges. 'The arrival of the work party in the women's cells, when Raucous or Shrill were on shift, could have provided the soundtrack for the arrival of the damned in apartheid hell. Both these wardresses shouted instructions uninterruptedly in Afrikaans' (35).

What exempts the 'I' from this inferno is precisely why she is under detention in the first place – apartheid itself, against which First committed her life in the struggle. References to Dante, to 'suspension' and forced inactivity, all proceed from the whiteness of this isolated inmate segregated from a darker sea of humanity, here converted directly into labour power. The logic of the social system is inscribed ineluctably into the regime of incarceration, which privileges the white subject despite everything she has done to abolish it.

> I, a prisoner held under top security conditions, was forbidden books, visitors, contact with any other prisoner; but like any white South African Madam I sat in bed each morning, and Africans did the cleaning for the 'missus'. Should a spot appear on the floor during the day the wardress would shout to the nearest African warder *'Gaan haal my 'n kaffer'* [Go and get me a k . . .], and once again all would be well in South Africa's forced labour heaven. (35)

Like James Joyce, First is uncomfortable with the idea of ascribing to her isolated character (herself) any thoughts that would not naturally spring from the situation itself, and that situation tends always to the matter of personal deprivation.[3] So, the matter of expressing political criticisms of the system in which she is ensnared is left principally to the scenes of interrogation, where her character can freely, if impotently, vent in dialogue. Absent those scenes, the criticism is left implicit in the language of descriptive narration, as with the following account of the new model prison in Pretoria to which First is moved in the third chapter:

> All week gangs of African convicts laboured in preparation for the weekends, sweeping, hosing, planting, weeding, rolling the grass, and trimming its edges to nail-scissor-clipped neatness. Armed guards stood duty over them as they worked at the bent, half-running jog which seems to be required prison posture and pace for African men. They wore dirty off-white singlets and shorts and were shoeless.

---

[3] See the discussion of Joyce's reticence in Hugh Kenner, *Ulysses*, revised edition (Baltimore: Johns Hopkins University Press, 1987), 31–42.

> Lean to the bone, they were animated stick figures, incongruously subservient to the watching, armed guards in such carefree surroundings. By the weekends the convicts had been herded back into their jail; their labour was done and the water and the lawns lay invitingly at the feet of their guards. (67)

The model prison is nothing less than a model of the ideal apartheid state, with only the guns and the emaciated figures of forced labour to attest to the cost of that veneer of 'carefree neatness' the National Party used to advertise itself to the world. First is at her sharpest and most satirical when detailing the function of the women's prison as the laundry of the Pretoria governing class.

> There was every conceivable article of clothing, mostly in good condition. Each item was marked with a number and a well-known Afrikaans name. [. . .] Suddenly the shot went home. The prisoners were earning the jail's keep by taking in the washing of Cabinet Ministers, important civil servants, and well-to-do Pretoria families who were having a good laundry job done cheaply and were at the same time aiding the rehabilitation of the country's reprobates. The women scrubbed for their sins the sheets of the Director of Prisons and the hand-towels of the myriads of civil servants who stamped, cancelled, and countermanded their passes and their permission to remain in the city; and I took my exercise amidst the underpants of the Minister of Agriculture. (73)

What marks First out as a distinctive prison writer is this capacity to seize on a vivid detail that represents (and mocks) the critical place of the prison-industrial system within the apartheid state, synecdochally drawing the connections between 'inside' and out. Her sharpened journalistic talents for following the trail of money, labour and interest out from a nucleus of imprisoned immediacy (a pair of underpants on a line; a well-clipped lawn; external plumbing) into a vast system of interlocking privileges and abuses, are peerless. By placing the 'I' in the midst of these mediations, First makes clear the importance of the trained subjective place where 'the shot goes home', but also establishes a plane of immanence in which all are related by contiguity and implication in the open prison of state-sponsored racism.

However, because the secret subject of this text is not apartheid per se, but the evolving geopolitical weaponisation of prison against the organised Left, many of the most powerful passages in it concern the interpersonal drama that takes place between the prisoner, Ruth First, and her inquisitors – detectives Van der Merwe,

J. J. Viktor, and Van Rensburg, Special Branch officers Swanepoel and Van Zyl, Warrant Officer Lanky, and Sergeant Smit. One clear signal that, despite our attention being claimed by the graphic synecdoches and satiric thrusts of First's seasoned campaign against apartheid, something more disturbing to the 'I' is taking place in the background, is the stylistic worry triggered any time the narrative voice is preoccupied with the trials of interrogation. This worry takes the form of a dramatic shift into conditional and subjunctive modes:

> If they would permit me no legal aid, I would tell them, whenever they came, that I would have to do the best I could helping myself. So I could not possibly answer any questions till I knew if the police were in the process of collecting evidence against me. Nor, for that matter, I decided to tell them, would I say that I would not answer questions. [. . .] This cat and mouse game could go on for a limited period, I knew, but it was worth playing until I found out how the interrogation sessions were conducted, and whether there was any possibility that I might learn something of the state of police information. (8–9)

The auxiliary verbs do a tale unfold. Three 'woulds' and a 'could' in the first sentence; another 'could' in the second; and two 'woulds' in the third, followed by another 'could' and a 'might'. In sharp contradistinction from her stylistic confidence in descriptive parataxis, passages like this one throw the subject into a state of anxious irresolution and second-guessing conditionality. The conditionals dictate terms: 'If they would', 'till I knew if', 'until I found out', 'whether there was'. Such uncertain rehearsal of the various possibilities latent in the upcoming interrogation make clear the unpreparedness of First's persona for what is really at stake in the ninety-day detention: not the idea of criminality or punishment, but precisely the horror of betrayal, of inadvertently compromising the freedom of one's comrades. This is the aching political concern of *117 Days*, an attempt to recreate the chronic unease and self-doubt that attends a historic transformation in the very mechanics of information-extraction by the state.[4] First plays with the irony of her convictions about her own

---

[4] This transformation was in the news as First's book was being written, in the wake of the break-up of the African Resistance Movement in mid-1964 (after Adrian Leftwich gave up his comrades under interrogation), and after the Park Station bomb outrage (John Harris, July 1964; he was hanged 1965). See also David Attwell, 'Writing After the "Poor Little Bomb": Fictionality and Sabotage in Nadine Gordimer's *The Late Bourgeois World*', *ELH* 87.1 (Spring 2020): 273–91. Thanks to Andrew van der Vlies for these references.

intellectual superiority: 'As on the previous night I rehearsed again the imaginary first confrontation with the Security Branch. I was warming to my role in the encounter and was becoming master of the ambiguous and evasive reply to the questions I invented for my unseen interrogators' (13). In this imaginary rehearsal of a confrontation that hasn't taken place, she masterfully executes her role as the foxy, superior radical running rings around her witless inquisitors, whose lines she has 'invented' for them out of a third-rate spy novel.[5] Indeed, it is just such a novel that First plans to write when she is finally given a pencil.

> I devised a plot for a novel. The characters were me and my friends, all cast in heroic mould. We planned and organized in opposition to the Government, called for strikes and acts of civil disobedience, were harassed and chivvied by the police, banned, and arrested. Then we were locked in prison cells and here I was again, grappling with life in a cell. I did better than that. I spent hours getting behind the political declarations of my characters, dissecting their private inclinations, scrutinizing their love affairs and marriages, their disillusionments and idle talk. (77)

Prison engenders a two-dimensional political idealism that ramifies itself in formal cliché. *117 Days* is pitiless about this tendency of the isolated radical to relapse into culture-industry stereotypes once disconnected from the living cellular organism of a revolutionary network and movement. It critically performs the weakness of the segregated subject in terms of an emphatic discursive strength – the strength of genre. But what pulverises genre, invalidating it from the inside, is the infinite elasticity of time itself in the context of an indefinitely renewable ninety-day detention. 'Minutes, hours, days, weeks are measurements of time for normal living. For the prisoner in idle isolation, hours and days go by too slowly for them to be acceptable measurements of time' (81). 'Like sand dribbling through an hourglass the passage of time became a physical act dribbling through my consciousness. It seemed I had to push time on for it to move at all, for in my cell it had lost its own momentum. [. . .] Feeling, experience, accumulated, but without relation to days or nights or artificial markings of time' (81). It is a constant of prison literature, to be sure, but here what we find is that this steady erosion of the contours of phenomenological duration effectively disables the

---

[5] Accounts of her comparable courtroom presence come later in many of the Rivonia Trialists post-release memoirs. See, too, Hilda Bernstein, *The World that Was Ours* (London: Heinemann, 1967).

generic confidence that undergirds First's robust initial sense of her own endurance.[6]

> I had had ninety-one days of floating in suspense, hanging in inde-terminate doom. I would rather hear a verdict than face continued suspension. How could I get events round me to move? For ninety-one days I had been stubbornly impenitent, obdurate in making no attempt to draw them on in their questioning of me. I was still stub-bornly uncontrite but now my impatience was stretched to the point of snap. I could no longer bear to sit and wait while events moved around me; I had to provoke them. (129)

Floating, suspension, indeterminacy, inaction: against these ambient atemporal forces, the subject marshals her will, deciding to temper her stubbornness and resistance in order to provoke an event. But the authorities, having power over the nature of incarcerated time, are able at every turn to stretch impatience beyond its limit and create an entirely new temporality. For the new detention regime, the radical subject's expected obduracy and impenitence are part of a much longer game, in which the subject's fortitude and will are snapped, rendered impotent in a directionless, momentumless con-tinuum where false hopes and periodic upsurges of optimism have finally ceded to a mindless eternal present. As Special Branch officer Swanepoel puts it: "'You're an obstinate woman, Mrs Slovo. But remember this. Everyone cracks sooner or later. It's our job to find the cracking point. We'll find yours too.'" (57) That cracking point is a moment when all the resources at the disposal of an intellectual dissident – courage, solidarity, commitment, pride, tradition, train-ing, superiority, faith and selflessness – have been depleted by an indefinite solitary detention where time has collapsed in upon itself.

This is, in fact, the underlying purpose of *117 Days* as a critical text in the tradition of prison literature: not as yet another autobio-graphical, ethnological account of time spent behind bars, though it is that too, but as a historical document in the record of prison as a weapon against the organised Left in the twentieth century. For what transpires as the book approaches its end is that First has in fact arranged her memoir to reflect the precise moment at which

---

[6] 'Prison narratives more than any other bear the representation of time and space and the gap between the narrative and narrated chronotopes as a special burden, since the passage of time and the restrictions of space are themselves the very substance of the story.' David Schalkwyk, 'Chronotopes of the Self in the Writings of Women Political Prisoners in South Africa', in *Apartheid Narratives*, edited by Nahem Yousaf, *DQR Studies in Literature Online*, vol. 31 (Leiden: Brill, 2001): 1 [1–36].

the South African Left found itself outwitted and, indeed, defeated by a superior force made manifest in the prison regime itself. In making sense of this chilling transformation, the extreme contrast with Joe Slovo's imprisonment in 1960, just three years earlier, is particularly telling. Constantly surrounded by a retinue of fellow detainees, Slovo frequently provided much-needed services as a jailhouse lawyer, listened attentively to Eli Weinberg's wonderful stories, participated in a prisoners' choir and a performance of Shakespeare's *Midsummer Night's Dream*, and held court on 'Joe's Throne' – an outdoor toilet around which dozens of comrades would gather daily. Ruth was led to write to him: 'By the sound of it your wonderful company have the best brought out of them by confinement; though it's largely the company, not the confinement.'[7] In *117 Days*, she reflects that, going into prison, she 'had always been contemptuous of the state security apparatus' (153) because stories like Joe's were the rule, not the exception.[8] The 'bumbling methods' of the security apparatus 'brought them ridicule', but even better, they led to improvements in the morale and solidarity of the Left:

> Those held in prison pending political trials, or during the 1960 State of Emergency and the days of the 1961 Mandela strike, had emerged from a spell of community jail life with morale marvellously unimpaired. Every new stretch of prison for a group of political prisoners gave birth to a new batch of freedom songs. Jail spells had not broken us; they had helped to make us. (153)

But then, just as the Ninety-Day Law became enforceable and solitary rather than group incarceration the norm, the interrogation techniques also shifted, clearly informed by some toolkit of psychological torture drawn up by the CIA but with deep roots in the fascist and Stalinist experiments in state power. Where before there had only been crude threats, taunts and simple appeals to personal interest, now there was a battery of new tricks and cunning devices toggling between flattery, promises, cajolery, generosity and concern, callousness, official propriety, screw-tightening, jokes and laughter,

---

[7] See Wieder, *Ruth First and Joe Slovo*, 116.

[8] This is only true for political prisoners, of course. For the general, mostly Black prison population, 'the authorities contrived a state of nature, making prisons an arena that was permanently dangerous for inmates, an arena in which the prospect of being murdered was perpetually in play. In the circumstances of a racial dictatorship, this was deemed the best way to exercise control. It was thus left to inmates to constitute the basis for order in the most difficult conditions.' Jonny Steinberg, 'Writing South Africa's Prisons into History', in Michelle Kelly and Claire Westall, eds, *Prison Writing and the Literary World* (London: Routledge, 2021), 168.

bait-and-switch, good cop bad cop, appeals to conscience, ominous warnings, mysteriousness, and above all a sense of endless unurgency in a context of indeterminate solitary confinement – a vast repertoire of psychological manipulation presided over by discipline, order and trained role-playing officers. Having 'studied its texts carefully', the Security Branch launched a deliberate plan of attack against the well-springs of radical fortitude.

> After the first score or so of detentions, the Branch began to work with some measure of confidence. The key judgement was when to apply really stiff pressure, at what moment the victim was emotionally most fragile. People's 'cracking points' did vary; some were demoralized quite early on in their detention; others took longer; many lasted out altogether. [. . .] Men holding key positions in the political movement, who had years of hard political experience and sacrifice behind them, cracked like egg shell. (154)

This is, for First, one of the more significant turning points in twentieth-century history at which she was personally present, when the state's available instruments of torture were greatly expanded from the physical to the psychological, and applied in principle to any member, white or Black, of the organised Left in order to shatter its integrity and coherence. And because it was fully bureaucratised, this development was immediately disavowable by any of its individual perpetrators, a great advantage for the long-term suppression of radical political currents around the world, and a refinement of fascist political repression, as First outlines with great clarity:

> Perhaps one day the South African Security Branch will plead that it used psychological torture for the benefit of science; that from its files one can study the case histories of its victims to discern 'cracking points', resistance to suggestion, the correlation of psychological types with will and ability to exist over long periods of time in isolation. Beside longer experienced inquisitors, the South Africans might be amateurs just beginning to learn the methods of psychological warfare; but they are learning fast. Give them time: they have the eagerness to outdo any Inquisition. Because, they tell themselves, they are only doing their duty. They all talked like little Eichmanns. There was rarely a Security Branch detective who did not say: 'It's the law, we're only doing our job.' This is the danger. Like Eichmann they will do anything in the name of their job. They will be answerable for nothing. Torture itself becomes no more than the pursuit of their daily routine. (154–5)

This warning, sounded in 1963, has an extraordinary prescience and marks a decisive moment in the history of a nascent prison-security complex – the moment at which the concentration camp, the political detention facility, the Gulag, is normalised as a moment of the modern capitalist state's perfection of 'security' against internal enemies. We begin to detect a clear geopolitical arc of transmission, of fascist and Stalinist methods of direct political suppression, and state-sponsored American psychological techniques of control and conditioning, feeding into an apartheid state's internal mechanisms of communist containment and extirpation, all through the emergent apparatus of the prison-security system. We shall see subsequently both how this was to feed back into an ever-expanding American regime of mass incarceration and took its ultimate bearings (via Hitler's obsession) from the systems of African plantation slavery and Jim Crow in the American South. We can also speculate about its dissemination into right-wing dictatorships in South America, Western Africa and South-East Asia, especially Indonesia: First's razor-sharp observations mark the point of no return for the Left's laissez-faire contempt for any state intelligence focused through the prison.

Her decision to cooperate with her captors, her voluntary statement, subsequent self-revulsion, existential crisis and attempted suicide all follow First's exemplary account of being ensnared in an unprecedented web of new disciplinary structures and processes for which even her extraordinary militant self-control and extensive preparation was unprepared. 'I was appalled at the events of the last three days. They had beaten me. I had allowed myself to be beaten. I had pulled back from the brink just in time, but had it been in time? I was wide open to emotional blackmail, and the blackmailer was myself' (145). This cruel intersection of autobiography and history charges *117 Days* with the crackle and hum of political electricity: as testimony, her account amounts to a critical self-reckoning by a Left stranded in pre-Second World War practices and sensibilities, coming to terms with a new world order. 'I had presided over my collapse with a combination of knowingness and utter miscalculation. My conceit and self-centredness had at last undone me. I had thought to pit myself against the Security Branch in their own lair. What had I hoped to learn?' (148) Confession tilting over inevitably into allegory, this account obliges a searching recalibration of tactics, expectations and attitudes. It is at this point that First's memoir tessellates with that archaic Christian-Stoic tradition, insofar as it presents a subject 'more uncertain, more frequently apprehended as misguided and aberrant [than the main line of twentieth-century prison writing], and her individual interior life is disclosed to the reader for scrutiny, judgement and perhaps absolution'.[9]

The prison is a microcosm of the wider social experiment of apartheid, with its draconian restrictions against movement, speech, gatherings and intercourse, between 'races', of course, but also more generally (like fascism) as a fist to break the Left once and for all. First accounts for what has already happened to her profession, her livelihood, before she landed in jail, as an escalating series of ministerial bans on the conditions of her existence: bans against her leaving Johannesburg, reporting on forced labour conditions, entering townships, attending meetings, writing anything for publication.

> Then finally the bans stopped every literate or available Congressman from writing, and the printer, the last one we could find in the country to publish our notoriously outspoken copy, gave us notice that he could no longer take the risk. We sold the paper to a new proprietor whom we hoped would assemble a fresh team of writers. We were not to know until almost a year later but 'Babla' Saloojee, the new owner, was himself detained under the Ninety-Day law, and, driven to despair by the interrogation methods of the Security Branch, he hurled himself to his death from the window of the very room where I was being questioned. (134–5)

The addition of ninety-day prison terms without charge and new interrogation methods to the already debilitating ministerial decrees against organised resistance is here framed as a death sentence for the free exchange of information and the egalitarianism it promotes.

This sense of a terminal moment, an irreversible catastrophe immanent in the experience being narrated, is doubtless what prompts First to use her always relatively privileged, relatively safe position as a middle-class white woman as a frame to house seven distinct sub-narratives, in italics, of men, most of them Black, having it much worse. The stories of Arthur Goldreich, Dennis Brutus, 'W', Looksmart Solwandle Ngudle, James April, Isaac Tlale, William Tsotso, John Marinus Ferus, all of them victims of the Suppression of Communism Act, ring with the blows of physical and mental torture

---

[9] Daniel Roux, '"I speak to you and I listen to the voice coming back": Recording Solitary Confinement in the Apartheid Prison', *English Academy Review* 22.1 (2005): 23 [22–31].

far more severe than Ruth First's.[10] Brutality of this sort, familiar from Levi's ruminations on Auschwitz, is the 'extensive' aspect of the 'intensive' disciplinary forms put to work on First; and the willing participation of the judiciary and press in the general farce of misrepresentation that attends such torture and murder drives more nails into the coffin of civil society under apartheid. Looksmart's death by excessive electrical shock and beatings is wrapped up thus:

> The magistrate returned a verdict that Looksmart Solwandle Ngudle had committed suicide by hanging himself, and his death was not due to 'any act or omission involving or amounting to an offence on the part of any person'. The verdict ended the attempt to produce further evidence of the treatment of detainees but it was too late for officialdom to try to stifle that. Looksmart by his death and Tlale by his courage had lifted the lid for the first time on the systematic resort to the torture of Ninety-Day detainees by the Security Branch. (113)

But the defiance in this last, typical Ruth First sentence, which hinges on exposure and the spread of knowledge, is undone in advance by all the various acknowledgements of banning orders and impediments to press freedom already vouchsafed. The lid, precisely, would not be lifted; stifling of evidence was written into the social contract now prepared for an entire citizenry by the machinery of apartheid. The bars of a social prison had already swung shut.

Yet *117 Days* sparkles with a mordant, tonic wit and worldly insouciance despite all this narrowing of the chinks in its narrator's cavern. There is a goodly amount of amusing play with the question of prison literature, or at least of the kind of literature permissible in an apartheid jailhouse. Determinedly clutching a copy of her favourite novel as she is admitted to prison, First is initially obliged to bid it farewell: 'No pencil. No necklace. No nail scissors. No book. *The Charterhouse of Parma* joined bottles of contraband brandy and dagga [marijuana] in the police storeroom' (6). But this is scarcely the end of the issue. First demands reading material and is fobbed off with the Good Book, which she reads and rereads diligently.

> I revelled in the energy of the Creation and the narration of the exile, in the tumultuous Revelations; I skipped with impatience through the elaborate collection of taboo and ritual, the wearisome census

---

[10] See the discussion in Jamie S. Scott, 'Space, Time, Solitude: The Liberating Contradictions of Ruth First's *117 Days*', in Gordon Collier, Marc Delrez, Anne Fuchs and Bénédicte Ledent, eds, *Engaging with Literature of Commitment, Vol. 1: Africa in the World* (Amsterdam: Rodopi, 2012), 71–80.

reports of the Book of Numbers, the bewildering time sequences of the Chronicles. I felt close to the melancholy of Jeremiah and Lamentations. I wondered how comfort could be found, by those who use the Book for refuge, in the baleful and avenging God of the Old Testament. (69–70)

And she memorises psalms and proverbs ('A fool's mouth is his destruction/And his lips are the snare of his soul' [69]), unaware that it is she herself who will tremble in the glare of this judgement. And then, like the clockwork of some new psychological method, the Stendhal returns.

> One morning Viktor came to ask me what I would like to read. 'What's come over you people now?' I asked. He was behaving like a smug Father Christmas. No, he said, it's just that the colonel said I could have books, one at a time, and all the titles had to be approved by Pretoria. I asked for *The Charterhouse of Parma* which I had been longing to get my hands on for over three months, and I had to give him a potted summary of the plot. The next day he brought it to me. (158)

But most of the book's humour revolves around the matter of First's gender, which she both performs with aggressive swagger, and ridicules mercilessly in her account. Having won her battle for her suitcase in the opening scene, First ironically glories in the difference it allows her from her fellow prisoners: 'Their lipsticks were taken from them, and their combs, to be restored only when they were fetched to appear before a magistrate in court. The casuals were booked in from the police van in the clothes they had worn when arrested, and if they wanted a clean blouse they had to plead with the wardress to get the cell warder to telephone a relative. I could go to my suitcase' (12). Refusing to urinate or defecate in her prison-supplied 'po', she uses her white middle-class gender to win rights over a public facility by day, and to boast about her iron-clad bladder overnight. Admitted to Pretoria Central Women's Prison, she allows herself this comic pratfall: 'I minced in my high heels and thrust my bosom out firmly in my charcoal suit, free to impress them, I thought, while I was still outside a cell. I was so preoccupied with making a dignified exit that I dropped the biscuit tin I was carrying and had to get down on hands and knees to scoop up the biscuit pieces' (64).

It is her gender that makes First particularly vulnerable to the authorities' repeated threats over the visitation rights of her three daughters, which is presented as an acute source of pain. Yet it is her gender, too, that precipitates the book's most affecting scene of interpersonal contact, which takes place due to the solitary nature of First's visits to the bathroom and consists in a momentary revelation of what it is she is fighting for in the first place: a vanishing sense of community and belonging.

> There was generally a delay while the wardresses went to await the arrival of the doctor, so I moved to the bathroom window to gaze at the African women. They wore coffee-brown wrap-around overalls and bright red doeks, and, under their brown skirts, short petticoats of striped white and blue flannel. Several of the women had young babies on their backs. Tied to their skirts were mugs and spoons. When there were no guards standing over them they relaxed in their own company and talked and laughed together. Several of them would generally catch sight of me staring at them through the grille of the bathroom and point me out to the others, and we would make gestures to one another across the yard. (71–2)

Through steel bars and in the few, meagre seconds of a relaxation of oversight, First rediscovers her journalistic impulse as a mark of solidarity with the women for whose freedom she will ultimately give her life. Her memoir, which has been pulled in every direction away from them, and been obliged to take on the burdens of a terrible political document and historical marker, here snaps back to a peaceful enclave of African women carved out within the belly of the carceral beast – a space of mutual recognition and regard, a laugh, a gesture, a contact beyond race, beyond class, but made possible by a sisterhood that apartheid itself was never able to expunge.

Chapter 8

House Style: Black Prison Writing of the 1970s

Angela Y. Davis, who had campaigned as a student for the release of South African political prisoners including Ruth First, first met her in exile shortly after Davis's own release from prison in 1972, 'when I travelled to London during the mid-seventies to participate in an antiapartheid solidarity event. At the time I remember thinking that she seemed to possess the very best qualities of the most brilliant and driven scholars/activists/organisers I had encountered in my then relatively young political life.'[1] This close contact secures a vital link in an increasingly integrated story about the transformation of political imprisonment across the arc of the twentieth century. For Davis, a cosmopolitan communist and antiapartheid intellectual, the solidarity with First was a realisation about the spreading universality of a new social form in which she herself was ineluctably enmeshed. As First had already made clear in her memoir, the South African apartheid prison system had open affinities with the National Socialist carceral regime, on which various of its aspects (the psychology of the prison staff, the use of torture, the racialisation of the prison population) had been modelled. During her eighteen months held in the Women's Detention Center, New York, and the Marin County Jail in California, Davis would conduct research and write trenchantly about what she saw as the fascist tendencies in contemporary America. Considering the Folsom Prisoners' Manifesto of Demands and Anti-Oppression Platform as a lucid account of the structures of oppression within the US prison system, Davis notes,

[1] Angela Y. Davis, 'Introduction', in Ruth First, *117 Days: An Account of Confinement and Interrogation under the South African 90-Day Detention Law* (London: Penguin, 2009), 5.

'Their contention that prisons are being transformed into the "fascist concentration camps of modern America", should not be taken lightly.'[2] She writes: 'The government is not hesitating to utilize an entire network of fascist tactics [. . .], a system of "preventive fascism", as Marcuse has termed it, in which the role of the judicial and penal systems loom large' (30). Written in prison, this incendiary account of 'the world's greatest democracy' sought to extend the lessons of what happens in the jailhouse to the broader citizenry:

> Although the most unbridled expressions of the fascist menace are still tied to the racist domination of Blacks, Chicanos, Puerto Ricans, Indians, it lurks under the surface wherever there is potential resistance to the power of monopoly capital, the parasitic interests which control this society. Potentially it can profoundly worsen the conditions of existence for the average American citizen. Consequently, the masses of people in this country have a real, direct and material stake in the struggle to free political prisoners, the struggle to abolish the prison system in its present form, the struggle against all dimensions of racism. (35)

The twentieth century's first strident call for prison abolition was sounded in a California prison cell by a philosopher and social researcher who was using her time behind bars to connect the dots in what was disclosing itself as a wave of neofascist carcerality crashing very precisely on this American state just as Davis was bearing witness to it. The cry would soon be taken up by Norwegian researcher Thomas Mathiesen's 1974 work *The Politics of Abolition* and activist Fay Honey Knopp's 1976 book *Instead of Prisons: A Handbook for Abolitionists*.[3] The metaphor of choice for what was about to happen to California and to America more generally over the next three decades was eventually crystallised by Ruth Wilson Gilmore, another woman scholar of colour, and cousin of a murdered Black Panther, who coined the Solzhenitsyn-like phrase 'Golden Gulag' to account for the extraordinary explosion and intensification of racialised imprisonment in California since the early 1970s.[4] In this our midway chapter, which, due to the very explosivity and communality of its context, cannot be restricted to a single author or text,

[2] Angela Y. Davis, in Davis and Bettina Aptheker, eds, *If They Come in the Morning: Voices of Resistance* (University Park: Pennsylvania State University Press, 1971), 30.

[3] Thomas Mathiesen, *The Politics of Abolition* (New York: John Wiley & Sons, 1974); Fay Honey Knopp, *Instead of Prisons: A Handbook for Abolitionists* (Syracuse: Prison Research Education Action Project, 1976).

[4] Ruth Wilson Gilmore, *Golden Gulag: Prisons, Surplus, Crisis, and Opposition in Globalizing California* (Berkeley: University of California Press, 2007).

we seek to reconstruct this fateful moment in the history of prison writing, as, one after another, Black political intellectuals used their time in the California prison system to publish on a turning point in the life of racial capitalism – a point at which the question of what to do with surplus populations was 'solved' by a redoubled application of strategies deployed in Nazi Germany, Stalinist Russia and apartheid South Africa; which it turns out was not-so-secretly a reapplication of the very plantation system of chattel slavery that 'America' was supposed to have dismantled a century before.[5]

At issue here is the historical contradiction between a nascent intensification of the Western liberal carceral state, specifically its American epicentre, along lines pioneered by autocratic regimes, and the collective appropriation of prison conditions by prisoners of colour to accelerate and deepen an intensive research-based radicalisation programme. Reading Fidel, Che, Ho Chi Minh, Nkrumah, Võ Nguyên Giáp, 'Marx, Lenin, Trotsky, Engels, and Mao' behind bars,[6] a generation of incarcerated Black men and women leveraged the inbuilt paradoxes of postwar America's justice system – increasingly draconian at the level of judicial and legal racial profiling, but still residually stamped by the liberal rejection of the Auburn system under which generations had suffered before the Second World War – to transform the jail cell into a monastic scholarly retreat, with recommended reading lists, reading groups, tutorial assistance, and a distributed hermeneutics the likes of which no prison system on earth had ever tolerated. Thanks in part to the legend of Malcolm X's education while serving time at the Norfolk Prison Colony (1948–52), and to the wide dissemination of Martin Luther King, Jr's 'Letter from Birmingham Jail' (1963), the association of prison with radical critical discourse had gained ground over the 1960s. The specific conditions for Malcolm's remarkable transformation were acknowledged as exceptional to Alex Haley during the writing of the *Autobiography*: it 'was an experimental rehabilitation jail [. . .] whose penal policies sounded almost too good to be true.'

> In place of the atmosphere of malicious gossip, perversion, grafting, hateful guards, there was more relative 'culture', as 'culture' is interpreted in prisons. A high percentage of the Norfolk Prison

---

[5] Davis's developed position on this question is articulated in her two later volumes, *Are Prisons Obsolete?* (New York: Seven Stories Press, 2003) and *Abolition Democracy: Beyond Empire, Prisons, and Torture* (New York: Seven Stories Press, 2005).

[6] George Jackson, *Soledad Brother: The Prison Letters of George Jackson* (Chicago: Lawrence Hill, 1994), 16.

Colony inmates went in for 'intellectual' things, group discussions, debates, and such. Instructors for the educational rehabilitation programs came from Harvard, Boston University, and other educational institutions in the area. [. . .] Norfolk Prison Colony's library was one of its outstanding features. A millionaire named Parkhurst had willed his library there; he had probably been interested in the rehabilitation program. History and religions were his special interests. Thousands of his books were on the shelves, and in the back were boxes and crates full, for which there wasn't space on the shelves. At Norfolk, we could actually go into the library, with permission – walk up and down the shelves, pick books. There were hundreds of old volumes, some of them probably quite rare. I read aimlessly, until I learned to read selectively, with a purpose.[7]

Over the subsequent two decades, what had struck Malcolm as exceptional and rare became increasingly standard in US federal prisons. There took place 'an unprecedented growth in prison libraries' after the Second World War thanks largely to the crusading efforts of reformer Austin MacCormick, who saw the well-stocked prison library as 'an instrument of wholesome recreation, of direct and indirect education, and of mental health. Books are for many prisoners a bridge to the free world.'[8] State judiciaries adopted various, less liberal programmes, until Congress passed the Library Services and Construction Act in 1964, which specifically funded State prisons in areas historically more likely to have greater populations of inmates from 'disadvantaged communities' (Black, Hispanic, disabled) to provide them with meaningful library services. These were the objective conditions in which a generation of Black activists, incarcerated on the flimsiest of pretexts in the states' reactionary recoil from the Civil Rights agenda, enriched their radical education on the state's dime from 1964 to 1980.

George Jackson had been calling his prisons (Folsom, San Quentin, Soledad) 'concentration camps' since 1967 and would eventually sign off letters with the phrase 'From Dachau with Love'.[9] He entered San Quentin a politically innocent, undereducated eighteen-year-old

---

[7] Malcolm X, *The Autobiography of Malcolm X*, as told to Alex Haley [c.1964] (New York: Ballantine Books, 1992), 157–8.

[8] Austin MacCormick in the 1950 American Prison Association's Library Manual for Correctional Institutions; qtd in Vibeke Lehmann, 'Challenges and Accomplishments in US Prison Libraries', *Library Trends* 59.3 (2011): 492 [490–508].

[9] He uses the phrase 'concentration camps' repeatedly; see Jackson, *Soledad Brother*, 17, 29, 115, 140, 234. Huey P. Newton had used the phrase to characterise the coming American mass incarceration of Black citizens in the Black Panthers' Executive Mandate Number One on 2 May 1967, and we can safely assume that this is the source

in 1961. Nine years later, as the result of a fiercely accelerated educational drive undertaken with his comrade W. L. Nolen, and mere
weeks after a yard brawl with the Aryan Brotherhood ('Hitler's
Helpers') took the life of Nolen and precipitated his own brutal
demise, Jackson could run off the following definition of fascism to
his lawyer Fay Stendar: 'the definition of fascism is: a police state
wherein the political ascendancy is tied into and protects the interests
of the upper class – characterized by militarism, *racism*, and imperialism' (18; emphasis in original). Jackson's account of the transformation of the enlightened prison population into a vanguard of the
Black revolutionary forces at large in 'Amerika' by the turn of the
decade in 1970 is historically acute:

> We're something like 40 to 42 percent of the prison population.
> Perhaps more, since I'm relying on material published by the media.
> The leadership of the black prison population now definitely identi-
> fies with Huey, Bobby, Angela, Eldridge, and antifascism. The savage
> repression of blacks which can be estimated by reading the obituary
> columns of the nation's dailies, Fred Hampton, etc., has not failed to
> register on the black inmates. The holds are fast being broken. Men
> who read Lenin, Fanon, and Che don't riot, 'they mass', 'they rage',
> they dig graves. (27)

That Huey P. Newton, Bobby Seale, Angela Davis and Eldridge
Cleaver would all have served significant jail time by the time of
Jackson's murder in prison (Newton: 1964–5 and 1968–71; Seale:
1969–72; Davis: 1970–2; Cleaver: 1958–66) focuses our attention on
the role of the institution itself as a spur and accelerant of Black militant knowledge and leadership at this moment in American history.
The California Statewide Prison Strike of 1970, led by Folsom prisoners with their articulate manifesto of demands,[10] demonstrates the
degree of coordination and leadership at this time between institutions and across regional lines among what Jackson calls 'the black
prison population' – coordination and leadership with open lines
of communication to extramural associations like the Panthers and
beyond, ultimately to 'the other colonies, those in Asia and Latin
Amerika, in Appalachia and the southwestern beanfield [. . .] a true
internationalism with other anticolonial peoples' (264). For the first

---

of Jackson's deployment of the term. The phrase 'From Dachau with Love': 304, 307
and 313.

[10] See the Folsom Manifesto at https://sfbayview.com/2018/10/folsom-manifesto-for-the-
california-statewide-prison-strike-1970/ and in Davis, *If They Come in the Morning*,
57–63.

time in history, the prison had become a pivotal, perhaps the most important node in a distributed network of sites of critical inquiry investigating how racist state apparatuses and the institutions of racial capitalism used prison itself – among other techniques and systems – to punish, disrupt and subject to surveillance the organised political representatives of surplus populations.[11]

Consider the difference between this and what Ruth First described nostalgically as the reparative use of prison time by first-generation antiapartheid activists:

> Those held in prison pending political trials, or during the 1960 State of Emergency and the days of the 1961 Mandela strike, had emerged from a spell of community jail life with morale marvellously unimpaired. Every new stretch of prison for a group of political prisoners gave birth to a new batch of freedom songs. Jail spells had not broken us; they had helped to make us.[12]

This collaborative cultural work in confinement, under the disorganised conditions of detention in the early apartheid state, depends upon extensive time together out of the cells and is focused on minor acts of morale-boosting solidarity. It does not amount to significant radical research and development, let alone meta-carceral analysis or theory, the conditions for which were simply lacking in community jails. Another comparison, with Rosa Luxemburg, will help draw out the specificity of what was happening in the California prisons of the late 1960s and early 1970s. Luxemburg had of course treated her isolation cells – at Barnim Street, Wronke fortress and Breslau – as places of theoretical reflection and scholarship, penning her great 'Junius Pamphlet' during her near four-year stretch of detention and using her correspondence to flesh out a comprehensive humanist vision and social-democratic ethos. But it was not until after her release that she turned her critical eye on the prison system itself as a mode of social control. Standing with the 'thousands of pale, emaciated figures who have been incarcerated for years behind the walls of the gaols and penitentiaries in expiation for petty offences', it was only once she was free herself that she took up their cause in her writing.[13] The prison cell as a scholarly space was never used by Rosa Luxemburg to reflect theoretically or politically on the prison

---

[11] For a discussion of relative surplus populations in relation to prison growth, see Gilmore, *Golden Gulag*, 70–8.

[12] First, *117 Days*, 153.

[13] Rosa Luxemburg, 'A Duty of Honor', in *Rosa Luxemburg: Selected Political Writings*, edited by Robert Looker (London: Jonathan Cape, 1972), 259 [258–61].

itself; rather, a division of labour opened up between situation and object of research during her prolonged detention.

Here stands the true distinction of Newton, Jackson and Davis in the annals of prison writing. The American dialectic of what Davis called 'prisoners who have attained political maturity during the course of their imprisonment for non-political crimes and against whom prison authorities have consequently launched political vendettas'[14] led to rapid radicalisation among imprisoned Black cadres and the production of cogent anti-prison discourse by those same prisoners and their legal counsel (including Bettina Aptheker, part of Davis's defence committee). Repeatedly, the state's use of incarceration to manage surplus populations yielded the unwanted product of critical carceral state theory emanating directly from the cells, connecting what Newton called the 'black colony' to wider anti-imperial struggles and revolutionary processes in the Third World, as well as the whole of Black history.[15] Huey Newton, who lovingly recalled George Jackson's request to join the Panthers while Newton was in the California Men's Colony and Jackson at Soledad, eulogised his fallen comrade as follows: 'He was one of the few prisoners who was shackled and heavily guarded for his infrequent trips to the visitors' room. Attempts on his life became almost daily occurrences. But he never gave in or retreated. Prison was the crucible that shaped his spirit,' as it had been for generations of communists and radicals before him; 'George often used the words of Ho Chi Minh to describe his resistance: "Calamity has hardened me and turned my mind to steel."'[16] But within this tradition of resistance, there was also a difference. It took Black autodidacts to articulate the specific continuity of their oppression through the lens of prison itself, as Etheridge Knight put it in his introduction to *Black Voices from Prison*: 'From the time the first of our fathers were bound and shackled and herded into the dark hold of a "Christian" slave-ship – right on up to the present day, the whole experience of the Black man in America can be summed up in one word: prison.'[17] Bobby Seale separated Black American life into two carceral camps: 'maximum security' (prison

[14] Davis, *If They Come in the Morning*, 68.

[15] Huey P. Newton, 'Black Panther Party Platform and Program: What We Want/What We Believe' [c.1966], in *The Huey P. Newton Reader*, edited by David Hilliard and David Weise (New York: Seven Stories Press, 2002), 56.

[16] Newton, 'Fallen Comrade: Eulogy for George Jackson, 1971', in *Huey P. Newton Reader*, 241 [241–7].

[17] Etheridge Knight, *Black Voices from Prison* (New York: Pathfinder Press, 1970), 5.

as such) and 'minimum security' (the policed streets and ghettos).[18] And Malcolm X, another prison autodidact, put it most simply: 'Don't be shocked when I say that I was in prison. You're still in prison. That's what America means – prison.'[19]

Ishmael Reed wrote of Cleaver: 'As in the case of his hero, Malcolm X, Eldridge Cleaver went to school in jail, reading, writing, meditating, and practicing his intellectual style on mentors, who were obviously no match for his probing, hungry intellect.'[20] The quality of that education was exceptionally high, especially relative to the official curriculum of the various schools these inmates were sent to as children. As Huey Newton wrote in his memoir:

> During those long years in the Oakland public schools, I did not have one teacher who taught me anything relevant to my own life or experience. Not one instructor even awoke in me a desire to learn more or question or explore the worlds of literature, science, and history. All they did was try to rob me of the sense of my own uniqueness and worth, and in the process they nearly killed my urge to inquire.[21]

Indeed, George Jackson had not yet finished high school when he was sentenced to San Quentin for one year to life, for robbing a gas station of $70 at gunpoint, and was obliged to complete his schooling to be eligible for parole (which was never granted). His critique of that experience is sobering. In one of the longest narrative scenes written during his ten years in prison, Jackson recounts his altercations with the 'patriotic and Republican' Colonel Davis, sent into maximum security to run the schoolroom with 'the same fascist textbooks that contain the same undercurrent of racism and overtones of nationalism' that his brother Jonathan was using in public school outside.[22] Their argument, presented in great detail, demonstrates the remarkable power of prison autodidacticism against prescribed pedagogy, as Jackson breaks down every puerile, sanctimonious bromide of state-and-capital logic with his rigorous radical critique. 'We don't want people like Davis teaching the children,' he concludes, 'he has himself been educated into inanity' (262). This stylised scene crystallises,

---

[18] Qtd in H. Bruce Franklin, 'The Literature of the American Prison', *Massachusetts Review* 18.1 (Spring 1977): 59 [51–78].

[19] Qtd in Nicolaus C. Mills, 'Prison and Society in Nineteenth-Century American Fiction', *Western Humanities Review* 24.4 (1970): 325.

[20] Ishmael Reed, *The Reed Reader* (New York: Basic Books, 2001), 274.

[21] Huey P. Newton, *Revolutionary Suicide*, with the assistance of J. Herman Blake (London: Penguin, 2009), 20.

[22] Jackson, *Soledad Brother*, 256. The nature of Jonathan's education was a long-standing issue in the correspondence between Jackson and his father, Robert.

in blazing cadences, the self-evident truth that Jackson had already taken his own education leagues further than anything the state could have wished; and done so precisely in the absence of what passes for pedagogy in school. 'Reading, writing, meditating, and practicing his intellectual style' in prison was a self-confirming exercise in spiritual liberation, undertaken by this generation of incarcerated Black men alongside punishing physical regimens (Jackson regularly completed four to five hours of physical exercise in his cells, using books as weights [104]; he also smoked seventy-five cigarettes a day). To Angela Davis Jackson wrote:

> They send us to school to learn how to be disgusting. We send our children to places of learning operated by men who hate us and hate the truth. It is clear that *no school* would be better. Burn it; all the fascist literature, burn that too. Then equip yourself with the Little Red Book. There is no other way to regain our senses. We must destroy Johnson Publications and the little black tabloids that mimic the fascist press even to their denunciations of black extremists. Burn them or take them over as people's collectives, and give the colonies a dynamite case of self-determination, anticolonialism, and Mao think!!!!! (255)

Prison would become an alternative academy of radical studies not administered by the enemy but managed internally by the learners themselves – provided the curriculum could be shaped and the library stocked. Jackson's letters to his parents include various requests for new reading material, on which prison rules permitted inmates to spend as much money as they liked to supplement the library. He requests precise publication details of all Mao's available books, Du Bois' *Encyclopedia Africana* (a late work, because 'Du Bois was a mere fool in his earlier days,' 62), a textbook on the Swahili language to teach himself (102); asks Angela Davis to send him 'Lenin, Marx, Mao, Che, Giap, Uncle Ho, Nkrumah, and any Black Marxists. Mama has a list' (301); reads St Augustine and Leibniz (87), and legal textbooks pertinent to his case (231); painstakingly builds his vocabulary out of 'small paperback pocketbooks' (135); and requests one correspondent to get copies of Fanon's and Malcolm X's works for his brother Jonathan (294). Soledad will become an academy of Black history, because 'We have no knowledge of our heritage. Our economic status has reduced our minds to a state of complete oblivion. The young black who comes out of college or the university is as ignorant and as unlearned as the white laborer. For all practical purposes he is worse off than he went in, for he has learned only the attitudes and ways of the snake, and a few well-worded lies' (62). But Black history only makes sense in relation to what encages it; of Davis he also asks that 'With each load of heavy stuff throw in a reference book dealing with pure fact, figures, statistics, graphs for my further education. Also books on the personnel and structure of today's political and economic front. I am doing some serious theory work for you concerning the case, dedicated to Huey and Angela' (302). Altogether, this improvised syllabus vies with graduate courses in the major universities, and the specific place of Angela Davis in this remarkable complex now requires some consideration.

Angela Davis is, of course, no autodidact. Her remarkable scholarly pedigree is among the most prestigious for a Black American woman in her lifetime: scholarship student at Brandeis, where she first meets her mentor Herbert Marcuse; Hamilton College exchange student to undertake advanced study at Biarritz and the Sorbonne; converted philosophy major back at Brandeis, under Marcuse's supervision; graduating *summa cum laude* as a member of Phi Beta Kappa; graduate student at the University of Frankfurt, where she attends classes led by Theodor Adorno; a master's from the University of California, San Diego, again under Marcuse's supervision; a Doctor of Philosophy from Humboldt University. In 1969 she took up her controversial Assistant Professorship in philosophy at the University of California, Los Angeles, as a member of the Communist Party USA and an affiliate of the Black Panther Party, Los Angeles chapter. With repeated attempts to terminate her contract led by then-governor Ronald Reagan, the university administration eventually succeeded in firing her on the grounds of 'inflammatory speech'. It was this fabled figure, an intellect of the highest calibre with extensive Continental training by some of the world's most important radical theorists, who, due to her support for the Soledad Brothers from January 1970, began to feed the already prodigious knowledge-thirst of George Jackson. Their ardent communication would lead to a situation in which Jonathan Jackson, George's younger brother, effectively became her armed bodyguard – a role made necessary by the clear and present danger of far-right threats to her safety – and so indirectly made her a fugitive when Jonathan led an armed assault (using guns purchased by Davis) on the Marin County courtroom and took five hostages (a judge, a prosecutor and three jurors) to use as bargaining chips for releasing the Soledad Brothers, an effort that cost him and four others their lives. After escaping to New York and making the FBI's Ten Most

Wanted fugitive list, Davis was finally apprehended on 13 October 1970, and herself became a prisoner, first in the state of New York and then on remand in California, awaiting a trial eighteen months after her arrest that ultimately acquitted her of all charges.[23]

Clearly a very different figure from that of Jackson, Newton, Seale or Cleaver, Davis on one level represented the very elite educational system that these men had explicitly condemned as reproductive of the social relations of racial capitalism, the system that Diane di Prima, under the influence of the Panthers, would denounce in one of her revolutionary letters:

> schools
> where all our kids are pushed into one shape, are taught
> it's better to be 'American' than Black
> or Indian, or Jap, or PR
> [. . .]
> degrees from universities which are nothing
> more than slum landlords, festering sinks
> of lies, so you too can go forth
> and lie to others on some greeny campus[24]

And yet, just as clearly, Davis had already become a deeply contradictory member of the scholarly elite, openly acting as an 'enemy within' and conducting radical research on the very conditions that had led to the growing incarceration of Black men, and their conscription into a war machine in Vietnam, in the years leading up to her own arrest.

The point of these paradoxical relations is that prison functioned at this moment as a levelling power, cancelling out the distinction of 'education' from 'reform', and so the distinction between 'criminal' and 'political prisoner'. Consider the very different backgrounds of the protagonists of this chapter at the moment they entered incarceration: Davis's exemplary story we know; Jackson was a boy with a rap sheet not yet graduated from high school; Bobby Seale was a sheet-metal mechanic who attended community college to study politics and economics; Eldridge Cleaver was a high school dropout petty criminal who graduated to rape and attempted murder and described himself as having had 'a Higher Uneducation';[25] and Huey Newton,

---

[23] This story is told phlegmatically in Davis's *Autobiography* (New York: Random House, 1974).

[24] Diane di Prima, *Revolutionary Letters*, 50th anniversary edition, Pocket Poets #27 (San Francisco: City Lights Books, 2021), 28, 29.

[25] Eldridge Cleaver, *Soul on Ice* (London: Penguin, 1999), 37.

though poor and carrying a rap sheet, graduated from high school and community college, where he studied philosophy. All bar one had merely scraped the dregs of an education off the very bottom-tier state schools; yet in prison, all worked on an equal footing as articulate spokespeople and theorists of the Black carceral condition in America. At the core of this levelling-up was the shared realisation that, as Davis put it, 'the army of Blacks, Chicanos, Puerto Ricans immured in the nation's dungeons are largely victims of an exploitative, racist socioeconomic arrangement', and that 'crime' was the judicial fig-leaf for this profoundly antidemocratic truth.[26] That political leaders, activists and rebels were specifically targeted and framed over drug charges, or for standing up with force against racist policing, is the burden of Davis's sober anatomy of the situation of Black prisoners in *If They Come in the Morning*; but she means this analysis to be understood in relation to the prevailing norms of a 'racist socioeconomic arrangement' where prison is used to dispose of surplus labour *tout court*. The unique conditions inside American jails were optimal for this surplus population to become conscious of itself. As Davis writes of the Chicano revolutionary prisoner Luis Talamantez, held in San Quentin, 'Like so many other captives, Talamantez acquired his political understanding and first expressed his commitment while in prison' (85). For, despite the fact that 'being lynched under the color of law' is endemic to the American carceral system (96), and that 'Black people emerged from slavery only to encounter the prison labor system as one element of the new apparatus of exploitation' (127), the prison had also become an enclave where, spared the necessity of working eight hours a day to earn a minimum wage (added to two hours' commuting), and granted access to well-stocked libraries, prisoners of colour were radicalised at pace and attained a highly sophisticated grasp of their situation.[27]

In marked contradistinction to all the other material covered in this book, what is significant about this American prison writing of the early 1970s is that it does not have a single author, and so

[26] Davis, *If They Come in the Morning*, 67. George Jackson: 'Most crime, however, is clearly the simple effect of a grossly disproportionate distribution of wealth and privilege, a reflection of the state of present property relations.' In Davis, *If They Come in the Morning*, 142.

[27] On the libraries, however, we should note Davis's report on hers: 'To talk a little about the library, they have a collection of adventure stories and romances which they have designated the library. It is important to realize that although the prison population is 95 per cent Black and Puerto Rican, I found only five or six books about Black people and literature in Spanish is extremely scarce.' Davis, in *Selections from the Black: Purple Book* (Jamestown: Jamestown Publishers, 1974), 147.

is not marked by idiosyncratic stylistic concerns. To the contrary, what distinguishes this body of writing is the steely depersonalisation of its voice, in a collective effort to construct an acephalous intellectual idiom with one foot in the academy, and another behind the bullhorn. At once scholarly and hortatory, pedantic and passionate, scrupulous and sensational, this prose avoids the pitfalls of a personal voice of pathos, even in letters, in order to forge a shared militant persona capable of carrying forward the struggle irrespective of who fell to the violence of the state (as George Jackson would within months of his first book's publication). From inmates like Davis, it borrows the impersonal accents of the academic researcher; while from those like Bobby Seale and Huey Newton, it takes the fearless *parrhesia* of the street leader, rousing the masses to action. In neither speech genre is there any room for personal phenomenology or rumination. Such was at any rate a luxury scarcely to be afforded by what inmate Erika Higgins distilled as the needs of the hour: 'No heroes, no rhetoric, but massive educational rallies and street politicizing, showing how POW's are examples of the situation every one of us face. [. . .] So we all really have to get to work and focus on the people, not individuals.'[28] The shared voice of this school of writing is the voice of a vanguard intellectual formation, thinking on behalf of a toiling, racially profiled public, deliberately suppressing the temptation to individualise its utterances in order to meet the objective demands of the situation – and doing so from a cage.

Take the voice deployed by George Jackson in his contribution to *If They Come in the Morning*. On the one hand, we read impersonal statistics and plain speaking:

> There are more prisons of all categories in the United States than in all other countries of the world combined. There are at all times two-thirds of a million people or more confined to these prisons. Hundreds are destined to be executed outright legally and thousands quasi-legally. Other thousands will never again have any freedom of movement barring a revolutionary change in all the institutions that combine to make up the order of things.[29]

On the other, incendiary exhortation:

> As it stands above us monopoly capital is an obstruction that leaves us in the shade and has made us its servant. It must be completely

---

[28] Erkia Higgins, 'Message from Prison', in Davis, *If They Come in the Morning*, 107.
[29] George Jackson, 'Towards the United Front', in Davis, *If They Come in the Morning*, 141–2.

destroyed, not rejected, not simply transformed, but destroyed utterly, totally, ruthlessly, relentlessly – as immediately as possible terminated! (144)

In his quest for a 'unitarian' approach to the prison problem in America, drawing together all elements of the Left, lies a less apparent quest – for a new speaking position, a new post-identitarian voice, which has taken wing from the carapace of the former individual in order to weave together an unprecedented collective expressive capacity out of the available rhetorical resources. Jackson was able to articulate what he understood this to mean:

> At the end of this massive collective struggle we will uncover our new man; he is a creation of the process, the future, he will be better equipped to wage the real struggle, the permanent struggle after the revolution – the one for new relationships between man. (147)

The question we must answer is how and why prison became the institutional space from which this voice strove to make itself heard, and did so with extraordinary levels of popularity and public success. It bears remembering that *Soledad Brother* sold half a million copies, and *Soul on Ice* and *Revolutionary Suicide* were million-plus bestsellers: something about the voice towards which these writers were striving – didactic, impassioned, disciplined, tactical, resolute, without a trace of self-pity (except in Cleaver's frequent and lamentable lapses from radical taste[30]) – resonated with a reading public hungry for information and organisation. And perhaps a first glimpse of the answer to our question is aired in a letter from Eldridge Cleaver to Beverly Axelrod, a lawyer he was courting several years into his time in San Quentin. Cleaver writes:

> I was 22 when I came to prison and of course I have changed tremendously over the years. But I always had a strong sense of myself and in the last few years I felt I was losing my identity. There was a deadness in my body that eluded me, as though I could not exactly locate its site.[31]

---

[30] Indeed, it is worth suggesting that the only salvageable elements of *Soul on Ice* are those in which we detect the least of Cleaver himself, where the circulating impersonal voice colonises his sensibility and attains a grandeur otherwise inaccessible to this fatuous egotist, homophobe, misogynist and future far-right apologist.

[31] Melanie Margaret Kask, *Soul Mates: The Prison Letters of Eldridge Cleaver and Beverly Axelrod*, vol. 1 (Berkeley: University of California Press, 2003), 232.

Prison, then, engenders an existential subsidence, a wasting of the resources of selfhood and identity. It wears away the muscles of resilient self-fashioning and espouses the individual to a death-in-life that eats away at the living fibres of the body. Bestowing numbers rather than names upon inmates, separating them from their sexual partners, dressing them in institutional uniform, encaging them and radically hampering their freedom of movement, the jailhouse takes the 'strong sense of myself' that I enter with and negates it. But this very assault on the body as a source of selfhood also makes possible the fructification of a spiritual regrowth not grounded in corporeality but in discourse, the archive, information and the rhetoric of collective aspiration. Huey Newton grasped the fundamental lesson about the prison as a space of spiritual resistance in his own contribution to *If They Come in the Morning*, where he writes:

> The prison cannot gain a victory over the political prisoner because he has nothing to be rehabilitated from or to. He refuses to accept the legitimacy of the system and refuses to participate. To participate is to admit that the society is legitimate because of its exploitation of the oppressed. This is the idea that the political prisoner does not accept, this is the idea for which he has been imprisoned, and this is the reason why he cannot cooperate with the system. The political prisoner will, in fact, serve his time just as will the 'illegitimate capitalist'. Yet the idea that motivated and sustained the political prisoner rests in the people. All the prison has is a body.[32]

Here we rencounter a much older, stoic idea about imprisonment and morality; only it has been completely transposed from a religious to a political frame of reference.[33] The specific genius of Black prison writing in the early 1970s is that it rediscovers one of the oldest and most resilient forms of prison discourse – the self-hardening, disciplined, morally sharpened, stoical language of political prisoners facing execution and excommunication – and breathes into it a new set of resources: research, communalism, Black consciousness, internationalist political awareness and direct links to the broader extramural population. In the event, an especially evolved aspect of twentieth-century prison writing to date – the phenomenological registration of prison experience as an embodied, affective, perceptual complex, in writing that strains towards the outer reaches of human expressivity – suffers a notable setback.

---

[32] Huey P. Newton, 'Prison, Where Is Thy Victory?' [c.1970], in *Huey P. Newton Reader*, 156.

[33] See the discussion of Oscar Wilde's *De Profundis* in Chapter 1, above.

Nowhere is this better exemplified than in Davis's autobiography, whose language (relative to her crisp and electrifying theoretical texts written from jail) is slack and imprecise, just exactly where we might have expected it to attain its maximal stylistic force: in its descriptions of prison experience. Lacking Ruth First's laser-like exactitude and insouciant irony, Luxemburg's ecstatic reveries of perception and reflection, Levi's mordant observational minimalism, Pound's brimming phenomenology or Berkman's engrossing characterisations, Davis writes about her time inside with a tin ear and a lacklustre effort to raise herself to the trials of description. Riddled with clichés, stocked with two-dimensional portraits, using irony only in the most overblown ways, and missing all salient sharpness of detail, these episodes could not be further removed in tone and voice from her own contemporary theoretical interventions, with their brilliant syntheses, ease with potent abstractions, methodological flexibility, stylistic rigour, muscular sentence constructions, judicious rhetorical devices and thoroughly depersonalised accounts of processes, institutions and structures. But so it is across the board with the 'house style' of this particular moment in the history of prison writing: description is demoted in favour of analysis, subjunctive existential meditations making way for political intervention and the imperative mood. Literature itself is reconceptualised as a sharpened instrument in the radicalisation of a vanguard, not the entertainment of dead and empty hours. Novels are scarcely mentioned, and the only pre-existing poem that merits quoting at any length is Claude McKay's 'If We Must Die', a copy of which was found in an Attica cell in the aftermath of the uprising, and which George Jackson quotes in full.[34] Looking back three decades later at the miraculous elaboration of a distributed radical voice in prison cells at this time, Davis wrote:

> Literature has continued to play a role in campaigns around the prison. During the 1970s, which were marked by intense organizing within, outside, and across prison walls, numerous works authored by prisoners followed the 1970s publication of George Jackson's *Soledad Brother* and the anthology I co-edited with Bettina Aptheker, *If They Come in the Morning*. While many prison writers during that era had discovered the emancipatory potential of writing on their own, relying either on the education they had received prior to their imprisonment or on their tenacious efforts at self-education, others pursued their writing as a direct result of the expansion of prison educational programs during that era. The contemporary

[34] Jackson, *Soledad Brother*, 103.

disestablishment of writing and other prison educational programs is indicative of the official disregard today for rehabilitative strategies, particularly those that encourage individual prisoners to acquire autonomy of mind.[35]

'A new consciousness had taken root,' she wrote in her *Autobiography*. 'It was not simply the consciousness of those who were in prison for political reasons. This was a mass phenomenon. Prisoners – particularly Black prisoners – were beginning to think about how they got there – what forced them into prison.'[36] What H. Bruce Franklin calls the 'two overlapping groups of prison authors' who coalesced while incarcerated at this unique juncture in American history – 'the political activist thrust into prison, and the common criminal thrust into political activism'[37] – made for a searching reconsideration of literature itself, not as expressive or individualist, but as the collective property of an unending educational initiative in a call and response between the formally educated and the autodidactic. Literature was, indeed, the medium in which the 'distinction between these two groups tend[ed] to dissolve' (55), providing 'a major catalyst for intensified political action in and around prisons'.[38] What Davis described as 'the transformation of convicts, originally found guilty of criminal offenses, into exemplary political militants' took place and was propagated in the medium of literature. 'Their patient educational efforts in the realm of exposing the specific oppressive structures of the penal system in their relation to the larger oppression of the social system have had a profound effect on their fellow captives' (26). Prison writing is thereby transformed from a reportorial, testimonial function into a didactic and rhetorical function, which explicitly makes of its very conditions an occasion for the radical self-education of a population now aware of its status as a 'surplus' in relation to the available social product.

[35] Davis, *Are Prisons Obsolete?*, 54–5.
[36] Davis, *Autobiography*, 249.
[37] Franklin, 'The Literature of the American Prison', 55.
[38] Davis, *If They Come in the Morning*, 26.

Chapter 9

Living Hell: Bobby Sands' Prison Writing

Wouldn't it be a relief and delight to stroll through a lush green field and touch the blades of shining grass and feel the fresh texture of a leaf on a tree or sit on a hill and gaze upon a valley filled with the buzzing life of spring, smelling the fresh, clean, healthy scent with nothing but miles of space around me.

Freedom: that was it. Freedom to live again. I turned from the window to continue my relentless pacing, disheartened a little by the thoughts of freedom. I looked at the stinking, dirt-covered walls, the piles of disease-ridden rubbish and decaying waste food that lay scattered in the corners on the damp floor. The mutilated, filthy mattress, torn to shreds by a thousand searches. The tea-stained ceiling, to cut the glare reflecting off the bright light, the scraped and scarred door, and the disease-ridden chamber pot that lay beside the door. It was getting harder and harder to conjure up the picture of that beautiful lush green field. Every minute my nightmarish surroundings screamed at me. There was no escaping this nightmare unless I gave up! A few – a very few – had already given up. They had put on prison clothes and conformed. Not that they had wished to do this. They just couldn't bear the unrelenting burden of torture, the continued boredom, tension and fear, the deprivation of basic necessities like exercise and fresh air, no association with other human beings except through a shout from behind a closed heavy steel door.

The depression, the beatings, the cold – what is there? I said to myself. Look out the window and concentration camp screams at you. Look around you in the tomb that you survive in and you are engulfed in hell, with little black devils in the forms of A—, B— and C— ready to pounce on you each minute of each stinking nightmare-ridden day.[1]

---

[1] Bobby Sands, *Writings from Prison* (Cork: Mercier Press, 1997), 37–8.

The compulsive rhythms of Bobby Sands' prison writings, their wild swings between utopian reverie and sudden disenchantment, political hymn and savage realism, lyricism and satire, take their measure from an existential torsion wound around a Gordian knot: the 'unrelenting burden of torture' is suffered solely as a consequence of the blanketman's unyielding subjective militancy. It could all be ended at a stroke: don prison clothes, conform to the status of common criminal, and the immediate torture will evaporate. The 'escape' betokened by simple accommodation dangles as a constant prospect. Some comrades will have already made the choice, which the narrator understands perfectly, without any judgement. There are only good objective reasons to make it; every living moment is saturated with the pestilential stench of excrement smeared over the walls and spilling from the pot, and of rotten maggoty food heaped in corners of the cell, and further laden with the sensory menace of harsh overhead light, freezing temperatures for the naked prisoner shivering on punishing concrete floors, and the endless screams of anguish and agony from other cells, as the gaolers do their routine work. All of it is itching with its own negation, ready to be transformed into cleanliness, order and a measurable duration; but only at the price of a total collapse of the subjectivity that has conjured these 'nightmarish surroundings' into existence in the first place, and daily, hourly, minutely continues to will their being. This is the excruciation out of which the unique expressive idiom of Sands' writings is wrought: at the intersection of temptation and resignation. In a parallel text, he muses further on this crux: 'During moments of weakness I try to convince myself that a prison uniform and conforming wouldn't be that bad. But the will to resist burns too strong within. To accept the status of criminal would be to degrade myself and to admit that the cause that I believe in and cherish is wrong. When thinking of the men and women who sacrificed life itself, my suffering seems insignificant.'[2] It is ever thus: the sage counsel of the dead keeps the blanketman nailed to the cross where his very life is made a medium for the sacred cause.

Upon the walls of this psychic and physical dungeon, the subjunctive is scrawled in vivid characters of green. 'Wouldn't it be a relief . . .?' Always bucolic, generally enlivened with animal and avian life, the 'freedom' conjured by the subjunctive is a shimmering vision of now distant youth, a nostalgic reminiscence of days spent

---

[2] Sands, 'The Harvest Britain Has Sown', *Writings from Prison*, 93.

running wild through field and wood.[3] 'A happy boy through green fields ran,' as one of his H-Block ballads puts it (13), and the insistence here on 'exercise and fresh air' as 'basic necessities' tells a vital story about wasted Irish potential. The promising athlete Sands once was, 'who ran miles in gruelling cross-country races and swam miles and kicked football' (192), visits the cell in the form of an aching optative mood, a vibrant antithesis of the present suffocating nightmare. In 'a valley filled with the buzzing life of spring, smelling the fresh, clean, healthy scent with nothing but miles of space around me', the traumatised militant takes imaginary refuge from filth and pain, only to find that doing so redoubles his torment, as 'thoughts of freedom' are as a rule 'disheartening' in Hell. This utopian seam, by turns openly sentimental and piercingly affective, is a vital element of Sands' style, striving to relativise the surrounding brutality, to keep the muscles of the mind flexed, and to recall to consciousness the ultimate reason for the patriot's sacrifice: a free country. Nature is a perduring ground-note throughout the prison writings of Her Majesty's Maze, as it symbolises the object of contention between an occupying force and a native population; but it just as well stands as allegorical signifier for lost youth and innocence and the physical torture of enclosure on a once-healthy body rapidly losing its vitality and sinking inevitably into death. We shall find further reasons to consider one particular metonym of Sands' green fields, its trilling birdlife, below.

* * *

Yet the surest rhetorical point of this recourse to the natural, the open, the free, is of course to set off the more infernal aspects of Sands' incarceration, whose Catholic identity supplies him with readymade visions of what it is to be 'engulfed in hell, with little black devils' on all sides. H-Block itself is described as 'the gate to hell' (62, 98, 116), one narrative episode is entitled 'And so Life in the Living Hell Goes On', and more generally 'hell' peppers the pages of these prison writings, appearing over fifty times. 'I must have died last night, because when I awoke this morning I was in hell,' one

---

[3] In this, of course, it reprises some of the affects of Alan Sillitoe's great story, 'The Loneliness of the Long-Distance Runner'. See the discussion of this as a prison text in Claire Westall, 'Literary Studies and the Teaching of Prison Texts', in Michelle Kelly and Claire Westall, eds, *Prison Writing and the Literary World: Imprisonment, Institutionality and Questions of Literary Practice* (London: Routledge, 2021), 327–33.

vignette opens (178); and the most typical rhyme in the ballads runs: 'Four bare walls make this prison cell/The eight by eight space the prisoners call hell' (169). The tone is more Miltonic than Dantesque, with Sands adopting the outraged Satanic idiom of unconstrainable defiance rather than indulging in any hint of naturalisation. Yet damnation and its torments are only escapable via the proffered pact with the British devil: a signature in blood, a shameful agreement, a disavowal of the cause. Failing that, the minor salaried demons are unfailingly 'ready to pounce on you each minute of each stinking nightmare-ridden day'; their pitchforks, batons and pistols, their methods steeped in the pitch of Tartarus:

> A demon came his eyes aflame
> And round him was the law.
> They danced like in Hades and rats in plagues
> And Christ I froze in awe.
> They spun a cord this gruesome horde
> On loom of doom and sin,
> To make a noose that would induce
> A tortured soul within.
>
> Oh! Gorgons and Morons
> And vipers danced a ball,
> Ugly beasts and Satan's priests
> Stood naked 'pon the wall.
> Crude and lewd the spectres spewed
> And goblins jigged in rage,
> While snarling shrimps and imps and pimps
> Threw sins onto the stage.
>
> Wizards, Lizards, Sins in Blizzards
> Swirled round above their head,
> Squealing bats and snapping gnats
> Would suck the bloody thread.
> And all spat hate to that man's fate
> And all cried, 'Satan come!'
> All praised the law in evil awe
> For evil is but one. (125–6)

Sands is then ready to segue from this conventional Gothic idiom into the political register of anti-fascism and the 'concentration camp' itself, now stamped on the twentieth century as the default technique for containing the threat of political resistance (as we shall explore further below). Evocations of 'the stinking, dirt-covered walls, the piles of disease-ridden rubbish and decaying waste food that lay scattered in the corners on the damp floor' conjure up strong memories of the closing passages of *If This Is a Man*, its nightmarish descriptions of dysentery-befouled wards and corpses piling in the corridors. The concentration camp is personified here, 'screaming' its baleful imprecations at the inmates, and through association with the British state's policies in Northern Ireland, these screams enter a chorus with the historical howls of Auschwitz and the Gulag (and so with the neofascist carceral yelps of First's Johannesburg jail and Angela Davis's California cell). Throughout his testimony, Sands is explicit in his nomination of analogues for his treatment as a political prisoner of an imperialist state, all fetched from the recent annals of fascist mass incarceration. One guard is described as a 'straight-out-of-Belsen type' (31); a morning cavity search 'was like something last seen in Stalag 18 or Dachau' (37); the approach to H-Block reminds Sands 'of a clip of film I once saw, when I was young, of a Nazi concentration camp in winter' (61). Pivoting between sacred and geopolitical frames of reference, he can write:

> And I think of those long lines of naked, ragged Jews in the midst of a jungle of grey gruesome barbed wire and I can hear their feet, the almost silent, shuffling, naked feet of wretchedness and inhumanity and the whispering, whimpering, weeping, shrieking, screaming sounds of torture and death and I hear them all right. They're screeching at me from all sides and the wolves of Dachau are no different from the wolves of this hell and, dearest Jesus, is this not hell? And I know I will die if I have to, we all will if need be to quench the flames of this hell . . . (202)

Without having read Levi, deriving the better part of his understanding of the Nazi death camps from films and comic books, the autodidact Sands can nevertheless raise himself to such rhetorical heights on the basis of his profound existential affinity with these 'naked, ragged Jews' who stalk his imaginary like premonitory ghosts of the genocidal dead. 'The H-Blocks could become the knacker's yard of the Republican Movement,' Sands said elsewhere.[4]

By this point in the twentieth century, every political prisoner is implicitly in conversation with this legion of the mass-incarcerated dead, their texts strewn with references, images, metaphors, figures fetched from the human abattoirs of national socialism; and so, a tradition is constituted out of these abiding geopolitical solidarities

---

[4] Sands, quoted in David Beresford and Peter Maas, *Ten Dead Men: The Story of the 1981 Irish Hunger Strike* (London: Grafton, 1987), 39.

with those whom the extreme right has jailed only to kill. Every reading of Sands' prison writing is, to be sure, conducted under the sign of his own avoidable death behind bars, his voluntary self-sacrifice via hunger strike in furtherance of the same cause that neither the blanket protest nor the 'no-wash' dirty protest was able to vindicate – and that the terrible hunger strike, too, could not make victorious. But the tradition of political annihilation to which First, Davis, Jackson and others would testify in their prison writings, the inescapable conclusions each would draw about the use of political imprisonment not just to frustrate but to exterminate the racialised left, ensures that Sands' death too is understood as part of the larger story as told by Levi, Berkman, Ngũgĩ and Luxemburg, among countless others: prison is the gateway to a political hell fashioned in the image of the world of property.[5] Sands is the most explicit since Levi in his convocation of a community of inmates who are neither living nor dead because they have been denied their status as people with rights by powers invested in negating their very existence. 'Sort of makes you think why they keep us locked up and naked and filthy in disease-ridden, smelly concrete dungeon like cells, unfit even for pigs. It is a mentality that makes it so easy for them to torture us, or butcher us when the opportunity arises. A mentality much the same as those who maintained and organised the Nazi concentration camps and the subsequent genocide of the Jews.' (95)

In the case of the Irish Republican Army volunteers who undertook paramilitary anti-British activities in the North and were apprehended for it, this denial of a certain set of rights was relatively recent. In 1972 the Special Powers Act empowered British forces with the extraordinary ability to arrest without a warrant and imprison without charge any persons suspected of this kind of action; but it also granted Special Category Status to those so detained, allowing them to wear their own clothes, to freely associate with one another, to undertake further education, and to be spared hard prison labour. 'The prison authorities implicitly recognised paramilitary command structures, conducting all communication with the POWs through the prisoners' officer commanding (OC). In the Cages of Long Kesh, prisoners endured communal

---

[5] Sands knew his radical and prison literature. 'He read voraciously – his favourites including Frantz Fanon, Camilo Torres, Che Guevara, Amilcar Cabral, George Jackson and, of Irish writers, Connolly, Pearse and Mellows – keeping a fast-growing pile of exercise books full of political analyses, quotations and notes. He was planning to write a book with it all, but they were destroyed in 1974.' Beresford and Maas, *Ten Dead Men*, 60.

incarceration in a compound reminiscent of the prisoner-of-war camps of World War II, each Cage housing about ninety POWs in Nissen huts: the POWs were locked into the huts only at night. In short, detainees with Special Category Status were treated as political prisoners in all but name.'[6] Enjoying conditions much closer to those endured by Ezra Pound than any other prisoner considered in this book, the early IRA prisoners were deemed military prisoners of war rather than common inmates. But with an ever-expanding prison population across the 1970s, as political resistance accelerated in the streets during the so-called 'Troubles', and following the Gardiner Report's recommendations in 1975, the British government abandoned Internment and Special Category Status towards the end of the decade. 'By phasing out Special Category Status and by creating the appearance of due process, the British state hoped to redefine paramilitaries not as guerillas but as gangsters.'[7] Now moved out of the Nissen huts and into the Maze of H-Blocks, prisoners were forced to undergo a radical redefinition of their status and institutional identity. 'The first IRA men to enter the H-Blocks encountered a regime that refused to recognize any social unit larger than the individual inmate. The depoliticization of the paramilitary's former political status conversely meant his extreme individualization and a refusal on the part of the prison administration to recognize his organizational affiliation.'[8]

This is how Sands puts it in his piece, 'Training Camp':

> H Block was blackly engineered to crush the political identity of the captured Republican prisoner, to crush his resistance and transform him into a systemised answering machine with a large criminal tag stamped by oppression upon his back, to be duly released back onto the street, politically cured – politically barren – and permanently broken in spirit. (225)

Most of his writings from prison are issued with the explicit intention of reversing these losses and reinstating the category of political prisoner: able again to wear their own clothes, avoid prison labour, freely associate with each other, and with rights to weekly visits and the remission of sentences. The proper context in which those rights are withheld are not criminal but political and military. The guards

---

[6] Lachlan Whalen, *Contemporary Irish Republican Prison Writing: Writing and Resistance* (London: Palgrave, 2007), 57.

[7] Whalen, *Contemporary Irish Republican Prison Writing*, 58.

[8] Allen Feldman, *Formations of Violence: The Narrative of the Body and Political Terror in Northern Ireland* (Chicago: University of Chicago Press, 1991), 152.

and the higher authorities who train and pay them are denounced, not as common thugs, but as 'War criminals! I said to myself. They're a stinking, dirty shower of war criminals, every last one of them' (36). The full description of the 'Belsen-type' guard runs as follows:

> He was heartless, sly and intelligent when it came to torturing naked men. There was no physical stuff from him. All purely psychological attacks and cunning tricks. He was a right-out-of-Belsen type, and like the majority of the screws he took great pleasure in attacking the dignity of the naked prisoners-of-war. He was on a constant ego trip, but then weren't they all once they donned their little black suits with the shining buttons, and were handed their baton and pistol? (31)

Fascinating here is the line of continuity with Ruth First's unhappy discovery of new techniques of psychological warfare, and their explicit association with Nazi concentration camp methods; but just as crucial is the insistence on the category of prisoner of war in the midst of this historico-psychological portrait of a now familiar type. It is precisely that category over which the struggles in the text are waged: the resistance to violent searches, the filthy cells, the urine pools, the shivering naked bodies, the clandestine writing, all are undertaken in the interest of re-establishing the right to be so identified. 'I was naive when I was young,' Sands writes. 'Here I was now going back to a filthy concrete tomb to fight for my survival, to fight for my right to be recognised as a political prisoner-of-war, a right for which I would never stop fighting' (62). And there is nothing the agents of the British state can do to end this multifoliate struggle, even to the limit of murdering all these blanketmen, or allowing them to die. At the end of his 'day in the life' narrative, Sands summarises the iterative nature of his story in accents that recall Solzhenitsyn:

> It had been a hard day but wasn't every day the same and God only knew what tomorrow would bring. Who would be the unlucky unfortunates tomorrow, supplying the battered bloody bodies for the punishment block? Who would be hosed down, beaten up or torn apart during a wing shift? Tomorrow would only bring more pain and torture and suffering, boredom and fear and God knows how many humiliations, inhumanities and horrors. Darkness and intense cold, an empty stomach and the four screaming walls of a filthy nightmare-filled tomb to remind me of my plight, that's what lay ahead tomorrow for hundreds of naked Republican political prisoners-of-war, but just as sure as the morrow would be filled with torture so would we carry on and remain unbroken. (79)

For the political prisoners of Long Kesh, individual identities, names and stories recede into relative indifference before the purely generic nature of their collective punishment for refusing to be labelled as criminals. It is the collective that supplies the bodies, suffers the pain, in a kind of hydra-headed endurance test subsuming their individual differences. The narrative voice aspires to speak the impersonal language of these 'hundreds of naked Republican political prisoners-of-war' thinking and acting as one, just as Levi's testament speaks from the empty point of view of the *musulmano*.

* * *

But it is ultimately as subjects that each of them must take the final step. As the inevitable conclusion draws ever nearer, there is a paradoxical insistence on the inverse relationship between a merely beaten animal body and a rapturous spiritual attainment of immortality:

> I was a skeleton compared to what I used to be but it didn't matter. Nothing really mattered except remaining unbroken. I rolled over once again, the cold biting at me. They have nothing in their entire imperial arsenal to break the spirit of one single Republican political prisoner-of-war who refuses to be broken, I thought, and that was very true. They can not or never will break our spirit. (80)

And so, we appear again to rejoin that older tradition of the self-hardening, disciplined, morally sharpened, stoical political prisoner facing execution and excommunication, affirming what is unbreakable in him: a spiritual fortitude in the face of death. But it is never only a question of strength and resilience, though this is the line most often taken by our narrator. Alain Badiou writes: 'All the affects are necessary in order for the incorporation of a human animal to unfold in a subjective process, so that the grace of being Immortal may be accorded to this animal, in the discipline of a Subject and the construction of a truth.'[9] These affects include rage, hatred, fear, impotence, futility, as well as the more usual courage and boldness; and the fact is that sometimes, in order truly to live, as an Immortal apart from suffering animal bodies (including one's own), it is necessary to undertake the task of dying, with all the affects that unleashes. A spirit, in order not to break, must learn to weep, to agonise, to

---

[9] Badiou, *Logic of Worlds*, translated by Alberto Toscano (London: Continuum, 2009), 87.

doubt, to tremble in mortal terror as the life is being drained from the animal one also is. The discipline necessary to become immortal requires all this of a subject; and when that discipline has been perfected, it is as Sands writes: 'They have nothing in their entire imperial arsenal to break the spirit' rendered so supple and smooth and free that it can relinquish all ties to the body and become a bird in flight, an ecstatic moment of truth.

Against this sublime tendency, the text constantly calls us back to the numbing routines and sensory punishments of the self-inflicted horror deemed necessary to attain the true cause.

> The stench rose to remind me of my situation and the floor was damp and gooey in places. Piles of rubbish lay scattered about the cell, and in the dimness dark eerie figures screamed at me from the surrounding dirty, mutilated walls. The stench of excreta and urine was heavy and lingering. I lifted the small water container from amongst the rubbish and challenged an early morning drink in a vain effort to remove the foul taste in my throat. (27)

The tone of the phenomenological in Sands' writing is disproportionately olfactory and excremental, in profound if unconscious sympathy with a long-standing Irish satirical tradition – that of Swift. But there remains an insistent association of the most private, loathsome, shameful bodily excreta, and the violent coercion of the state powers who seek so ardently the total transparency and permeability of the prisoner's body. If excrement is everywhere, that is in good part because 'anal retention' is a physical impossibility inside Her Majesty's Maze. The refusal to bend ('Bend over, you little cunt!' [35]) results in enforced cavity searches.

> Jesus, here it comes. He stepped beside me, still laughing, and hit me. Within a few seconds, in the midst of the white flashes, I fell to the floor as blows rained upon me from every conceivable angle. I was dragged back up again to my feet and thrown like a side of bacon, face downwards on the table. Searching hands pulled at my arms and legs, spreading me like a pelt of leather. Someone had my head pulled back by the hair while some pervert began probing and poking my anus. It was great fun; everybody was killing themselves laughing, except me, while all the time a barrage of punches rained down on my naked body. I was writhing in pain. They gripped me tighter as each blow found its destination. My face was smashed against the table and blood smeared the table under my face. I was dazed and hurt. Then they dragged me off the table and let me drop to the floor. (29)

This slaughterhouse trauma, experienced almost daily, is in dialectical-existential relationship with the anticipated tedium of another day just like the thousands that have gone before and will surely follow after. Numbing repetition and traumatic violence both annihilate the capacity for experience; Sands' typical day tilts dramatically between them, with the result that there is no life left to live, only a turbid vacancy where one might have been. And this is doubtless why the rectum comes to be a privileged allegorical lens on the whole complex of political imprisonment. With it fixed in place, Sands achieves one of the quintessential images of the twentieth century, an image that other scatological Irishman Samuel Beckett would have saluted as standing comparison with his own. Forced to defecate on the floor of his cell 'among the rubbish and dirt' where his stools will rot alongside dozens of others, Sands rouses himself to a rhetorical parenthesis:

> Who among those so-called humanitarians who had kept their silence on the H Blocks, who among them could put a name on this type of humiliation and torture, when men are forced by extreme torture into the position that they had to embark upon a dirt strike to highlight the inhumanity poured upon them! How much must we suffer, I thought. An unwashed body, naked and wrecked with muscular pain, squatting in a corner, in a den of disease, amid piles of putrefying rubbish, forced to defecate upon the ground where the excreta would lie and the smell would mingle with the already sickening evil stench of urine and decaying waste food. Let them find a name for that sort of torture, I thought, rising and moving towards the window to seek fresh air, the beatings, the hosing downs, starvation and deprivation, just let them bloody well put a name on this nightmare of nightmares. (42)

The best name we have for it is 'Bobby Sands', who gave his life to realise it in prose that ranks, in its grotesque extremity, alongside Dante and other sable chroniclers of the infernal depths of 'man's inhumanity to man'.

The story of that writing and its tortuous emergence into our world of letters is as excruciating as its diegetic narrative. As Richard O'Rawe, a fellow inmate of Long Kesh, was to put it later, 'Tiny comms were smuggled in and out every day. Appeals for support were written on cigarette papers and smuggled out in the mouths, foreskins and noses of prisoners. Our people outside then sent these appeals to every major newspaper in the world, as well as to colleges, trade unions, prominent foreign politicians and anyone else who could help build sympathy for our cause.'[10] This passage through the body, the ineluctable progress via which all prison writings from the Maze were fated to appear outside, vouchsafes an irreducible kernel of meta-literary significance to every one of Sands' scatological episodes, since O'Rawe was far too squeamish to mention the most obvious and frequently used orifice for literary storage. That inevitable destination was signalled, to be sure, by one of the three principal sources of paper available to the prisoners.

> We had one miserly pencil and a pen refill that were constantly in use around the wing, going from one cell to the next, back and forth from one side of the wing to the other, eating up sheets of 'bog roll' (toilet paper) for the wee smuggled notes to worried wives, mothers and girlfriends; for the letters to the newspapers and the quickly scribbled notes to the H Block Information Bureau telling of the beatings and horrors that took place every single day. I would have to wait my turn for the pen or pencil. (68)

Toilet paper was the medium of choice for this illegal testimony of prison life, along with cigarette papers and torn fragments of the Bible, and Sands learned an astonishing efficiency in exploiting every shred. 'No Republican POW was more adept at utilizing every available millimetre of paper than Bobby Sands. His prose manuscripts are astounding in their economy: Sands could easily fit three hundred words on a single cigarette paper.'[11] With the frequent cell searches and general filth of his environment making secure storage a constant problem, these letters minutely written on prison toilet paper were bound to meet their destination. 'Bobby kept the manuscript, written on dozens of sheets of toilet paper, stuffed up his anus, carefully folded like an accordion to keep it as small as possible.'[12] By a certain point, indeed, there was 'a considerable library carried around in his back passage' (215).

What does this anal gestation of Sands' prison writings entail for their reception? In the first place it means that Swift's excremental vision is not merely incidental but fundamental to everything published under the name of Bobby Sands: each missive, each article, each poem is a nauseating smear on all bourgeois propriety and good

---

[10] Richard O'Rawe, *Blanketmen: An Untold Story of the H-Block Hunger Strike* (Dublin: New Island, 2005), 48.

[11] Whalen, *Contemporary Irish Republican Prison Writing*, 61.

[12] Denis O'Hearn, *Nothing but an Unfinished Song: Bobby Sands, the Irish Hunger Striker Who Ignited a Generation* (New York: Nation Books, 2006), 213.

taste, bearing on its every word a smell of the underlying situation:
'To eat and sit where you've just shit!'[13]

> Then came the reek of stomach weak
> For some men retch with fear,
> And worse again and ne'er the shame
> The bowels of men appear.
> For listen, friend, we don't pretend,
> There are no heroes here. (150)
> [. . .]
> Shocked you are, by far, by far
> But shock you do now know.
> Perhaps you say this poet's way
> Is crude and very low?
> But in the blocks men have had shocks
> That filled the very po! (145)

Secondly, this passage through the body entails clear stylistic and generic consequences, as the 'crude and very low' way establishes a base of operations that the writing is compelled to return to in a manner unexampled in the prior history of prison writing. To an extent, every act of prison writing is a confrontation with the body, its limits and most basic needs; yet most writers considered in this book have striven to offset that preoccupation with various tactics of discretion and tact – best exemplified in First's witty excursions around the topic of her own bladder. Even in Levi's harrowing text, which details obscenities and desecrations of the flesh far exceeding Sands', there remains a delicate, polite effort to spare the reader any thought that the author remains trapped in the orbit of blasphemous ordure he is endeavouring to recreate. But in Sands, there is no exit, no reprieve from the formal 'shocks' of an obscene element that cannot be repressed from the text because it is the very element in which it has been inscribed.

And third, it all amounts to an implicit gendering of the IRA prisoner of war as feminine, invaginated, violable, constantly being forced open to the sexualised assaults of an aggressive male keeper.

> I felt the cold chamfered edges of the large mirror being pushed
> between my legs. They were scrutinising my anus, using the mirror
> to afford them a view from every angle. A foreign hand probed and
> poked at my anus and, unsatisfied, they kicked the back of my knees,
> forcing me down into a squatting position where they again used the
> mirror and, to finish off, they rained more kicks and blows on my
> naked, burning body for good measure. (60)

[13] Sands, *Writings from Prison*, 144.

In a sister passage from her own prison testimony, Assata Shakur tries to articulate what a fully feminised prisoner might feel like:

> The 'internal search' was as humiliating and disgusting as it sounded. You sit on the edge of this table and the nurse holds your legs open and sticks a finger in your vagina and moves it around. She has a plastic glove on. Some of them try to put one finger in your vagina and another one up your rectum at the same time.[14]

As Joshua Price argues, 'routine strip searches and cavity searches, as organized forms of sexual assault, cut to the core of citizenship in a democratic society. As a social practice, these searches, and their invasive, assaultive character, are at once well known to all and socially invisible.'[15] But when Sands writes about it as a blanket-man, and smuggles the evidence out through his own rectum, what Davis calls 'the gendering of state punishment' and 'the extent to which women's prisons have held on to oppressive patriarchal practices that are considered obsolete in the "free world"', go through a strange and immensely productive defamiliarisation.[16] For here the full obscenity of what goes unseen despite routine acknowledgement is laid bare: prison is an industry of the law predicated on violently sexualised invasive procedures that treat all bodies as a rapist treats his victim. The political prisoner, suspected of carrying contraband in any available orifice, is confronted with the kinds of sexual assault that women everywhere know as an ambient condition of life under patriarchy. That is to say, 'the institution of the prison has stockpiled ideas and practices that [. . .] retain all their ghastly vitality behind prison walls',[17] and that is one of the critical means at the disposal of the state for perpetuating its obscene tangle of unwritten codes and norms supporting the explicitly written laws in the unconscious. Žižek likes to write about 'the basic constellation of the social law as that of the "law in general and its obscene superego underside in particular"'.[18] Prison, the place where the law sends its offenders, is precisely where the obscene barbaric underside of our decorous world intrudes into the real and is visited on their bodies, but only on the condition of a total obscurity 'behind walls'. By passing his testimony through the rectum, by fecundating it and making it a

---

[14] Assata Shakur, *Assata: An Autobiography* (Chicago: Lawrence Hill Books, 2001), 85.

[15] Joshua M. Price, *Prison and Social Death* (New Brunswick, NJ: Rutgers University Press, 2015), 46.

[16] Angela Y. Davis, *Are Prisons Obsolete?* (New York: Seven Stories Press, 2003), 64.

[17] Davis, *Are Prisons Obsolete?*, 83.

[18] Slavoj Žižek, *Sex and the Failed Absolute* (London: Bloomsbury, 2019), 197.

womb of thought, Sands transforms sexualised terror into a mode of apprehension of the social law as such.

* * *

And always, yearning away from this filth, there is the siren call of a freedom the body has already adapted away from.

> What would it be like if they were to open the door now and throw me out to freedom? I wouldn't be able to cope with it. Dear God! I could hardly bear up to a visit. I just couldn't imagine what state I would be in if I were to be released from this torture. I knew how to appreciate small, seemingly unimportant things now that one time or another I would have taken for granted or probably not even noticed. When was the last time I received a decent warm meal? Funny how one can adapt to things – especially when you are starving . . . (65)

The horror of institutionalisation is the horror of adaptability, our innate animal ability to make a home in hell. The foreclosure of rich sensual experience, the daily exposure to torture, emaciation, cold and torment, spell the fatal closing in of an entire horizon of being, the 'world shrinking down about a raw core of parsible entities', as someone once put it – whether those entities are edible or sensory.[19] But Sands notes the dialectical complement to this starvation of the human appetite for freedom, and it resides in those 'small, seemingly unimportant things' that habitually fall below the threshold of perception, but which in prison (like Pound's insects) loom with breathtaking psychic enormity. And it is yet again with the visiting birdlife that this extraordinary prisoner's 'appreciation' is helplessly invested, to a degree that only Rosa Luxemburg can rival – for Sands had been, as he puts it, 'a once-upon-a-time budding ornithologist' as a youth (235), and it is to that amateur pastime that he returns as his flesh wastes away on hunger strike in the harrowing final diary entries.

The lark is the bird he first identifies with, since it carries him back to his grandfather's words in a small vignette about a captured skylark:

> My grandfather once said that the imprisonment of the lark is a crime of the greatest cruelty because the lark is one of the greatest symbols of freedom and happiness [. . .] the lark had spirit – the spirit of freedom and resistance. It longed to be free, and died before it would conform to the tyrant who tried to change it with torture

---

[19] Cormac McCarthy, *The Road* (New York: Knopf, 2006), 75.

and imprisonment. I feel I have something in common with that bird and her torture, imprisonment and final murder. (82)

This is somewhat too programmatic, too steeped in Shelley's lore and the obligatory romantic accents of song. Elsewhere the identification is more elastic and contextual:

> Many a day in the eternal hours, I stand watching the birds and listening to the lark, trying to discover its whereabouts in that stagnant blue ocean above me that represents the outside world, and I long for the liberty of the lark. I suppose, to many, a few birds, the sound of a lark, a blue sky, or full moon, are there, but stay unnoticed most of the time. But, to me, they mean existence, peacefulness, comfort, entertainment and something to view, to help forget the tortures, brutalities, indignities and evils that surround and attack my everyday life. (161)

But the symbolism is still too overt. It is with the starlings that Sands' budding ornithology takes wing.

> . . . it is soothing in many respects to spend a half an hour with one's head pressed against the concrete slabs, gazing in wonder, and taking in the antics of a dozen or so young starlings bickering over a few stale crusts of bread. Circling, swooping, sizing up and daring an extra nibble, continually on their guard, and all their tiny nerves on end, the young starlings feud among themselves, the greedy one continually trying to dominate and always wanting the whole haul to himself, fighting with his comrades whilst the sparrow sneaks in to nibble at the spoils. (160)

This deliciously Luxemburgian passage marks the rarest of all moments in the writings from Long Kesh, a moment in which sensory attention is fully captivated by something other than pain and takes the prose style places it is otherwise forbidden to go. Here we glimpse, in nuce, the writer that Sands could have been had he been granted the terms of liberty for which he fought: observant, playful, responsive, sly, and called to mimic what his senses conveyed. His characterisations do not capitulate to crude prison allegories but keep open the rushing confusion of animal behaviour. By the time he turns to the seagulls, Sands' ornithology is in full flight:

> But the ruler of the kingdom of my little twenty-yard arched view of the outside world is the seagull, who dominates, steals, pecks, and denies the smaller birds their share. The seagull takes it all. In fact, his appetite seems insatiable. He goes to any length to gorge himself.

Thus I dislike the seagull, and I often wonder why the starlings do not direct their attention to the predator, rather than each other. Perhaps this applies to more than birds.

During the summer months, finches were abundant, and the music of the lark a constant symphony of sound and a reminder of life. The various crows, the odd magpie, and the little wagtails are still to be seen and heard from dawn to dusk. (161)

Allegory is allowed its place here, to be sure, but it remains subsidiary to the accuracy and pleasure of observation itself, which discovers in the surprisingly rich avian polyphony an image of freedom otherwise forced to adopt the vestments of nostalgia and memory. Moral temptations and identifications are played with, but the minor world of animals is finally not assimilable through those categories and instead calls for its own impersonal language: the catalogue, the notation, the account. For it is through naming animals that the human comes into being as such: an affirmation of what sets us apart in the act of nominating the free and unfettered.

And then, in almost the very last words to make it out of Long Kesh in the handwriting of this great militant, inscribed in Gaelic on Friday, 13 April 1981, after forty-four excruciating days of nil-by-mouth, we read his magnificent valediction, the most moving words ever written in a prison and enough, in one ecstatic sigh, to etch his immortality on the granite of time:

> Bhí na héiníní ag ceiliúracht inniu. Chaith ceann de na buachaillí arán amach as an fhuinneog, ar a leghad bhí duine éigin ag ithe. Uaigneach abhí mé ar feadh tamaill ar tráthnóna beag inniu ag éisteacht leis na preácháin ag screadáil agus ag teacht abhaile daobhtha. Da gclúin-finn an fhuiseog álainn, brisfeadh sí mo chroí.
>
> Anois mar a scríobhaim tá an corrcrothar ag caoineadh mar a théann siad tharam. Is maith Horn na héiníní.
>
> Bhuel caithfidh mé a dul mar má scríobhain níos mó ar na héiníní seo beidh mo dheora ag rith' s rachaidh mo smaointí ar ais chuig an t-am nuair abhí mé óganach, b'iad na laennta agus iad imithe go deo anois, ach thaitin siad Horn agus ar a laghad níl dearmad deánta agam orthu, ta siad i mo chroí – oíche mhaith anois.[20]

---

[20] 'The birds were singing today. One of the boys threw bread out of the window. At least somebody's eating! I was lonely for a while this evening, listening to the crows caw as they returned home. Should I hear the beautiful lark, she would rend my heart. Now, as I write, the odd curlew mournfully calls as they fly over. I like the birds. Well, I must leave off, for if I write more about the birds my tears will fall and my thoughts return to the days of my youth. They were the days, and gone forever now. But I enjoyed them. They are in my heart – good night, now.' Sands, *Writings from Prison*, 242.

Chapter 10

'Free Thoughts on Toilet Paper!': Ngũgĩ wa Thiong'o at Kamĩtĩ

But we all shared a common feeling: something beautiful, something like the promise of a new dawn had been betrayed, and our presence and situation at Kamĩtĩ Maximum Security Prison was a logical outcome of that historical betrayal.

Irretrievable loss! Had we really come to this? Was prison our destiny as a Kenyan people? Fated always to plunge back to the days of the colony only hours after being tantalized with glimpses of new dawns? What of the million dead and maimed? Was it only to enable a depraved few to carry on the colonial philosophy for which the lives of countless poor men, women, and children had been sacrificed?

In the cell, each political prisoner would struggle against mounting despair – the inevitable outcome of bitter reflections churned over and over in the mind. For here one had no helper except one's own experiences and history. That, I would say, was the real loneliness of prison life. In the silence of one's cell, one had to fight, all alone, against a thousand demons struggling for the mastery of one's soul. Their dominant method was to show continually that there was only one way of looking at things, that there was only one history and culture, which moved in circles, so that the beginning and the end were the same. You moved only to find yourself back on the same spot. What was the point of making the effort? We were all the children of Sisyphus fated forever to roll the heavy stone of tyranny up the steep hill of struggle, only to see it roll back to the bottom.[1]

---

[1] Ngũgĩ wa Thiong'o, *Wrestling with the Devil* (London: Random House, 2018), 66–7. Although the primary prison text is Ngũgĩ's *Detained* (1981), this later, edited version remains in print and is more accessible to the reader, so it will be quoted first in this chapter, with sometimes (as here) an additional reference to the corresponding passage in *Detained: A Writer's Prison Diary* (London: Heinemann, 1981), 63–4. There are notable differences in emphasis, discourse and ideology between the two editions,

Ngũgĩ wa Thiong'o's prison writing turns in the gyre where the personal and the historical intersect. It is a vital, innervating cross-roads, where merely accidental, biographical facts are shot through with dynamic historical energies, rendering them salient in the fateful back-light of the 'million dead'. But this energising existential torsion is then rudely transformed into a logic of empty repetition and timeless futility by the state's instrumentation of prison time. One has, in the neocolonial state, been cast into the dungeon – here, Nairobi's maximum-security Kamĩtĩ prison – on the basis of one's identification with a 'betrayed' historical process; but, in embodying that betrayal (as an incarcerated intellectual in league with the socialist trinity of workers, peasants and students), one has effectively been ejected from history altogether into a Hades where 'the children of Sisyphus' toil in the gloom. Sisyphus is, in fact, the dominant allegorical figure for the African masses across the length of Ngũgĩ's prison memoir: 'the African Sisyphus' (67, 70, 86, 92) recurs as a potent personification of perennially disappointed political triumph, a fatality inscribed not in the genes of the continent's working people but in their leaders' spineless complicities and capitulations to imperial capital. It is a mythic figuration that works in a pointedly different register from Shelley's Prometheus or Blake's Orc, because it factors a pitiless, ironic temporality into the experience of heroic organised resistance. Note how, in this associated passage, the 'irony of history' is explicitly evoked to characterise Kenyans' damnation to repetition: 'Foreign-run private armies to protect foreigners and a handful of Kenyans from real or imagined wrath of fellow Kenyans: what an irony of history! The culture of silence and fear had achieved a dialectically opposite effect. Kenyan people had rejected the view of history that the colonial and neocolonial gods had tried to impose on rebellious Sisyphus' (74–5/71). Along with that other mythological figure, Tantalus ('*tantalized* with glimpses'), Sisyphus may 'reject' the version of history that imprisons him; but the rock continues to roll back to the bottom of the mountain, the fruit eludes his grasp, the water forever retreating from his lips. Dialectics have a way of reversing every gain and of negating that reversal – but the neo-colony remains an exemplary instance of 'dialectics at a standstill'.[2]

---

which can best be summarised by the fact that *Detained* uses variations on the term 'patriot' over a hundred times, while *Wrestling* uses it only six.

[2] Walter Benjamin, *The Arcades Project*, translated by Howard Eiland and Kevin McLaughlin (Cambridge, MA: Harvard University Press, 1999), 462, 463, 912.

There is an obvious grammatical emphasis on the first-person plural pronoun (stronger still in the first edition, *Detained*, 1981, where dozens of other inmates are named to flesh out its specificity) and Ngũgĩ puts its marvellous flexibility of inclusivity to work, encompassing now the political prisoners at Kamĩtĩ, and now the nation at large; and it resonates, too, with the impersonal pronoun 'one' and the generic second-person pronoun. We intuitively grasp its relation to another pronoun – a 'they', a 'them' – with whom it finds itself in perpetual dialectical tension. The 'we' stands poised on a mythic threshold where metaphors abound: 'new dawns' beckoning on one side, and 'a thousand demons' gibbering on the other. But historical stasis traps the plural subject at this excruciating juncture between revolutionary promise and reactionary betrayal; and that is precisely the existential condition of the neo-colony – having staged its revolution without extending its logic into the broad life of the people; perpetuating imperial models of discipline and control in order to forestall any lingering threat of that political contagion stimulated by the anti-colonial struggle of yesterday. This stasis is prison itself, both literally and figuratively: 'Was prison our destiny as a Kenyan people? Fated always to plunge back to the days of the colony only hours after being tantalized with glimpses of new dawns?'

Time at Kamĩtĩ, as in Kenya, is non-time. And in non-time, 'we' cannot be sustained. Segregation, separation, isolation dictate that Eliot's 'We think of the key, each in his prison/Thinking of the key, each confirms a prison'[3] is the name of the grammatical game: 'we' becomes 'each political prisoner', and 'the real loneliness of prison life' corrodes the political solidarities that precipitated it. Even thinking about the 'we' is a private undertaking, the very key each is meditating, confirming an 'I' that falls out of temporal sequence into the merely iterative and generic, into mythic temporality. The 'thousand demons struggling for the mastery of one's soul' claim this mythic, circular time as their own and lull the isolated subject into conformity with its rhythms, into accepting 'only one history and culture, which moved in circles, so that the beginning and the end were the same'. Prison is a space where time loops back onto itself, and where history yields to the privative temporality of infinite repetition. 'I find that here at Kamĩtĩ, in a certain sense, everything is so very ordinary – well, worse than ordinary, for time here is sluggish, space is narrow, and any action is a repetition of similar

[3] T. S. Eliot, *The Waste Land*, ll. 413–14 (New York: Boni and Liveright, 1922), 47.

nonactions – that I have nothing outstanding to record. Yesterday as today' (138). This tightens the remarkable figural resilience of Ngũgĩ's deployment of the conventional allegoresis identifying prison and state: in the neo-colony, everybody is a prisoner, and historical time cedes to the mythic temporality of a private and repetitive relationship with time. The African Sisyphus is '[f]ated always to plunge back to the days of the colony only hours after being tantalized with glimpses of new dawns', but only because it has been thoroughly atomised by the statewide carceral apparatus.

The terrible fate hanging over the 'African Sisyphus' in detention is his monstrous conversion into a 'colonial zombie, a total negation of his earlier predetention self' (88). This is the grim destiny awaiting those who succumb to the blandishments and entreaties of the 'thousand demons' who would lure him away from visions of new dawns and revolutionary solidarities. In his fifth chapter, Ngũgĩ treats this potential at significant length, going over the record of political detention in the British colony and considering anti-colonial heroes like Harry Thuku and Jomo Kenyatta who, after years in prison, emerged as lackeys of international capital and assumed positions of power in the independent Kenyan state – while arresting and torturing militants in the Kenya Land and Freedom Army (KLFA), the so-called Mau Mau guerrillas. Kenyatta, under whose orders Ngũgĩ himself was detained for over a year, is perhaps the starkest case of 'neo-colonial zombiedom' in need of diagnosis.

> What happened to that [heroic] Kenyatta during the ten years of prison life in lonely, dusty places? In the prisons, reading only the Bible and the Koran, with the district commissioner constantly calling him to private audiences away from the other four, did the demons, in the ghostly forms of Ross, Hooper, Barlow, and Arthur – all the early missionaries who used to write to him in the 1930s urging him to return to church fellowship and give up 'extreme' politics – did these now visit him and, raising him from the valley of dry bones, showed [*sic*] him the escape route from the ceaseless, fruitless labors of African Sisyphus? (92/86–7)

Prisons break the militant's resolve, his solidarity with comrades outside and in, because prisons are where the 'demons' of an undead colonial past stalk the conscience of the revolutionary subject and tempt it with a different kind of promise. The privatised escape velocity from the 'African Sisyphus' is measured in units of 'property' and 'personal gain' (93, 94), a path this kind of prison-zombie will cynically sell to the masses in mantras of toil and acquisition.

On the other hand, prison can be a place where fundamental commitments are tempered and strengthened; it is where the 'other type of political prisoner, typified by Waiyaki wa Hinga, Ngunju wa Gakere, Me Katilili, and Arap Manyei, never repudiated their former militant political stands' (98), and where the 'hard-core Mau Mau' (98) is forged in steel. Much as it had already been framed by Ruth First, Angela Davis, George Jackson, and by Bobby Sands most memorably, prison is the greatest trial of 'not being broken' for any political activist, and something which the militant must be expected to face when his name is cashed in for a number – in this case K6–77 – by arbitrary presidential decree. Ngũgĩ looks specifically to one former political prisoner, J. M. Kariũki, who wrote 'an account of his own wrestling bouts with demons in at least fourteen concentration camps all over Kenya. His autobiography, *Mau Mau Detainee*, is an important contribution to the Kenyan literature of struggle' (101). In that archly understated document, Kariũki details what it was like to be confined (amongst others) to the vast Manyani Special Detention Camp, where 'hard-core Mau Mau' fighters were held en masse. 'One thousand two hundred detainees were in each hangar. They never went out into the sun and they could never tell if it was day or night when they woke up. Because of the murmuring of innumerable voices it sounded like a huge market-place. [. . .] The detainees were very dissatisfied with the general conditions in the hangars.'[4] This camp alone held over twenty thousand 'hard-core' guerrillas by 1955; but there were many more camps. British policy towards the KLFA ranks among the most ignoble in the history of its empire, and Caroline Elkins has compiled blistering evidence of the long trail of blood, limbs, and death left by Britain's 'Gulag' in Kenya. In 1958, detainees at Marĩira detention camp penned a letter for *The Observer* detailing the authorities' 'many wonderful tortures and maltreatment': denial of water, denial of medical care, savage beatings, rampant disease, slave labour, murders. 'Here is a camp comparable to none – perhaps the Nazi Concentration camps could be better. The Government pays no heed whatsoever, although deaths after severe beatings have been reported by us.'[5] Ngũgĩ's purpose in referencing Kariũki's testimony and that of Makhan Singh, and connecting it to the combined witness of 'a

[4] Josiah Mwangi Kariuki, *'Mau Mau' Detainee: The Account by a Kenya African of his Experience in Detention Camps, 1953–1960* (London: Oxford University Press, 1963), 93.

[5] Qtd in Caroline Elkins, *Imperial Reckoning: The Untold Story of Britain's Gulag in Kenya* (New York: Henry Holt, 2005), 338.

common anti-imperialist national tradition that goes way back to the very early political prisoners – Me Katilili, Waiyaki, Ngunju wa Gakere' (101), is to establish a profound continuity in Kenyatta's new Kenya – of the old colonial carceral regime and its explicit use of detention as a deradicalisation technique. And it is also to draw upon that militant tradition as a source of resilience, a refusal to break, under today's somewhat milder conditions in Kamĩtĩ.

Such relative mildness is, however, contested by one of the living remnants of the colonial regime's punitive measures. The repressive efforts of Edward P. Lokopoyet, senior superintendent of prisons in charge of Kamĩtĩ Prison, had made the previous two years (1976–7) an 'actual hell'. 'Wasonga Sijeyo, the longest resident at the compound, confirms this: "I was in colonial detention for five years. And now, after Independence, I have also been in this compound for nine years. But these last two years have been the worst of all the previous twelve years!"' (134) The neo-colony was increasingly less tolerant of political dissidents and trade union organisers than their British forebears of the Mau Mau rebels; the difference between a guerrilla army in the bush and a cadre of militant organisers within the institutions of state is the difference between the extrinsic and the immanent, and immanence is always the greater threat to the accumulation of capital. And the latter was the raison d'être of the emergent ruling clique and its government apparatus.

> All agreed that inequality was growing as fast as the economy, if not faster. The inner circles were becoming rich. There was a tight network of directorships and hidden interests that ran through virtually every major company with local ownership, linking it with one senior politician or another through nominee accounts, Asian supporters or overt directorships. This elite, particularly the Kikuyu, were notorious for their closed business practices, their love of golf and their emulation of colonial British behaviour. There was a growing alignment of political, administrative and economic power, creating something close to a ruling class for the first time.[6]

It was as a detainee of this new ruling class's 'managing committee'[7] that Ngũgĩ came face to face with the real Kenya that independence had wrought, and, as a corollary, with the role of the artist in a state governed by what he called the 'comprador bourgeoisie' (84, 131,

[6] Charles Hornsby, *Kenya: A History Since Independence* (London: I. B. Tauris, 2012), 317.

[7] Karl Marx and Friedrich Engels, *The Communist Manifesto*, translated by Ben Fowkes (London: Penguin, 2004), 5–6.

163).[8] If the artist, the teacher, the union organiser and the activist were to be treated as the British had treated the KLFA, and some of their best years spent in prison, then that spelled out in no uncertain terms the state's direct *politicisation* of literature, education, organisation and cross-class solidarity. Ngũgĩ's career as a writer to this moment – the novels *Weep Not, Child* (1964), *The River Between* (1965), *A Grain of Wheat* (1967) and *Petals of Blood* (1977), and above all his play with Ngũgĩ wa Mirĩĩ, *Ngaahika Ndeenda: Ithaako ria ngerekano* (1977) – already showed a distinct escalation in political temperature as these broader national realisations became inescapable; but prison was to make the definitive difference between any lingering liberal Eurocentrism and the open commitment to a socialist Kenya that marked the next phase of his life as an artist.[9] 'Ngũgĩ now [wrote] about state power, not as something read in texts on authoritarianism, but from his own personal experiences in the dungeon of postcoloniality.'[10] In part this was due to the culture of Kamĩtĩ itself, where the bones of his beloved Mau Mau warrior Dedan Kimathi lay mouldering and whose walls 'still dripped with the blood of the many Kenyan nationalists, fighters, and supporters of the Kenya Land and Freedom Army' (31). In Kamĩtĩ a peculiar ethos took root:

> Strange how a place acquires its own personality, history, even culture and special vocabulary. All those who have been in this compound have become part of the spirit of our history as political prisoners. Those of us who are new can never hear enough about the personalities, characters, anecdotes, exploits, words, songs, and sayings of those who were here before us and have now left. Cyrus Jamaitta, Achieng Oneko, J. D. Kali, Ndhiwa, Mak'anyengo, Waweru Gĩthiũngũri, and the renowned *mganga* (medicine man) Kajiwe, etc. – all these acquire legendary proportions in our imagination. (145–6/131)

---

[8] 'It is difficult to find commonly accepted terms to best describe social class divisions in former colonies whose economy was and still is integrated into the Western imperialist economies. The word comprador, denoting a person or an economic class in a subordinate but mutually beneficial relationship with imperial corporate capital, as opposed to nationalistic capitalists, is still the most helpful term, particularly in the era of globalization.' Ngũgĩ, *Wrestling with the Devil* (189 n. 10).

[9] The general line is that Ngũgĩ 'successfully deployed Europhone writing as a strategy for contesting the authority of the former colonial masters', a claim that subtly associates him with the imperial enemy. Ode Ogede, *Intertextuality in Contemporary African Literature* (New York: Lexington Books, 2011), 72.

[10] Simon Gikandi, *Ngũgĩ wa Thiong'o* (Cambridge: Cambridge University Press, 2000), 199.

The act of assimilating oneself to a notable lineage of dissidents, all stamped by the fact of detention as crystals of political energy and so revered as *genii* of the place, is tantamount to redoubling one's solidarity with the oppressed. If prison exists to separate the organic intellectual from his community, to break the living bonds between theory and practice, then it also forges a higher-order collective within its walls, where those isolated representatives create bonds with one another to achieve a more 'totalising' relationship with the broadest cross-section of the population. This is a dialectic of the jailhouse that few writers have hitherto articulated so explicitly as Ngũgĩ does here. '[I]t wasn't easy for the warders to enforce total segregation. The other political prisoners would break through the cordon by shouting across to me or by finding any and every excuse for going past where I was sitting and hurriedly throwing in one or two words of solidarity. Or they might assure me of their solidarity as they walked past my cell [. . .]. This was always very touching coming from people who were in no better conditions' (33).

These others are then 'media' for the masses they represent by virtue of their imprisonment, serving as vital conduits to that wider world of heteroglossia now barred off from the writer's art. Ngũgĩ establishes a firmly Bakhtinian theory of literary production here.

> Writers need people around them. They thrive on live struggles of active life. Contrary to popular mythology, a novel is not the sole product of the imaginative feats of a single individual but the work of many hands and tongues. Writers just take down notes dictated to them by life among the people, which they then arrange in this or that form. In writing a novel, I love to hear the voices of people working the land, forging metal in a factory, telling anecdotes in a crowded *matatu* (public minibus), gyrating their hips in a crowded bar before a jukebox or a live band – people playing the games of love and hate and fear and glory in their struggle to live. (20/8)

In prison, however, it is the other prisoners who must offer up the deposits left in them of these dialogical strata of 'the people'. 'I am lucky to have for teachers the other political prisoners and a few guards, who are cooperative and very generous in sharing their different mines of information and experience. But mostly I pick a lot from ordinary meandering conversations, when in groups we talk of women of various careers – barmaids, secretaries, teachers, and engineers – as well as different aspects of social life and bourgeois rivalry in Nairobi' (21/9). The political prisoner becomes a political artist by virtue of his ability to mine these seams, the living discursive tissues of that teeming heteroglossia, of whose polyphonic dictation he has become the elective amanuensis. It is, indeed, precisely as a novel that the *genii* of Kamĩtĩ dictate their most adequate expression, and Ngũgĩ's prison memoir is at once an allegorical insider's account of the atemporal neo-colony, and a diary of the production of his literary masterpiece, written inside the walls of Kamĩtĩ: *Devil on the Cross* (1978).

* * *

Just as important to the overall evaluation of Ngũgĩ's prison writing is the writing that got him detained in the first place, 'the most important event on the African literary and cultural scene in the postcolonial period', according to Ugandan poet Okot p'Bitek: the extraordinary experimental theatre collaboration at the displaced persons' village of Kamĩrĩĩthũ (north-west of Nairobi), *Ngaahika Ndeenda: Ithaako ria ngerekano* [*I Will Marry When I Want*].[11] It was here in 1977 that Ngũgĩ's inveterate Anglophonism finally succumbed to the cultural-nationalist demand that the illiterate peasants and workers who spoke his native Gĩkũyũ have a literature and a theatre of their own. 'It was Kamĩrĩĩthũ which forced me to turn to Gĩkũyũ and hence into what for me has amounted to "an epistemological break" with my past; particularly in the area of theatre. The question of audience settled the problem of language choice; and the language-choice settled the question of audience. But our use of Gĩkũyũ had other consequences in relation to other theatre issues: content for instance; actors, auditioning and rehearsals, performances and reception; theatre as a language.'[12] Incorporating elements of song, dance, mime, ritual ceremony, as well as the language itself, *Ngaahika Ndeenda* became a *succès de scandale* on the basis of this thoroughgoing immersion in the lives of a proletarianised peasantry, and its radical aesthetic adaptation to the requirements of the audience for whom it was composed – leaving 'no barrier between the content of their history and the linguistic medium of their expression' (45). Ngũgĩ takes inordinate pride in the potent fascination for this achievement amongst his captors, detailing how copies of the play text are appropriated by each of his arresting officers (28), upbraiding the prison chaplain for not having read it (37), quoting the Kĩambu district commissioner who presided over

---

[11] As reported by Simon Gikandi in his *Ngũgĩ wa Thiong'o*, 195.
[12] Ngũgĩ wa Thiong'o, *Decolonizing the Mind: The Politics of Language in African Literature* (Harare: Zimbabwe Publishing House, 1987), 44.

the banning of the public performances of the play, Eliud Njenga, at length (75), and portraying the young prison superintendent who admits Ngũgĩ to Kamĩtĩ as a fan:

> Business over, he raises his head – he has been sitting, and I have been standing – and says, 'I have read all your books. I was planning to come to see *Ngaahika Ndeenda*. Then I read in the papers about the ban. Tell me, why really did they bring you to this place?' I say to myself, *Here now begins the long-awaited interrogation*. But his voice sounds sincere.
> 'I don't know,' I tell him, adding, 'but it could be because of *Ngaahika Ndeenda*.'
> 'What's wrong with the play? What was it about?'
> 'Our history. The lives of peasants and workers.'
> 'What's wrong with that?'
> 'I don't know!' (125)

The fact is that *Ngaahika Ndeenda* occupies a pivotal position, not just in Ngũgĩ's own trajectory as a writer, but in Kenyan, African and postcolonial culture more generally; and his extrajudicial detention because of its success announces one of those critical junctures between the personal and the historical where allegorical energies flood the mechanisms of sense, magnifying the trials of the individual artist into something properly emblematic and representative of the wider geopolitical situation. Prison is a concentrating spatial frame where these allegorical energies become even more exaggerated. 'Later, the political prisoners are let out in groups. They remove the piece of blanket covering the bars, they crowd around my door, and they ask me many questions all at once. But one question stands out above the others: "Is it true that *Ngaahika Ndeenda* was acted by peasants and workers?"' (126). Not only the detained, but the warders themselves find the question irresistible; and this is part of Ngũgĩ's strategy in *Detained* – his insistence that between the prisoners and the jailers there is only a thin and soluble membrane.

> Yes, *Ngaahika Ndeenda* has preceded me in prison. Throughout my stay, I'll get more inquiries about it. One comes from a warder of Kalenjin nationality who tells me the play was read and translated to him by his Mũgĩkũyũ friend who worked at a coffee plantation around Kĩambu. He tells me about the play and recounts the plot and mentions the names of several characters.
> 'I hope that I will one day be able to see a performance of the play,' he says wistfully. He is voicing the hope of many Kenyans, and it feels good. (126)

In various scenes, Ngũgĩ shows the Kamĩtĩ guards as reasonable interlocutors capable of argument and delighted by Ngũgĩ's wit and wordplay; they leak critical information to him, engage him in life-giving banter, and never indulge in wanton physical or psychological abuse. This marks a crucial distinction between Ngũgĩ's prison characterology and almost all other prison writing, especially that of Ruth First and Bobby Sands: in *Detained*, the guards and even many of the officials are comrades-in-waiting, because they all belong to the same national essence being sold to the highest bidder by the vampiric comprador bourgeoisie. Indeed, it is a guard who, astonishingly, reprimands Ngũgĩ for his Anglophone Europhilia and keeps him to the narrow path of cultural nationalism.

> The trouble with you educated people is that you despise your languages. You don't like talking to ordinary people. But what use is your education if it cannot be shared with your own people? Let me tell you. You may possess all the book education in the world, but it's we, ordinary people in tattered clothes with bare feet and blistered hands, who have the real knowledge of things.
>   It is an ordinary Mũgĩkũyũ warder talking to me, no, actually lecturing me, for I am speechless with disbelief. (143–4)

'I recall that two of my class of fifty-eight in Alliance High School opted for prison service,' muses Ngũgĩ (125), thereby underlining the continuity of himself with his gaolers, refusing to demonise them, keeping the rhetorical door open for a later solidarity that all along remains implicit. It is a rare and dangerous tactic, this eschewal of antagonism between prisoner and guard, but its purpose is to push the underlying antagonism outward in a national and international direction, where capital and labour lie coiled in a ceaseless embrace of struggle. Ngũgĩ is, of course, an artist of opposition and antagonism, and prison is a *topos* where the true fault lines of geopolitical struggle come into sharp definition – but only by thinking allegorically and not privately, not in the dimension of the merely visible or present-to-hand. Guards must be resolved into the paychecks that keep them at work, and the paymasters who sign them. 'At one time [. . .] a more sensitive warder breaks down and weeps: "Some of us are really sorry about all this. Please understand that we are only carrying out orders. If I should lose my job, what will my children eat, where will they get their clothes and school fees? Where will they sleep?"' (134). It is, to be sure, the alibi of the banality of evil the world over, but its pathos is real enough to the novelist who records it here. In the writings of Levi, Sands, First, Angela Davis and others, the warders are ontological *others*, representatives of a class, a racial faction, a sect opposed in essence to the civil and human rights of their captives; but Ngũgĩ approaches the problem more along the lines of a Luxemburg or a Solzhenitsyn: *there but for the grace of God go I*. The warders are first and foremost working Kenyans under the governance of a ruling class hell-bent on privatising the gains of an independent Kenya, robbing working people of their share of the common wealth and selling it instead to the bagmen of multinational capital.

It is here that Ngũgĩ stages his antagonism, in terms resounding with literary echoes.

> There was another side to my detention: the growing anti-imperialist consciousness among peasants, workers, university lecturers, and students, and I was the sacrificial lamb!
>
> Thought for despair? No! I am part of a living history of struggle. And without struggle, there is no movement, there is no life.
>
> The thought is not original – I once read it in William Blake: without contraries there is no progression; attraction and repulsion, reason and energy, love and hate, are necessary to human existence. And later in Hegel: contradiction is the root of all movement and all life, and only insofar as a thing incorporates a contradiction is it mobile, does it possess impulse and activity. But it is true! (131–2)

Within the general dialectic of forces that he puts into play in *Detained*, Ngũgĩ shows how a community theatre project written and performed in Gĩkũyũ can become a critical lens into the fault lines that run through the neo-colony. What casts him into prison, his allegiance with socialist cultural-nationalist practices, is also what brings out the underlying contradictions of the neocolonial prison itself, its constitutive and explosive ironies. Staffing penitentiaries and police forces with locals and putting them to work breaking down the most outstanding Kenyans is ultimately unsustainable, which is why the regime turns to mercenaries. 'Foreign-run private armies to protect foreigners and a handful of Kenyans from real or imagined wrath of fellow Kenyans: what an irony of history!' (74). At Kamĩtĩ, where all warders and the superintendents are Kenyan, the historical dialectics are yet alive with possibility, as menace morphs into mildness in a moment:

> The face of the guard fills the whole window: I know nothing so menacingly sinister in its silent stillness as that trunkless face glaring at one through the iron bars of a prison cell.
>
> 'Professor, . . . why are you not in bed?' the voice redeems the face. 'What are you doing?'

Relief! I fall back on the current witticism in the detention block.
'I am writing to Jomo Kenyatta in his capacity as an ex-political
prisoner.' (14)

Given this ambivalence, the work of art can be gestated within the
existential barrenness of prison life. It is the very phenomenological
emptiness of that quotidian grind – 'basically a cliché: dull, mundane,
downright monotonous, repetitious, torturous in its intended animal
rhythm of eating, defecating, sleeping, eating, defecating, sleeping'
(124) – that surcharges every interaction with allegorical significance, and saturates the creative intellect with the blood and sweat
of history in its longue durée. Not the 'I' but the echo chamber one
has become for ghosts of the civil dead ('I am part of a living history
of struggle'); not the immediate animal functions of mere being but
the reasons for their exclusive imposition by illegitimate authority –
dialectical negation compensates for the 'degree zero' of being
'completely quarantined from everything and everybody, including
convicted prisoners in all the other blocks' (13). If prison annihilates
experience, then let imaginative nihilation return the favour: 'To
hell with the guards! Away with intruding thoughts! Tonight I don't
want to think about guards and prisoners, colonial or neocolonial
affairs. I am totally engrossed in Warĩĩnga, the fictional heroine of
the novel I have been writing on toilet paper for the last ten months
or so!' (16). Just as Bobby Sands would transfigure the excremental
into the literary and the sublime, so Ngũgĩ joins a notable lineage of
African political prisoners in his daily effort to wrest truth from the
latrine of lost hopes, on 'the same good old toilet paper – which had
served Kwame Nkrumah in James Fort Prison, Dennis Brutus on
Robben Island, Abdilatif Abdalla in G Block, Kamĩtĩ, and countless
other persons with similar urges' (18).

* * *

As a writer's notebook, *Detained* includes explicit thematic and
formal statements on the origins of *Devil on the Cross* which are
profoundly Brechtian in orientation. Brecht's poem 'A Worker's
Voice' appears in *Detained* as its concluding quotation, Brecht's
'Questions from a Worker Who Reads' is used to explain the literary
politics of *Petals of Blood*,[13] and in *Decolonising the Mind*, Ngũgĩ
answers a question posed by the Guatemalan poet Otto René Castillo

---

[13] Ngũgĩ wa Thiong'o, *Writers in Politics: Essays* (London: Heinemann, 1981), 97–8.

('What did you do when the poor/Suffered [. . .]?') with the exhortation, 'we, who teach literature, history, the arts, culture, religions, should be able to answer proudly, like the Brechtian intellectual, we helped turn the struggles into the spheres of common knowledge and, above all, justice into a passion'.[14] Brecht is generally associated with Ngũgĩ's supreme pantheon of Western artists (Blake, Whitman and Sartre) and belongs in any general consideration of the work of Soyinka, Ousmane Sembène and Chinua Achebe, but particularly of Ngũgĩ.[15] The Brechtian trick of turning the problem of aesthetic epistemology around on an audience, prompting them to pose to themselves what the underlying political issues are in any text or production, informs Ngũgĩ's strategies here: 'Those outside the barbed wire and the stone walls must ask questions and demand answers. It's the only way to defeat the culture of fear and silence. And if a community of millions were to ask questions and demand answers, who would deny them?' (122). 'Brecht is constantly aware of the masses,' observed Walter Benjamin, 'whose conditioned use of the faculty of thought is surely covered by this formula [epic theatre addresses itself to those "who do not think unless they have a reason to"]. His effort [is] to make the audience interested as experts.'[16] So it is with Ngũgĩ. The lessons of Kamĩrĩthũ, where 'the whole project became a collective community effort as peasants and workers took more and more initiative in revising and adding to the script, in directing dance movements on the stage, and in the general organization' (81), dovetail with Brecht's explanations of his practice. The question of how to adapt this process to novel-writing hangs over the intermittent reflections on composing *Devil on the Cross*.

Cultural nationalism and the matter of language are easily dealt with:

> I would write in Gĩkũyũ, a language that did not yet have a modern novel, as a challenge to myself, a way of affirming my faith in the possibilities of the languages of all the different Kenyan nationalities, languages whose growth as vehicles for people's struggles and development had been actively suppressed by the British colonial regime (1895–1963) and now its postcolonial successor. (19–20)

[14] Ngũgĩ wa Thiong'o, *Decolonizing the Mind*, 106.
[15] '[I]t is largely in his theoretical writings that Ngugi has again and again cited Brecht poems and has paraphrased Brecht. [. . .] Brecht is the single most cited and referred to author.' Georg M. Gugelberger, 'When Evil-Doing Comes like Falling Rain', *Comparative Literature Studies* 24.4 (1987), 370–86.
[16] Walter Benjamin, *Understanding Brecht*, translated by Anna Bostock (London: Verso, 1998), 16.

These residues of Kamĩrĩthũ are henceforth indelible; but the novel's fundamental dialogism entails pushing the epistemological ambitions further still, into a strategy of totalisation implicit in the material itself.

> I would not avoid any subject – science, technology, philosophy, religion, music, political economy – provided it logically arose out of the development of the novel's theme, character, plot, story, and world view. Furthermore, I would use everything I had ever learned about the craft of fiction – allegory, parable, satire, narrative, description, reminiscence, flashback, interior monologue, stream of consciousness, dialogue, drama – provided it came naturally in the development of character, theme, and story. Content – not language and technique – would determine the eventual form of the novel. (20)

The result is Brechtian above all in its refusal of standard aesthetic categories of value judgement; that it is a kind of miscellany or hodgepodge of materials is perfectly justifiable on the basis of the absence of any secure bourgeois vantage point in the new Kenya from which to insist on something like 'organic unity'. Furthermore, as an artistic cross-section of a society whose historical engines are stalled, the novel must give form to the 'content' of a wildly uneven social development: neo-imperialist disdain for locality; fading energies of anti-colonial struggle; a seam of cultural-nationalist affirmation; proletarianisation as a fact of life; and the deep residua of immemorial folkways and mythopoetics. Perhaps above all, as a fugitive act of prison writing, scrawled on toilet paper and secured from the attentions of the Kamĩtĩ guards (indeed, a major point of drama in the prison memoir concerns the discovery, appropriation and return of the almost-complete manuscript), *Devil on the Cross* must project the underlying allegoresis of the situation (Kenya as a prison) onto the general material without deforming it from within.

It is no accident, then, that one of the genres it most resembles is the Brechtian *Lehrstück*, the Learning Play (Marxist parables meant for workers' collectives), in which we find 'a reduction of action and gesture alike to the very minimum of decision as such, within a situation itself reduced to the most minimal machine for choosing', 'the primacy of the collective situation over individual ethics',[17] and where a perdurable folk wisdom, wise to the slimy importunities of capital, stages its superior moral energy against cynical reason. *Devil on the Cross* is not a novel in any conventional sense. Translated

[17] Fredric Jameson, *Brecht and Method* (London: Verso, 1998), 61, 63.

from its Indigenous tongue in such a way as to perform its alienness from Western models, and dressed head to toe in the regalia of its proverbial Gĩkũyũ folk knowledge, the text demands assent from its readers, 'an assent that endows the story with communal cultural authority'.[18] That assent is solicited with the larger aim of conditioning the reader to identify with the central figure of Warĩĩnga herself, who experiences the road-trip-cum-satanic-allegory with all the wide-eyed reluctance to take sides that this didactic novel assumes as a given. While other characters come with a definite quotient of prior commitment and orientation – two are veterans of the struggle against colonialism, one is a cultural-nationalist composer, one is a bourgeois nationalist, one is a petty-bourgeois opportunist and cynic – only Warĩĩnga represents the function of choice, which it is the purpose of this *Lehr-roman* to foreground above all other effects. Allegory drenches every stray datum of novelistic observation with various levels of signification, from the road trip in the *matatũ* [minibus] to the culminating spectacle of the devil's competition in a modern version of Plato's cave; and all of it relates back to the presupposition of Kenya as an open-air prison. The *matatũ* is figured as prison-like ('When you are in my *matatũ*, you could be inside a prison or a grave'),[19] and prison is to the fore in the discourse of the thieves and robbers who compete for the title of Devil's favourite ('But there are a few blackguards who have had the audacity to talk about removing the scales from the eyes of the masses. Those who want to awaken the masses should be shown the whip – detention or prison – just like the fellows you all know about' [130]). Warĩĩnga's parents, who took up arms against the colonial government, were both sent to jail (Manyani, Langata and Kamĩtĩ; see 155–6), and her two militant friends from the *matatũ* will also serve time for their attempts to interfere with the Devil's feast. One of the contenders for the crown of best thief offers a vampiric vision of the ruling class whose deepest desire is to farm the workers and peasants like cattle:

> Kĩmeendeeri intends to fence off the farm with barbed wire, just like the wire that was used to fence off detention camps during the state of Emergency in colonial Kenya. He plans to pen the workers in there like animals. He will then fix electrically operated machines to their bodies for milking their sweat or the energy that produces the sweat, their blood and their brains. The three commodities will then

---

[18] Gikandi, *Ngũgĩ wa Thiong'o*, 211.
[19] Ngũgĩ wa Thiong'o, *Devil on the Cross* (London: Penguin, 2017), 57; see also 74.

be exported to foreign countries to feed industries there. For every gallon of sweat, or blood, or brains, Kĩmeendeeri will get commission at a fixed rate. (212)

The open-air prison of the neocolonial state is gothically troped as a facility for farming workers' 'brain[s], nerves, muscles and sense organs'.[20] But nothing clinches the presiding allegorical framework as surely as the description of the nearby slum Njeruca [New Jerusalem], lying cheek by jowl with the Ilmorog Golden Heights residential area, a ruling-class enclave – for it is here that the open-air prison comes most sharply into view as a geographical destiny stamped on the working poor by the production of social space itself:

'Sometimes I think of Njeruca as the Hell described in the Christian Bible . . .'

'Why?' Gatuĩria asked. 'What does the place look like?'

'How can you ask that, as if you were a foreigner in Kenya? Have you never visited the slum areas of Nairobi to see for yourself the amazing sight of endless armies of fleas and bedbugs marching up and down the walls, or the sickening, undrained ditches, full of brackish water, shit and urine, the naked children swimming in those very ditches? A slum is a slum. Here in Njeruca we don't have any drainage. Human shit and urine and the carcases of dead dogs and cats – all these make the area smell as if it were nothing but pure putrefaction. Add to this decay the smoke of dangerous gases from the industrial area – all these are blown toward Njeruca by the wind – and add too the fact that all the rubbish and waste from the factories is deposited there, and you'll see why I compare Njeruca with Hell. To bury a people in a hole full of fleas, lice, bedbugs – what hell could be worse than that?' Warĩĩnga ended her narrative with bitterness.

'Fleas, jiggers, bedbugs . . . are there more of those in Ilmorog's slums than the human parasites we have left behind in that cave?' Gatuĩria asked slowly, as if he were talking to himself. (146)

Rhyming with Ngũgĩ's evocation in *Detained* of Kamĩtĩ in olfactory terms ('the smell of shit and urine' [127]), this great description crystallises the continuity between the neocolonial house of detention and the neoliberal sentencing of the world's poor to physical conditions scarcely more salubrious than Kenya's most infamous prison. Ngũgĩ's prison writings, acutely literary in their ruminations on the occasion for his arrest and their account of how he spent his

---

[20] Karl Marx, *Capital*, vol. 1, translated by Ben Fowkes (London: Penguin, 1990), 164.

year in detention writing a novel, are literary above all in this sense of enacting seamless allegorical transductions from one region of postcolonial experience to another, in a viral contagion of tropes linking life under late capitalism to the life-depleting confinement of indefinite detention.

Chapter 11

Antigone Evolved: Nawal El Saadawi's *Memoirs from the Women's Prison*

Over the ground, my fingers sketch letters and interlacing circles. My hand trembles with anger, and my heartbeat quickens. If my fingers had not come to know the pen, perhaps they would have known the hoe. The pen is the most valuable thing in my life. My words on paper are more valuable to me than my life itself. More valuable than my children, more than my husband, more than my freedom.

I prefer my place in prison to writing something which has not originated in my mind. The sincere word demands a courage akin to that needed to kill – and perhaps more.

My fingers chisel the letters in the dirt. I contemplate the words which are circling round in my head. What appeared to me as certain a moment ago I see now as surrounded in the fog of doubt. To this moment, I don't know why I am in prison. I have seen no investigator or prosecuting attorney or lawyer. I heard the *shawisha* say that she heard they were saying I entered prison because of my writings . . . my crime, therefore, comes under the rubric of crimes of opinion.

Is free opinion a crime? Then let prison be my only refuge and my final fate![1]

The writing of Nawal El Saadawi, Egypt's incendiary feminist icon,[2] is so suffused with her metatextual personality, her highly cultivated, extroverted character, that its flagrant egotism comes to seem more like a grammar all its own. Seventeen times in some 220

---

[1] Nawal El Saadawi, *Memoirs from the Women's Prison*, translated by Marilyn Booth (London: Zed Books, 2020), 116–17.

[2] Nawal was 'the first Arab woman to raise the issue of sexual oppression publicly in a daring manner; before her, only forms of social, economic, and political oppression were discussed by Arab feminists'. Nawar Al-Hassan Golley, *Reading Arab Women's Autobiographies: Shahrazad Tells Her Story* (Austin: University of Texas Press, 2003), 131.

words here the first-person singular possessive pronoun rings out, joining the ranks of ten first-person singular pronouns, and various implied uses nestled into clauses otherwise bereft. This is a translation, of course, but it is in much the same voice Nawal uses for her English prose and her spoken interviews and speeches in English: adverting compulsively to itself, its quality as 'personné' in the body of its speaker, an ego compacted of so much mass and substance that language finds itself, its very parts of speech and lexemes, held fast in orbit around that lively, imperious Self. No other prison writer takes such abundant refuge in the safe harbour of her own person.[3] If prison is typically a place where the consistency of the social person is battered and broken, where the contours of the self are grated down to raw fibres of animal being, then Nawal's prison writing exists to defy that dictate above all. Her 'I' will be superimposed on the prison, emitting the steady ray of its judgement on all it touches, such that by the end of her memoir you may feel that she has invented it purely to provide a suitable allegorical schema for her inexorable self-transcendence.

Like others before her – Wilde, Pound, Ngũgĩ, First, Luxemburg – Nawal is a detainee on the basis of her writings: specifically, a string of published pieces directly questioning the putative democratic status of Sadat's regime in 1980 and 1981.[4] Her detention is so immediately political (stemming from a direct order from the president) that there is not even the pretence of a crime she is supposed to have committed beyond the very capacity to think outside the decrees of an authoritarian regime: thought crime, or as she puts it here, the criminality of 'free opinion'.[5] Crimes of opinion manifest

---

[3] Ahdaf Soueif objects that, in *Memoirs from the Women's Prison*, the other political prisoners housed along with Nawal are effectively 'reduced to the role of a chorus providing backing for Saadawi's courageous outspokenness'. See her 'In the Beggars' Cell', *New Society* 15 (August 1986): 23–4.

[4] 'Sadat introduced the Law for the Protection of the Internal Front and Social Peace, which became known as the "Law of Shame". Among a range of new restrictions, the law essentially criminalized opposition to the government, which, according to the statute, could be interpreted as just about anything and outlawed violation of public, religious, and national morals.' This was the law that provided the blanket Sadat needed to round up intellectuals like Nawal. See Steven A. Cook, *The Struggle for Egypt: From Nasser to Tahrir Square* (Oxford: Oxford University Press, 2012), 153.

[5] 'Over a thousand people representing all the supposed opposition forces in the country – right and left wing, radicals and moderates, civilians and religious figures, politicians and intellectuals – were thrown in jail on September 5, 1981, accused by Sadat of plotting to overthrow him. The communists along with the Muslim extremists were accused of incitement, aided and abetted by the Soviet ambassador, who was expelled a week later.' Alain Roussillon, 'Republican Egypt Interpreted: Revolution and Beyond', in *The Cambridge History of Egypt, Volume Two: Modern Egypt*

in her published writings, Nawal's offences are inseparable from her public persona, her larger-than-life role as an intellectual dissident, medical doctor, director of the Ministry of Public Health (sacked), chief editor of a medical journal (sacked), feminist, socialist, controversialist, speechmaker, and multipurpose gadfly to the all-male regime of liberators who took Egypt out of the hands of the British and the puppet monarchy.[6] This is doubtless the condition of possibility for the extravagant valuation placed here on Nawal's 'words on paper': the degree to which she already knows the disproportionate effect they can have on the world – including, obviously, her imprisonment for them.

The quoted passage establishes a trope that serves across the length of Nawal's prison memoir: a figural affinity between pen and hoe, paper and soil, precluding any categorical distinction between manual and intellectual labour. Her peasant stock, on one side of her family (her father's),[7] is a source of pride throughout her memoir, and the hoe is a critical metaphor of that class origin and class solidarity (much as the shovel is for Seamus Heaney) in the cell she shares with other political and religious dissidents. The hoe tends to locate Nawal's identity outside the cage reserved for the 'politicals' (it was formerly the beggars' cell; these lumpens now dwell in a tiny hut in the main courtyard), in that it creates a palpable distance between her fellow intellectuals and the *munaqqabas* (women who wear the hijab), none of whom would be caught dead wielding one, and explicitly associates her with the most memorable of the general prisoners with whom she comes into contact. This is Fathiyya-the-Murderess (there are so many prisoners sharing the same names that they come to be distinguished by epithets that describe their crimes), an arrestingly beautiful inmate who has killed her husband after discovering him raping their nine-year-old daughter.[8] The murder

---

from 1517 to the End of the Twentieth Century, edited by M. W. Daly (Cambridge: Cambridge University Press, 1998), 372 [334–3].

[6] 'But the greatest crime is that I am a free woman at a time when they want nothing but woman servants and slaves; and I was born with a thoughtful brain when they are trying to deform minds. [. . .] The most dangerous men of politics and of the press live in all ages. They sit on the thrones of the press, politics, arts, literature, and medicine, as firm as the sun in its center.' Nawal El Saadawi, 'Translation of the Introduction to the Arabic Edition of *Memoirs from the Women's Prison*', Appendix in Golley, *Reading Arab Women's Autobiographies*, 185 [185–8].

[7] 'Saadawi's acknowledgment of her father rather than her mother is not so much a sign of sexual discrimination as it is a sign of alliance with working-class positions.' Golley, *Reading Arab Women's Autobiographies*, 132.

[8] The figure of Fathiyya shares a certain similarity with the heroine of Nawal's earlier novel, *Woman at Point Zero* (1975).

implement was, of course, a hoe; as the likeable *shawisha* puts it, she 'gave her husband a blow on the head with her hoe then cut up his body into little pieces which she gathered in a sack and threw into the river so the fishes would eat him' (66). In the complex gradation of criminality this *shawisha* recognises in the women's prison, murderesses always come out on top – 'They're the best ones. A murderess comes straight from her home to prison, doesn't even know the meaning of dodging or evading. Murder is unlike all other crimes – in fact, it isn't a crime, but a moment of anger which passes. The murderess kills for the sake of her children and her honour' (70). This admiration is particularly felt for the hoe-wielding Fathiyya:

> Fathiyya-the-Murderess was a poor miserable woman, planting and harvesting with her own hands, while her husband lounged around the house, a lazy bum. Eating, burping, smoking his waterpipe. One day, she came back from the field and found him on top of her daughter, her nine-year-old daughter. She struck him on the head with her hoe and got a life sentence. She's been with us here for ten years now. Her heart is as sweet and gentle as the spring breeze, and it's impossible to believe that she would kill a mosquito. (73)

One's sense is that the murder weapon is such an immediate extension of the working woman's identity (as her crime is an extension of her honourable character), that it certifies and emblematises a primordial innocence, a spiritual sanctity that goes with immemorial peasant customs dating from a well-nigh matriarchal prehistory. There is an *Antigone*-like subtext at work in passages like this, stipulating a woman-guarded sacred justice anterior to the man-written laws that send the admirable Fathiyya to prison for life, away from her children. But the real purpose of this elaborate preparation is that it should serve as a justification for Nawal's taking up the hoe in prison, both literally in the passage (for which, see below) where she turns the soil of the exercise yard for fruitful planting, and figuratively in this passage where the pen and the hoe are thought together as the recto and verso of a peasant-intellectual's working tools.

'If my fingers had not come to know the pen, perhaps they would have known the hoe,' she sketches her alternate history, the becoming-peasant that class destiny had arranged for her sister and would have for Nawal, had not the pen asserted its superiority as instrument of fate. As she thinks this, she is using her fingers to draw letters and circles (not yet punishable words) in the dirt of the prison enclosure: an inveterate, incurable need to write, to trace, to 'chisel' signifiers into any available surface. There is always inside her 'the words which are circling round in my head', a mounting material pressure requiring expression; and any resulting 'words on paper are more valuable to me than my life itself. More valuable than my children, more than my husband, more than my freedom.' The association between pen and hoe cuts deeper than a mere assertion of class origins; it also slices into the body of the husband and the bodies of the children left on the outside of the prison, as Fathiyya's hoe had done, in the name of honour and the supreme value of truth. The pen will sever the closest family bonds, writing words whose value supersedes any sentimental, affective familial ties, because they espouse 'Egypt' itself. 'For I am come to set a man at variance against his father,' speaks the truth, 'and the daughter against her mother, and the daughter in law against her mother in law.'[9] Only this is not the truth of an unlimited universal, but the particularised universal of nationality. '"My reputation as a nationalist is worth my life to me!"' Nawal cries later (187). And it is here that the relationship with *Antigone* assumes a much more powerful charge, as the 'ethical life of the woman' in Hegel's scheme, and represented here by Fathiyya's illiterate hoe, is sublated into the 'citizen's self-conscious power of universality' by Nawal's literate performance of the nationalist moment where 'the self-contained life of the Family breaks up and goes beyond itself'.[10]

Like Antigone before her, but for crimes of a very different nature, Nawal will go to gaol. This is because her words, more important than her family, are also more important 'than my freedom'. Antigone's courageous stance on behalf of the immemorial gods of the hearth is transposed into Nawal's commitment to the abstract principles of nation, law and civil governance. Sadat, the Creon of this drama, has corrupted those sacred ordinals of the modern state through the imposition of an arbitrary personal will (authoritarianism), a corruption which then inverts every remaining loyal nationalist's ongoing commitment to them into a subversive criminality. The jail cell is the fate of all who, refusing to put family before citizenship, stay faithful to the 'Event' of national liberation under Nasser.[11] 'Then let prison

[9] Matthew 10:35.

[10] G. W. F. Hegel, *The Phenomenology of Spirit*, translated by A. V. Miller (Oxford: Oxford University Press, 1977), 274–5.

[11] 'The central creed of the revolution, then, was not simply that it would act in the people's interest but that it would speak with their voice. Socially and politically dominant elites could no longer rule for their own benefit; they had to account for their actions to the people.' Nathan J. Brown, 'Nasserism's Legal Legacy: Accessibility, Accountability, and Authoritarianism', in Elie Podeh and Onn Winckler, eds, *Rethinking Nasserism: Revolution and Historical Memory in Modern Egypt* (Gainesville: University Press

be my only refuge and my final fate!' Nawal declares, inhabiting the topsy-turvy legal logic of the authoritarian betrayal, and distancing herself from all those who would defend their complicity by appeals to the need to feed their families.[12] In a false state, the family is not a refuge but an inward-looking cancer cell of the general untruth, and prison is the refuge of the sane and sincere.[13] Summarising this chain of inference and implication, Nawal again takes up the association between pen and hoe-as-weapon: 'I prefer my place in prison to writing something which has not originated in my mind. The sincere word demands a courage akin to that needed to kill – and perhaps more.' There is writing and writing; the only writing that matters is 'sincere', and it requires more courage than killing because it can place you in prison alongside murderers without the serene inner peace of having executed your tormentor, who lives on, in all the pomp of state, to rape the people with impunity. Fathiyya has the holy vindication and solace of her act: '"Regret? Never! Impossible for me to feel any regret about it! By God, if I saw him in front of me now I'd kill him again"' (114). Nawal's published sincerity leaves the tyrant untouched – though, in obliging him to imprison her, it has exposed him precisely for what he is. Writing what is true may place one behind bars; but that effect illuminates the falsity of the law, the state and the legitimacy of the government itself. The 'sincere word' does not kill, but its dauntless *parrhesia* helps foment a situation in which millions may be willing to die to transfigure the coordinates of reality. 'Danger has been a part of my life ever since I picked up a pen and wrote. Nothing is more perilous than truth in a world that lies.'[14]

of Florida, 2004), 133 [127–44]. 'Sadat, faced with fissures in the social fabric along lines of relative wealth and relative piety, from the outset cast himself in the role of the nation's father. That role, moreover, was openly modeled on the image of the village headman.' John Waterbury, *The Egypt of Nasser and Sadat: The Political Economy of Two Regimes* (Princeton, NJ: Princeton University Press, 1983), 383.

12 A nameless old employee in the bowels of a dungeon of the state explains to the detained Nawal: 'marriage costs money, and I, praise be to God, have only enough to get by. I feed her and the six kids, through honest work, and they are all in school, praise the Lord' (14–15).

13 'For the word has lost its meaning. To be safe is to be in prison. Revolution means nonrevolution or aborting the revolution. Food safety means food poisoning. I said to myself, I will stop writing until I find new words, words that have not been devalued yet.' Nawal El Saadawi, 'Translation of the Introduction to the Arabic Edition of *Memoirs from the Women's Prison*', 188.

14 Qtd in Kalpana Sharma, 'Egypt's Face of Courage', *The Hindu* online edition (Saturday, June 3, 2001), https://web.archive.org/web/20041030002518/http://www.hinduonnet.com/2001/06/03/stories/13030786.htm.

All this would explain the great lengths to which the prison authorities must go to ensure that no writing invades or escapes from the politicals' cell. 'We were meant to know nothing of what was going on outside prison, or inside either. We were meant to remain inside the cell, behind the two steel doors, without newspapers' (47). And if a request is made for materials to write home, the reply is immediate:

> 'No pen and paper' [. . .]. 'That is utterly forbidden. Anything but pen and paper. Easier to give you a pistol than pen and paper.' The comparison between a pistol and a pen and paper rang in my ears oddly, like a line from a farce. I thought I must be sitting in a theatre. I had not imagined that pen and paper could be more dangerous than pistols in the world of reality and fact. However, this seemed to be the case – or the least of it. We had seen women prisoners undergoing body searches. If the female warden or *shawisha* happened to find a scrap of paper as she poked her fingers inside a woman's body, the gaol was turned upside down. (49)

The figural play between pen and hoe is here shifted up a gear, into an explicit hierarchy of potency between pen and pistol, where the pistol is the less dangerous implement. Of course, it is prison itself that creates the conditions for this strange, 'farcical' transvaluation, this 'theatre of the absurd' (165), because prison exists to incapacitate the 'sincere word' and its truant universalism. Prison's absolute particularisation of space – *this* cell, *these* walls, *these* inmates, *these* warders – is paradoxically a global abstraction by 1980: all over the world, the same designs, the same basic conditions, the same principles of management, the same cynical use-values to the state, have congealed into a unitary archipelago of sites, none more distant from any other than they all are, as one, from the liberty they supposedly protect. To write from prison is therefore to articulate a dangerous, communal universal at one of its most generative nodes, where the state suborns its own stated values. Nawal uses the same figure of the cavity search, deployed by Bobby Sands and Angela Davis before her,[15] to work at this troubling seam between the 'secret' of the written word and the regime of incarceration – the sense that even the most intimate, most private spaces of the body may, in prison, be harbouring the script of a new universal language, a promiscuous, penetrative word capable of turning the inside out and the upside down.

---

[15] She seems to have been aware of Davis's prison writings; see Golley, *Reading Arab Women's Autobiographies*, 149.

And, inevitably, like Sands and Ngũgĩ, she turns to the only available paper, again cementing the lively association between language
and the bodily interior in modern prison writing. 'It's after midnight,
now, and I'm seated on top of the overturned bottom of the jerry
can, ready to write. Since entering prison I've done my writing on
toilet rolls and cigarette papers. Toilet paper isn't against the rules:
we buy it from the canteen with our identity cards, like we do cigarettes' (81). Toilet paper will receive the fugitive script of Nawal's
memoirs and be stored in a secret hole near the latrine. Though it is
just as important to point out that even this now traditional resource
was a latecomer with regard to the composition of the *Memoirs*
themselves, which were rather written on that primordial writing
material, the whorls and folds of the human brain, projected onto
the very walls of the cell by the power of inward attentiveness.

> I began inscribing these memoirs while I was in prison, without
> benefit of paper or pen. I was not permitted to bring such dangerous
> things into my cell. I used to sit on the ground, leaning against one
> wall and facing the other, and write in my memory, without need for
> pen or paper. I wrote page after page in my imagination, virtually
> able to see the words before me, written – or perhaps engraved – on
> the wall itself. By night I would reread from memory, reviewing my
> writing, adding sections and deleting others, as if I were putting
> pen to paper. Eventually my memory became incapable of retaining
> all these pages, and I began to feel the need for a real pen and real
> paper. With great effort I was able to acquire a stubby black eyebrow
> pencil. One of the prostitutes incarcerated in the cell next to mine
> smuggled it in to me, along with a small roll of old and tattered toilet
> paper. (199)

That the supplement should arrive via the services of an imprisoned
sex worker seems perfectly apt: yet another blameless victim of the
hypocrisies and double standards of the patriarchal ruling class,
whose illiteracy intuits a binding solidarity with the incarcerated
medical doctor over the question of written witness and appeal –
not to Sadat's judiciary, to be sure, but to a global readership who
will ultimately vouchsafe the broadening and internationalisation
of a broken nationalist enterprise. In her striking Afterword, Nawal
details the Hegelian *Aufhebung* that underlies this radical expansion
of a hitherto limited universalism.

> And so nothing can alarm me. Writing is my life. There is no power
> in the world that can strip my writings from me. They have been
> printed and published; they have thousands – perhaps millions – of

readers in the Arab world and across the globe. Since childhood a dream has inhabited my imagination: I write my words and people read them – today, tomorrow, the day after. When does not matter, for people will read them. Those are the people who make a home-land, and my homeland has become those people. (204)

Writing, the medium of the universal, transcends all particulars in a frog-leaping of time and space that spreads from the carceral cell to colonise the conscience of a world. The very same process that has led to Bobby Sands', George Jackson's and Rosa Luxemburg's prison writings now standing as monuments of a new international – the international of the detained, the dispossessed, the homeless and the stateless – envelops Nawal's memoirs and transfigures their egotism into sociality. 'Nothing matters except the birth of words on paper, the dawn's birth, the gloom dissolving' (83): because words on paper are a social contract *in embryo*. 'Writing is my life' means, very pre-cisely, *Je est un autre*. It is something that prison has already taught her.

* * *

'In prison,' Nawal writes, 'I found my heart opened to love' (39), and the object of her love is herself magnified in the community of incarcerated women.[16] Overturning the social alienation of the iso-lated intellectual, prison restores to Nawal the communal dimension of all institutional life. Prison itself makes 'all the faces around me beloved and near to my heart. Even those faces hidden under the black veils . . . when the *niqaabs* were lifted I could see faces that were shining, clear, overflowing with love, a cooperative spirit, and humanity. Among the women and girls, I lived a communal life' (39–40). Of course, true to its deeply Hegelian engine, the memoir also depicts the radicalisation of isolation and alienation behind bars: 'In prison time extends,' she writes, 'on and on, as though it were timelessness' (56); 'In prison, night is longer than day, but daytime is more repulsive than the night, for the darkness conceals the blackened cracks, the garbage in the corners, the fingerprints and spatters of blood dotting the mattresses, walls, steel bars, bed posts, waterpipes, toilet doors and water spigots' (87); 'In prison, one does

---

16 'These new social ties among the women prisoners challenge not only the prison appa-ratus, which tries to separate political from common prisoners, but also the whole social apparatus which is built on familial or biological filiation.' Golley, *Reading Arab Women's Autobiographies*, 155.

not die of hunger, or from the heat or the cold, or from beatings or sicknesses or insects. One might die of waiting, though. Waiting transforms time to timelessness, the tangible object to nothingness, and meaning into meaninglessness' (99). The existential and phenomenological dimension of Nawal's writing is pointedly alive to the negativity of prison time, its annihilation of experience and sensory richness, and its asphyxiation of temporal dynamics. But the political engine of her prose revs in the intervals between this empty nihilism and the individual and collective praxis that overcomes it in solidarity and futurity.

Nawal, a practising doctor, has a name for this, and it is *health*. Early in her incarceration, she begins daily exercises, walking fifty laps of the enclosure and performing 'shameless' calisthenic exercises – exposing her knees and without any brassiere. The effect is a 'contagion of athletic exercise spread[ing] through the bars to the prisoners in the courtyard.'

> As soon as they saw me hopping up and down in our enclosure, they would stand in front of me in a long row and jump like me. When I raised my arms high, their arms went up. When I clapped my hands together above my head, their hands clapped. When I bent my torso, they folded their torsos. When I raised my head high, their heads went up. When I jumped into the air, they jumped. If I stamped the ground with my feet, they did the same. If I called out 'one, two' they shouted with me. 'One, two!' (96)

In a spontaneous recreation of the avant-garde utopian athleticism of the early Soviet state, Nawal's prison exercises stimulate the dormant collectivism of the serialised inmates.[17] Where there was one body asserting its physical refusal to be broken, now there are many: 'I began my exercises. I moved my legs and arms in that regular rhythmic movement which resembles dancing. Before me I saw a long line of arms and legs, moving through the air, striking the ground with the same, regular rhythm. As if my body and theirs are one. As if there are no bars or steel partitions between us. As if we are one body' (97). The barrier being breached here is the one between the political prisoner's yard and the much larger general prisoner enclosure, and the contagion is doubly dangerous for this unification through the bars of class and education. Nawal's diagnosis is inevitable: 'Any

---

[17] See Yana Grigoryan and Kira Bogatyreva, 'Physical Culture and the Process of Human Improvement in Post-Revolutionary Russia', *International Journal of the History of Sport* 39.2 (2022): 127–47.

organised group movement, even if it be merely bodily exercise or dancing, establishes a rhythm in the mind and body which resembles the pattern of revolution or revolt' (97). It is the same kind of rhythm she enjoys with her writing ('Writing slices time, slashing it sword-like into pieces,' 56) and then again with her prison gardening, as she picks up an actual hoe and uses it to break up the soil of the yard and remove the embedded stones. Here the rhythm of physical labour abolishes the grip of prison time over the body:

> I raised the hoe above my head, bringing it down on the rocky ground until the stones were in pieces. The blood flowed from my hand. I tied it up with my white handkerchief and went on digging. Energy stored since childhood welled out from somewhere deep inside me, and I felt a tremendous pleasure at being totally involved in something, absorbed as I was in extracting the rocks from the ground.
> How many hours of that day passed as I worked with the hoe? I don't know. But I was oblivious to time, as one hour followed another. I forgot that I was in prison. (85)

Hoeing, like writing, is a perfectly self-sufficient activity ('Writing in itself is pleasurable, and so is planting. Work is inherently a source of pleasure,' 98), but there is a different form of solidarity at work in this apparently individual exercise, as she explains to a sceptical fellow inmate.

> 'Planting without a yield is no pleasure,' she said. 'It's meaningless.'
> 'For me, planting is an aim in itself, and it is enjoyable. Anyway, what do you mean by "yield"?'
> 'Will we stay here until we're eating grapes and oranges from these seeds?'
> 'If we stay, we'll eat them,' I replied. 'If not, whoever comes here after us will eat them.' (98)

It is that casual but deeply felt solidarity with future inmates, Nawal's sense of belonging to a numberless community of women entombed by men of a certain class and sexual ascendancy, that will drive her to form the historical organisation for which she is best remembered – the Arab Women Solidarity Association, founded in 1982 in direct response to her time in prison. It is one of the perverse benefits of sexually segregated prisons that time inside them engenders critical reflection on the nature of sexual differentiation more generally as an instrument of social domination. It forges solidarities that are peculiar to the arbitrary legal and political antagonisms defining a state's lack of coincidence with itself, but which exceed their local conditions in international directions irreducible to any particular judicial and legal apparatus.

* * *

The true specificity of prison solidarity may well consist in the politicisation of its auditory dimension, an aspect of her experience that Nawal, as a novelist, proved supremely capable of registering in her memoirs. Sound is, indeed, the most unsuspected source of torture in a prison like Qanatir [سجون القناطر] (Nawal calls it Barrages Women's Prison), with its decaying infrastructure and chronic overcrowding. 'I enjoyed neither solitude nor silence [. . .]. I could not pull a door shut between me and the others, even when I was in the toilet [. . .]. I came to understand that in prison, torture occurs not through solitude and silence but in a far more forceful way through uproar' (128–9).

> Never in my life had I heard such voices – like millions of hammers striking blows over one's ears. And the voices, all of them, were transformed into a single, thick, scorching voice, almost a tangible one, like a cauterising fluid [. . .] which spread through the ears and head, attacking every nook and cranny, and pressing on the brain like poisonous gas. (44)

And yet, despite this terrible sonic overload, what Nawal learns to perceive through prison's hubbub is nothing less than a vision of the 'other Egypt' her working life had been dedicated to treating via medical and literary care. The 'strange voices, the shouting and wailing and howling and sobbing, were all coming from the cell of mothers imprisoned with their children who had been born in prison. Three hundred mothers, and three hundred children, inside one cell the size of ours . . .' (43) – the auditory vision rapidly gives onto a feminist analysis like no other in the annals of prison literature, where the nightmare is reflected back on its source:

> The bodies of women pressed together, and clinging to children . . . insects biting the bodies of newborn infants . . . children screaming . . . mothers fighting for buckets of water, for bread, for a bit of sugar to dissolve in the water so the child could drink . . . one grasping the hair of another, fighting with hands and legs . . . cracked bare feet pressing on the bellies of children, their bare bottoms on the ground . . . eruptions of cursing, woman cursing woman, cursing her mother, her genitals, herself, the day her mother was born and

the day her child was born, poor illiterate women, who had entered prison because of poverty or ignorance or oppression by men. Behind every one of these women prisoners is a man: a father branding his daughter for a life of thievery, a husband beating his wife into practising prostitution, a brother threatening his sister so she will smuggle hashish and hard drugs for him, the head of a gang stealing a young female child and training her to beg in the streets ... the pits of society, the very lowest of the low. The tortured on earth. The other face of the system. (43–4)

The great force of Nawal's writing is crystallised in these perfectly judged transitions from a breathless paratactic montage of close-up sensory images to a rational survey of reasons and causes and then to a metaphoric crescendo which, again paratactically, summarises the social function of prison in such powerful and economic terms. Prison performs the inner truth of a social order, condensing its pitiless logic into malefic friezes of the damned: hellscapes even Dante could scarcely have imagined.

Lest, however, we leave her exquisite acoustic imagination twisting at this political nadir, it is again remarkable how the minor creatures of prison life intrude upon Nawal's memoirs as they did upon Pound's Pisan cantos and Luxemburg's prison letters and Sands' excruciating missives from the Maze: 'creatures who crawled by night from the enclosure into the cell. Small animals and insects entering through the bars ... chirping, whistling, squeaking, biting' (86), and generally claiming the senses for the inhuman.

> From where does all of this come? Do these sounds pass through the four walls, the ceiling, the earth's depths, to arrive here? Human and non-human voices alike. A sharp scream like that of a newborn child; wailing and moaning akin to the howling of wolves, quarrelling and cursing and a stifled sobbing. Raspy coughing, hands slapping and the sound of kicking. The whinnying murmur of water, what sounded like pleas of supplication, and chanting like the ritual of prayer. Frogs croaking, cats meowing and dogs barking, and over all a sharp whistling, the cockroaches' calls. (32)

Nawal's acoustic sensitivities are second to none in the annals of prison literature, and they achieve optimal focus on a creature known equally to Bobby Sands, who wrote as he was dying, 'Now, as I write, the odd curlew mournfully calls as they fly over. I like the birds.'[18] So it is again with Nawal; and we might learn to track the

---

[18] Bobby Sands, *Writings from Prison* (Cork: Mercier Press, 1997), 242.

migratory path of these birds from Egypt along the Mediterranean up through the Iberian Peninsula into the British Isles and Ireland, as they unknowingly articulate two of the major sites of suffering under two punitive regimes and offer solace to their greatest ear-witnesses.

> Suddenly, I heard the voice of the curlew. My heart beat forcefully, and I jumped on to the bars, clambering up them with my bare feet, stretching my neck skyward, jamming my head between the two steel bars.
>
> I can't see him. The voice, though, affects me as if it's me that he's calling. A sweet, sad voice, piercing the silence. A lone flute in the darkness. Singing like a mother's voice, like offering a prayer of supplication, like weeping, like a child's abrupt, long laugh, or like a single scream in the night. Or an uneven sobbing which goes on and on.
>
> Every dawn, I wait for that voice, and I hear it. Every dusk, too. The curlew sings only in the stillness and the dark. Only in this moment which falls between night and day. A single bird in the universe . . . I raise my head toward the sky. I want to see him. Never in my life have I seen a curlew. The sky, though, is surrounded by walls and wires, and in prison we hear the curlew without seeing him. That's enough, to hear him without seeing him. (83)

It is as acousmatic song that this invisible avian visitor exerts his magic influence over the text – not subject to the kind of ornithological disquisitions that were Luxemburg's favourite distractions, but left to symbolise the new life, 'the fresh, moist dawn breeze . . . the morning light creeping in from afar . . . the voice of the curlew resounding, like broken sighs, pleas, sobbing, like a child breathing laughter . . . or crying' (189). Or, indeed, writing itself, caught on the cusp between laughter and tears, and signalling in its impertinent affirmation of being nothing less than the jubilee that must follow the long night of tyranny. 'Hope is revolution, it is the singing of the free bird.'[19]

---

[19] Nawal El Saadawi, 'Translation of the Introduction to the Arabic Edition of *Memoirs from the Women's Prison*', 188.

Chapter 12

So Much Malice: Behrouz Boochani's *No Friend but the Mountains*

One month has passed since I was exiled to Manus. I am a piece of meat thrown into an unknown land; a prison of filth and heat. I dwell among a sea of people with faces stained and shaped by anger, faces scarred with hostility. Every week, one or two planes land in the island's wreck of an airport and throngs of people disembark. Hours later, they are tossed into the prison among the deafening ruckus of displaced people, like sheep to a slaughterhouse.

With the arrival of newcomers, the prison reaches peak tension; people stare at them like invaders. They are mainly taken to Fox Prison because it is large and tents for the newcomers can be assembled in that isolated corner. On the western side, two prisons stand opposite each other: Delta and Oscar. But from Fox Prison only Delta Prison is visible. It looks like a cage, like a hive full of bees. There isn't the slightest room to move within these two adjacent prisons. The prisons are a confrontation of bodies, a confrontation of human flesh. Friction from their breathing, breath that smells like the sea, smells like the deadly journey.

In Fox Prison nearly four hundred people are kept in an area smaller than a football field. The spaces between the rows of rooms and the corridors are streams flowing with disenfranchised men, coming and going from all directions. The atmosphere in the prison is made up of scenes of famished people, provocative and deafeningly boisterous. No-one knows anyone else. It is like a city in which a plague has sent everyone into a frenzy. The crowd is frantic. It seems that if one stood still, one would be carried away by the motion.[1]

---

[1] Behrouz Boochani, *No Friend but the Mountains: Writing from Manus Prison*, translated by Omid Tofighian (Sydney: Picador, 2018), 116–17.

Translated from the lyrical Farsi by a close collaborator, Behrouz Boochani's intensely metaphorical prose – all tapped methodically into the text app of a mobile telephone – oscillates between the deracinated perspective of a damaged first-person participant and an objective, journalistic eye for the systems, patterns and structures that define the obscene reality of Australia's 'offshore detention'. The tropological operators of choice for these frenetic transits between memoir and critique are metaphor and simile, figures whose quest for imagistic singularity is conducted through the medium of generality. Consider only the liquid metaphors here: the 'sea of people' into which the 'I' has been cast, an element of drowning vastness, next modulates into a way of thinking about the humidity and tang of collective exhalation ('breath that smells like the sea, smells like the deadly journey'), before culminating in a riparian figure for multitudinous institutional life: 'streams flowing with disenfranchised men, coming and going from all directions'.[2] Natural figuration at once stabilises the contingent forms of this malevolent experiment in human sociality, makes them familiar and cognisable, and simultaneously renders them strange and hostile, as the ocean has already served as an immense presence across the opening chapters of the book – which detail the adversities faced by a boatload of migrants attempting to cross the stretch of Indian Ocean that separates Java from Christmas Island. There, the ocean in its rampant state was figuratively commingled with the presiding metaphor of mountain ranges (*'The mountains, the waves/The chain of mountain ranges/ The waves, the mountain ranges . . ./The boat is a wreck'* [34]), and served to divide Asia from Australia, past from present, life from death, in an accelerating series of separations that culminates in the disaster of Manus Prison itself. The recurrence of oceanic metaphor in that 'living hell' (171) cannot help but recall the scenes of traumatic nautical passage that inaugurate this memoir, and so the figuration is multifaceted and layered in a way unique to this prison writer, who writes as a poet in the discursive idiom of expository prose.

Our chosen passage, at the head of the sixth chapter, has the specific function of an 'establishment shot' in the context of the memoir, which has already moved us from Indonesia aboard a sinking boat to a rescue by a British container ship to a capture by the Australian

---

[2] For more on liquid metaphors and their personal resonance for Boochani, see Frances Egan, 'Resisting Confinement through Translation: Behrouz Boochani's *No Friend but the Mountains*', *Auto/Biography Studies* 36.3 (2021): 523–42, esp. 527–8.

border patrol to Christmas Island for processing and finally here, to the prison topos itself, a militarised (or 'securitised') offshore island detention camp located on foreign soil (Papua New Guinea) but owned and operated by the Australian government for purposes of punitive deterrence. During his detention, Boochani will witness the construction of a fourth compound, 'Mike', which will hem in Fox on the eastern flank, but what matters here is the perfectly modular design, the a priori representation of carceral space that imposes itself ineluctably through the very intention to use detention as a default technique of discipline, control and punishment. Over the course of a century or more, this technique has leapt the traces of a local solution to the problem of 'criminality' in a bourgeois social space, to become the key strategy of modern governmentality in dealing with all kinds of 'undesirables': ethnic minorities, dissidents, descendants of slaves, the underemployed, activists and 'illegal immigrants' (otherwise known as asylum seekers and supposedly protected under the toothless UN charter of human rights). It has a spatial logic all its own, a globally leapfrogging template elaborated from site to site in perfect indifference towards locality, tradition or history, perpetuating the dark lessons of the Gulag, the concentration and extermination camps, and industrialised American prisons in a resistless cancer of biopower. We note, again, how Boochani takes this form and processes it through the alembic of metaphor and simile: 'It looks like a cage, like a hive full of bees. There isn't the slightest room to move within these two adjacent prisons. The prisons are a confrontation of bodies, a confrontation of human flesh.' The apian simile (elsewhere, the prison is 'a hive of killer bees' [173]) recalls an ancient georgic tradition of reflecting on human industry,[3] but inverts it – in the absence of any meaningful work or collective project, the 'bees' merely mill around on an increasingly aggressive footing, stingers out. The point of the carceral hive is not to yield honey, but simply to 'confront' masses of human bodies with each other, obliging them to come face to face with themselves as cellular images of a generalised non-aesthetic 'purposiveness without a purpose'. It is a blueprint for a riot, which duly comes in the book's cathartic climax.

'It is like a city in which a plague has sent everyone into a frenzy. The crowd is frantic. It seems that if one stood still, one would be

---

[3] Stretching from Virgil and Hesiod through Mandeville, Shakespeare and beyond; see, e.g., Rachel D. Carlson, 'The Honey Bee and Apian Imagery in Classical Literature', PhD dissertation, University of Washington, 2015; Richard Grinnel, 'Shakespeare's Keeping of Bees', *ISLE: Interdisciplinary Studies in Literature and Environment* 23.4 (November 2016): 835–54.

carried away by the motion.' For the first time since Solzhenitsyn, an imprisoned writer has elected to meditate explicitly on the civic dimension of the prison camp: its distributed functions and responsibilities in relation to the regulative idea of a populated geographical location, its built space and public facilities, its infrastructure and salaried 'public servants' (all privatised, of course), its logistics and scheduling, its demographics, neighbourhoods and (vexed term) culture. Boochani is a writer many of whose better tendencies lead him away from the 'I' towards the underlying civic ground in which it is enmeshed – the carceral city itself, where plague has struck and all stability is jeopardised by the absence of a viable social contract. Boochani's carceral city is one comprised of 'crowds', not individuals, and these crowds are (as we shall see) constituted around overlapping modes of identification (principally: the boat one arrived on, and the national language one speaks) which are decidedly 'extra-familiar' and non-nuclear. Amidst their contrapuntal fields of gravity, the individual is incapable of making a stand apart ('one would be carried away by the motion'), and civil bonds are provisionally woven around passional and irrational nodes of attention and interest: hunger, disease and the various presumed 'rights' that haunt the camp like dream vestiges of the real city of which this is but the nightmare reflection.

Boochani's sociological talents as an observer of prison life are unrivalled, and it is worth making the distinction that the other major sociological thinkers in this tradition (Angela Davis and George Jackson foremost amongst them) tend to situate their prison analyses within a broader diagnosis of racial capitalism and the long-term legacies of slavery. The specificities of carcerality, not just as a privileged allegorical lens on social relations, are perhaps too quickly passed over by these great prison writers: the intricate institutional rituals, the regimentation of daily life, the peculiar social dynamics of the yard, the temporal exploitations of an indefinite detention, in all their semi-autonomous salience. For Boochani, meanwhile, all of this is the very polestar of his attention, never satisfied until it has explored the complex interweaving of all operational elements and resolved them into a peculiar modality of the logic of power. His sociological depiction of Manus Prison is properly multidimensional, offering a social mapping of the facilities as astute as it is exhaustive. The three major groupings are clearly demarcated: the motley tribes of Black and Brown inmates; the governing class of white Australian guards; and, in between them, local 'Papus' hired into contract work by an international agreement that puts interesting pressures on the essential two-class dynamic.[4] Of the prisoners themselves much more will be said, but that they resolve into a tapestry of many nationalities is of the essence of their status as a dissociated crowd: 'Afghan, Sri Lankan, Sudanese, Lebanese, Iranian, Somali, Pakistani, Rohingya, Iraqi, Kurdish', representatives of all the displaced peoples of the Middle Eastern, North-East African, and South Asian conflict zones on our planet (123), sharing little beyond their desperation and their sex (the women and children having been detained elsewhere), and the nature of the sea voyages that brought them to Australian waters. With the Australian guards, the stylistic emphasis is generally satirical, as the stored fury and resentment of a four-year detainee flood the prose with brickbats: 'bright-red faces ... blood-red faces. Australians with fat asses ... sweaty ass cracks flowing like rivers' (153); they are 'overweight' (144), 'dripping with sweat' (172); and nightly they 'flee the prison' (176) – 'Those Australians, those bastards' (341). At its zenith, this satirical impulse attains Orwellian registers of contempt: 'The Rhinos – basically I mean the officers. No, it's much better to say Rhinos because I think it's a more fitting name' (274). Beyond the satire, though, is a disabused view of the professionalised violence these men carry in their bones:

> G4S prison guards [. . .] are mostly overworked and have spent most of their lives working professionally in Australian prisons with different kinds of criminals. Without question, crime, criminal courts, jail, prison violence, physical violence and knife attacks have become part of their everyday routine and mindset. Many of the guards are ex-servicemen who have served for years in Afghanistan and Iraq; they have been waging wars on the other side of the world. They have killed humans. (142–3)

The routine employment of such men results in exactly the desired outcome for the Australian government: the criminalisation of the asylum seeker in a social space rendered invisible to the Australian public. This criminalisation is a military procedure, undertaken with a logistical and ruthless rigour in an unbroken chain of command extending up to the Minister himself.

---

[4] 'The agreement between the government of Papua New Guinea and the Australian Department of Immigration stipulates that a large percentage of local people must be employed. Therefore, the prison is forced to employ people who, until then, were the freest humans I have encountered. But now they are absorbed within The Kyriarchal System, absorbed into the prison structure, absorbed into a culture of systemic violence.' Boochani, *No Friend but the Mountains*, 144.

The Papuan local employees are thus conscripted within much larger geopolitical plate tectonics, their subservience to an imperial logic of control unhappily self-evident at every crisis. In times of relative normality, these employees are responsible for cleaning and routine surveillance, chewing betel nut and generally having as little as possible to do with any of the foreigners on their island; but as soon as a problem arises, an implicit command is issued: '"Let it be known that in this prison local people are nothing. They simply get instructions and follow them." This configures the relationships among the three basic elements in the prison: the prisoners, the local people, the Australians. The result is that the local people form alliances with us' (145). It is one of the more enjoyable aspects of the book, this intuitive sympathy between Papuans and refugees in an imperial non-space over which neither of them has the slightest authority; but more critical for us is Boochani's sociological insight into its causes, all of which inhere in the Australian state's regional hegemony and projected xenophobia.

> At the root of the orders and rules being blasted out are traces of the hierarchy of power. Without a doubt, this is an all-encompassing system of oppressive governmentality. This is clear from the way the Papus listen to everything the Australians dictate. The prisoners are nothing but a defeated and crushed division, nothing but captured soldiers, their bodies trembling with horror. We are prisoners of war. (329)

The overarching militarisation of this carceral situation recalls nothing so much as Primo Levi's harrowing reflections on Auschwitz, and the only real comparison with these 'Papus' in prison literature is the category of Kapos so ruthlessly outlined there.[5] Though, to be fair, the comparison is misleading in that the imperial logic of Australian domination does not here depend upon fostering internal 'class' distinctions among the detainees but upon regional power and the racist norms of 'international relations'. At any rate, in and amongst this essentially tripartite camp sociology we find other, less important categories of person: the translators, at once quietly sympathetic and pitilessly vituperated as collaborationists; the medical staff, hopelessly out of their depth and under-resourced; the visiting dignitaries and 'lawyers' who bring waves of hope and leave deep troughs of despair; the riot squad of 'Iron Men' who appear to quell the uprising (343–8); the 'bosses' who occasionally show their faces;

---

[5] See Chapter 5 in this volume.

and, most elusive of all, the ghosts of prisoners past, whose fading traces our narrator builds into moving portraits.

Boochani's name for this complex 'hierarchy of power' on Manus is the intriguing one of 'Kyriarchy', whose conceptual origins the text traces to work in feminist theology by Elisabeth Schlüsser Fiorenza and which is glossed: 'a theory of interconnected social systems established for the purposes of domination, oppression and submission' (124 n. 6). Boochani's use of the term in preference to other concepts nearer to hand (carcerality, biopower, and so on) permits him to focus not so much on the omnipresent capillaries of vertical control and the disciplinary saturation of daily life by regimentation and law, as on the fractured spatial and sociological zones where all of that breaks down without for a moment weakening the system of command.[6] In fact, quite to the contrary, the point of his theory of Kyriarchy is that camp power operates precisely through the implicit exploitation of gaps, breaks, leaks and malfunctions in the overt system of control, conducting the operation of power along relatively unconscious, instinctive and passional vectors that transform the detainees into agents of their own incarceration.

> The developments over the months slowly but surely prove to everyone that the principle of The Kyriarchal System governing the prison is to turn the prisoners against each other and to ingrain even deeper hatred between people. Prison maintains its power over time; the power to keep people in line. Fenced enclosures dominate and can pacify even the most violent person – those imprisoned on Manus are themselves sacrificial subjects of violence. We are a bunch of ordinary humans locked up simply for seeking refuge. In this context, the prison's greatest achievement might be the manipulation of feelings of hatred between one another. (124–5)

This remarkable realisation prompts a Freudian complication of the usual Foucauldian emphasis governing much prison literature today. For what it does is show that power does not function through discipline alone, but seeps into the deepest unconscious wellsprings of human sociality and subjectivation as Freud had depicted them in *Civilisation and Its Discontents*: structural antagonism, hatred for

---

[6] For a good account of the eroding distinction between biopower and necropower in Australia's 'kyriarchal system', see Samantha O'Donnell, 'Living Death at the Intersection of Necropower and Disciplinary Power: A Qualitative Exploration of Racialised and Detained Groups in Australia', *Critical Criminology* 30 (2022): 285–304.

the neighbour, hostility towards the Other, misogyny, and so forth.[7] The point of Boochani's disabused presentation of Manus camp life is that it demonstrates remorselessly how a system of domination and control refers many of its more nefarious internal disciplinary measures not to explicit rules but to the residual 'unwritten rules' brought with them by the asylum seekers themselves: tribal hatreds, ethnic chauvinism, homophobia, and religious intolerance between inmates, to name a few.[8] The twisted genius of the logic is that, by prodding and exacerbating these latent hostilities, the carceral system internalises itself in a 'pre-conscious' stratum of each imprisoned individual, leading to a general situation in which each of them can declare with Milton's Satan:

> 'Me miserable! Which way shall I fly
> Infinite wrath and infinite despair?
> Which way I fly is Hell; myself am Hell,
> And in the lowest deep a lower deep
> Still threat'ning to devour me opens wide,
> To which the Hell I suffer seems a Heav'n.'[9]

So it is with the Manus prisoners:

> In addition to the torment produced by the oppressive enclosure of the prison fences, every prisoner creates a smaller emotional jail within themselves – something that occurs at the apex of hopelessness and disenfranchisement. Most prisoners evaluate their health and vitality through regular close examination of their bodies, developing fragmented and disrupted identities, and a warped sense of self, that makes them cynical of everyone else. This is the objective of the prison's Kyriarchal System, to drive prisoners to extreme distrust so that they become lonelier and more isolated, until the prison's Kyriarchal Logic triumphs with their collapse and demise. (125)

Promoting the very opposite of a 'care of the self' and inverting all the loftier goals of nineteenth-century reformatory and penitentiary

---

[7] Sigmund Freud, *Civilization and its Discontents*, translated by James Strachey (New York: W. W. Norton, 1962).

[8] Omid Tofighian in his Afterword notes of the concept of Kyriarchy: 'it purposely encompasses multiple, interlocking kinds of stigmatisation and oppression, including racism, heteronormativity, economic discrimination, class-based violence, faith-based discrimination, coloniality, Indigenous genocide, anti-Blackness, militarism and xenophobia. The term also captures the way that the intersecting systems are perpetually reinforced and replicated' (370).

[9] John Milton, *Paradise Lost*, Book IV, ll. 73–8, edited by Gordon Teskey (New York: Norton, 2005), 79–80.

traditions, Manus Prison functions as a wrecking yard of the human being, disassembling him into incoherent fragments of his former 'self' and fostering widespread aggression both amongst these inconsistent part-objects of his dying personality and between all the other isolated, 'collapsing' monads of the camp community. '*This realm of the mind is itself a prison/His existence is splintered like a dry piece of wood/Bashed on the ground of a barren and vast desert/He is a small and rotting boat*' (132).

> The atmosphere in the prison is constituted by micro-level and macro-level disciplinary measures designed to create animosity between the prisoners. Hatred runs through every prisoner. In the prison, hatred makes prisoners more insular. The weight of hatred is so intense that the prisoners will suddenly collapse on a dark night and give up resisting ... surrender to a system that induces and amplifies hatred ... and accept refoulement. This basic aim reflects The Kyriarchal System of the prison: 'Returning the refugee prisoners to the land from which they came.' The only time the power of the fences can bring the prisoners to their knees is when it joins forces with those very people inside it. The prison is designed to breed hostility, animosity. (165)

The fences draw fracture lines within the camp, within each compound, and within each prisoner. It is this ramifying compound fracture of the self and the socius that defines Boochani's peculiar portraiture of daily existence on Manus. What keeps the four hundred inmates of Foxtrot Compound from forging any durable political or ethical bonds are the inherited intolerances of linguistic, religious and ethnic filial distinction, which rapidly but inevitably supplant the contingent affiliations of the sea-going passages that brought them together in the first place. 'With time, this group identity based on the boat experience shifts towards other identifiers, such as language and nation. After some time, groups become based on a single criterion: where one is from. Afghan, Sri Lankan, Sudanese, Lebanese, Iranian, Somali, Pakistani, Rohingya, Iraqi, Kurdish' (123). This reactionary recoil into chauvinism and national identity is a vital moment of the Kyriarchy, whose pulverising logic, atomising, separating, and further subdividing the inmates, is summarised in an industrial figure: '*To tame/To produce fragments of metal/A production line/A factory/We have become a replica of caged baby chickens/The prison has become a replica of a chicken coop/Modern/Industrial*' (210). And each social atom is further decomposed at an internal level, as prisoners are driven back by the system upon their

own psychological resources, all of which are irreparably traumatised and incapable of coherence.

In Boochani's case, of course, it is to 'Little Kurdistan' that his
filiative tendencies are drawn. The fierce patriotism manifesting
as 'repressed political aspirations', the 'miraculous' appearance of
a Kurdish flag on the door of the block masquerading as nation-
ally sovereign territory, the annexation of the compound's only
mango tree, and the emergence of a 'national hero' in The Gentle
Giant (235–40) – all gesture at the reparative logic in camp life of
national group belonging. It is something noted equally by Levi in
his Auschwitz memoirs, this clustering around residual linguistic
ties in terrible adversity. But of course 'Kurdistan' exists only as a
geopolitical cipher to begin with, and so 'Little Kurdistan' can only
be a frail shadow of a substanceless form, racked with agonising
existential pains that cannot be put aside in the 'unspoken fraternity'
of the experiment (240).[10] Each Kurdish inmate is forced to face
the broken, ravaged status of his national identity mirrored in the
memory bank of his own traumas and failures. For Boochani, the
meaning of 'Kurdistan' is forever fixed in memories of his childhood
during the devastating eight-year Iran–Iraq War, in a welter of vivid
horrors, flights to the mountains and desperate recriminations, as the
'two grand war elephants' of occupying military forces trampled a
nation's homeland into dust and mire.

> Do the Kurds have any friends other than the mountains?
> Horrified mothers . . . mothers wrapped their children within the
> instincts of motherhood and escaped to the mountains. Young girls
> were searching for their dreams within the hearts of men rounded
> up into groups – so many groups – and being led down a road
> to the front lines of war. Groups – so many groups – returned as
> corpses. (259)
> Animosities reached climax and teeth gnashed from extreme hate.
> Old wounds were opened and blades of battle tapped into the cess-
> pool of history, the history of hate, and disseminated its loathing,
> spread across what once were fields of goodwill; our vivid, green
> and bounteous homeland. A putrid smell came over the whole
> place. (261)

---

[10] 'Behrouz was writing in Farsi, not Kurdish. He was writing in the language of his
oppressors, even though he is a fervent advocate of Kurdish culture, language and
politics. And the book was being translated into the language of his jailers and torturers.' Elio Attilio Baldi, '(Meta)Physical Homelessness in Behrouz Boochani's *No Friend
but the Mountains*', *Forum for Modern Language Studies* 57.4 (January 2022): 400
[399–416].

There is no luxury of being a Kurd, when this 'being' is constituted principally of shocking international betrayals and openly genocidal intentions, a hatred so vast and distributed that it has conspired to this day – as with Palestine – to deny a population of forty million the simple dignity of a nation state. Every Kurd and every Palestinian is a stateless refugee from modernity itself, whose back has been turned on the cries of millions for a homeland since the imperial partition of the Ottoman Empire, in cynical betrayal of the provisions of the Treaty of Sèvres, and the Sykes–Picot and Lausanne agreements (1916–23).[11] Boochani occupies his Kurdish identity the way a starving squatter might occupy a condemned madhouse in a war zone, its masonry crumbling as the air-raid sirens scream in the night.

> I was born in the cauldron of this war. An abominable nativity that stank of cow dung. And so all the beings in existence joined forces; they conspired, and finally, their collective will hurled me into this world. Like an arrow released from the archer's bow and submerged into a chamber of afflictions. Suffering and revulsion. Arranged into a harmony of obscenities and configurations of pain. War. [. . .] And even the one-day-old child's psychological schema and mental state were traumatised . . . like shrapnel within critical parts of the body . . . imprinted . . . forever. (261–2; 263)

The harrowing fact is that Boochani himself is War, and like all Kurds his occupation of yet another war zone (this one the Australian government's against 'boat people') is another projected map of his already scrambled, dissociated and traumatised 'mental state'. He inhabits Manus Prison as he must inhabit that always-already stateless, homeless, pulverised 'harmony of obscenities and configurations of pain' that is his national and psychological condition.

> I feel that I am being taken over by multiple personalities: sometimes blue thoughts parade through my head, and sometimes grey thoughts. Other times my thoughts are colourblind. (130)

This remarkable accentuation of what we might call Boochani's 'dividuality', his tendency not to add up to a single figure, but constantly to deliquesce and disintegrate,[12] is prison writing's most disenchanted realisation of the fundamental goal of the 'Kyriarchal

---

[11] For more on this vital dimension of Boochani's writing, see Özlem Belçim Galip, 'From Mountains to Oceans: The Prison Narratives of Behrouz Boochani', *Biography* 43.4 (2020): 724–35.

[12] See Gerald Raunig, *Dividuum: Machinic Capitalism and Molecular Revolution*, translated by Aileen Derieg (Pasadena: Semiotext(e), 2016).

System' and of incarceration in general today. The polar opposite of Nawal El Saadawi's resilient egotism, we discover here a pitiless image of late capitalist sociality as comprised not of groups or even of individuals, but infinitely exploitable fragments of displaced persons. Boochani speaks for all who inhabit the 'worldless world' of limitless camps outside walled-off citadels of power:[13]

> I am disintegrated and dismembered, my decrepit past fragmented and scattered, no longer integral, unable to become whole once again. The total collection of scenes turns like pages of a short story, churned through with the speed of light. [. . .]
>
> I must confess that I don't know who I am and what I will become. I have interpreted my whole past over and over again. Parts of my past have been unlocked as a result of the death of my loved ones. And, in addition, other parts are frozen; they have become fixed in my mind. As I grow older, the images form into coherent islands, but they never lose that sense of fragmentation and dislocation. Life is full of islands; islands that all appear to be completely foreign lands in comparison to each other. (265)

There is, if you like, a kind of infrastructural logic to the presentation of such realisations in *No Friend but the Mountains*, a deep insistence on the dependency of 'identity' on the largely invisible, behind-the-scenes flows and impedances that make institutional life possible. If the Kyriarchal System works according to the planned breakdown of structures of power, stimulating dormant intolerances and hatreds, then that also extends to power's literal infrastructures, like sewage, electrical wiring, water supply and communications systems. The 'Oldman Generator' is one of the many personified objects in the text whose irregular breakdowns occasion spiralling rage and resentment among all the inmates. 'Those in charge of the generator are acutely

---

[13] 'For the crushing majority of men and women in the so-called world, the world of commodities and money, have not the slightest access to this world. They are harshly walled off from it, existing outside of it, where there are very few commodities and no money at all.' Alain Badiou and Clément Petitjean, 'True Communism is the Foreignness of Tomorrow,' Verso blog, 26 March 2014: https://www.versobooks. com/blogs/1547-true-communism-is-the-foreignness-of-tomorrow-alain-badiou-talks-in-athens. 'In its circumstantial aspect, capitalist nihilism has reached the stage of the non-existence of any world. Yes, today there is no world as such, only some singular and disjointed situations. No world exists simply because the majority of the planet's inhabitants today do not even have a label, a simple label. [. . .] Today, outside of the grand and petty bourgeoisie of imperial cities who proclaim to be "civilization", there is only the anonymous excluded. "Excluded" is the name for those who have no name, just as "market" is the name for a world that is not a world.' Alain Badiou, *Polemics*, translated by Steve Corcoran (London: Verso, 2006), p. 34.

aware of how easy it is to dominate the prisoners, simply by pressing a button. Everything is reduced to the generator – a mind made of machinery and wires. No-one knows its whereabouts in the prison, or maybe its location on the island – no-one knows where it is installed' (175). When it stops generating power, the air-conditioning fails, temperatures rise, the water ceases to pump, toilets overspill and all superficial civility dissolves into counter-flows of fury and violence. Boochani maps the dependency of psychic mood on infrastructural functionality, one result of which is the collective transference of psychic properties onto the 'mind made of machinery and wires'. 'The generator manipulates our minds to such an extent that it has morphed into some kind of agent; it has developed human motivations. Sometimes the prisoners select adjectives that ascribe human qualities to it: "That stupid generator", "The generator is a cunt", "Generator, you bastard", "You asshole of a generator"' (179). One of the author's many lyric episodes apostrophises the generator as a key character in the narrative:

> The generator has a face with the following features:
> *A device resembling someone of old age/*
> *Constituted by an intricate system of deteriorating wires/*
> *Poles and pipes of rusty metal/*
> *Probably within a dingy space/*
> *Somewhere worse than the prison/*
> *Covered by an old cloth/*
> *Under the protection of a rag/*
> *A rag that is withering away/*
> *The generator is withering away.*
>
> During these moments I want to believe the generator is a living being, with a soul, an organism that takes pleasure in throwing the prison into disarray whenever it feels like it. (177–8)

But it is the sewage system's dependency upon electricity that produces the most explosive commentaries on prison infrastructure, since even when they are working, the toilets and their effluent drains have nowhere near the capacity to dispose of the waste of four hundred angry bowels and bladders. 'A complex of maybe ten small rooms, a few of them without doors or, rather, a bunch of them that have just rotted away over time. It has become a region of humidity and cultivation, a lab for algae. The whole lot has turned green. The floor is always in the same state: piss up to the ankle. These toilets are so filthy that the toilet space has extended along the ground for a few metres. The toxic water has seeped into the surrounding area, penetrating the space where various species of plants are growing' (160). Forming their own nauseating ecosystem, the toilets have essentially fallen off the grid of infrastructure, into a 'rewilding' of basic excremental functions among camp inmates. The Freudian coordinates of the Kyriarchal System are nowhere better glimpsed than in this disgusting zone of filth and olfactory nightmare, since the first condition of 'civilisation' is a working cloaca.[14] Yet the prison population must queue, sometimes for hours at a time, for the privilege of urinating and defecating and masturbating and attempting suicide in filth unworthy of a pigsty, 'decaying concrete full of tiny crevices [. . .] full of accumulated grime and semen' (166), excreta slopping around the ankles.

Boochani's excremental vision rivals Bobby Sands' and ranks alongside the almightiest poets of the 'material bodily lower stratum', Swift and Rabelais.[15] One of the most humiliating passages in the narrative concerns the character known as the Prime Minister, a prisoner who holds himself with unparalleled dignity in the Kyriarchal System, refusing to be bowed or humbled, who has learned to regulate his bowels with military precision; which is all very well until a major infrastructural breakdown – 'in the end our renowned expert finds a spot behind one of the tanks, drops his pants with no regard for any set of norms, with no regard for any social customs . . . at that moment, with no regard for anything that he has until then identified with . . . and he shits out two heaps of dark, rotten faeces' (183–4). Overseen by the prison clown, Maysam the Whore, and subject to rounds of hilarious ridicule, the great man crumbles into a psychic ruin virtually overnight, swiftly signs the refoulement papers, and vanishes 'back home', where there is no home. The excremental is in many sense the key to Kyriarchal control on Manus: how better to motivate a recantation of the claim to refugee status than fanning the stench of other men's bowel movements? 'Within a few minutes the toilets cease to function and the smell of shit and piss sweeps the whole space from end-to-end. As time passes, the foul smell of human excrement worsens, contaminating the area with

---

[14] 'There is an unmistakable social factor in the cultural striving for cleanliness too, which was later justified on grounds of hygiene, but manifested itself before this connection was appreciated. The urge for cleanliness arises from the wish to get rid of excrement, which has become repugnant to the senses. [. . .] A person who lacks cleanliness – who does not hide his excrement – thereby offends others and shows them no consideration, and this is reflected in our strongest and commonest terms of abuse.' Freud, *Civilization and its Discontents*, 47.

[15] Mikhail Bakhtin, *Rabelais and His World*, translated by Helene Iswolsky (Bloomington: Indiana University Press, 1984), 368–436.

intensity' (174). Running throughout his psycho-topography of Manus Prison is a major emphasis on its offence to the sense of smell. 'The stench of hairy men's foul breath and sweat, sleeping alongside each other – this is more disgusting than the sewage gathered outside the tunnel. Like the smell of a dead dog, this stench sometimes combines with the smell of shit' (151–2).

In this noxious ambient olfactory pestilence, the hundreds of inmates are obliged to exist above all at the level of their most minimal and generic functions. As the metastatic 'representation of space' in the camp is abstract, ideological, operational, existing on a plane simultaneously material and symbolic, so too the inmates are caught by that space in a relentless logic of becoming-abstract, generic and iterative.[16] It is this very tendency towards the general and away from the particular that predisposes Boochani's narrative discourse towards the allegorical, even in the midst of his penetrating sociological analyses.[17] Allegory is, we may say, overdetermined in this text. Apart from these representational dimensions of its space and population, and the overtly satiric purposes already outlined, Boochani constantly emphasises his island setting (islands having, from More's *Utopia* through Golding's *Lord of the Flies*, promoted allegorical thinking), deploys animal metaphors and similes (bees, sheep, rhinos and so on) and specifically advises his reader that, in order to protect the identities of actual detainees, he has 'allegorized' the major personae of his account:

> No detainee or refugee in this book is based on a specific individual, however detailed their stories. They are not individuals who are disguised. Their features are not facts. Their identities are entirely manufactured. They are composite characters: a collage drawn from various events, multiple anecdotes, and they are often inspirited by the logic of allegory, not reportage. (xxxv)

So, in place of plausible, three-dimensional characters, we are presented with florid allegorical types: Maysam the Whore, who promotes carnivalesque abandon and lascivious sexuality ('Because we

---

[16] See the memorable discussion of 'representations of space' in Henri Lefebvre's opus *The Production of Space*, translated by Donald Nicholson-Smith (Oxford: Blackwell, 1991), esp. 40–6.

[17] '*No Friend but the Mountains* is [. . .] both a profoundly localized text responding to, making knowledge about, and exposing a highly specific and complex set of conditions, and [. . .] a uniquely transnational text that speaks to and about a global phenomenon.' Anna Poletti, 'Introduction: A Forum on Behrouz Boochani's *No Friend but the Mountains: Writing from Manus Prison*', *Biography* 43.4 (2020): 687 [724–35].

are incarcerated men and there are no women in this prison, from this moment on I hereby ordain gay sex completely permissible' [140]); The Prime Minister, dignified, upstanding, then broken; The Cow, who pursues the line of least resistance in his quest to consume as much food as possible; The Gentle Giant, a magnanimous and caring Kurd who serves to preserve the idea of the Good in impossible circumstances, and who is murdered in the final section of the narrative; The Prophet, who speaks truth to power; Grizzly, the self-harmer (one of many); The Father-of-the-Months-Old-Child, emblematising the pathos of all fathers separated from their families; The Smiling Youth, who observes contemplative silence by the side of our narrator; and The Hero, the half-inspired, half-moronic false leader of the final rebellion, with its gruesome body count and no-exit modus operandi.

This inveterate allegorical habit places Boochani well outside the main line of twentieth-century prison writers, who have generally preferred to individualise and particularise the portraiture of their fellow inmates (always excepting the guards and wardens, who have tended to remain in the orbit of satirical allegory). Yet, as this volume's only twenty-first-century text, perhaps *No Friend but the Mountains* is marking a determinate shift in the scope and scale of what today must stand as a global literary form without fixed national borders or populations. The local is precisely what is placed outside the generic spaces of Manus Prison: the island ecosystems and Indigenous population, the ocean itself, and all Papuan history remain strictly off limits to the camp's prisoners, who must dwell within a completely abstract system of rules, uniforms, infrastructures and schedules, projected by fiat from a distant Australian ministry upon a foreign soil to incarcerate the unwanted of the world. Allegory is the appropriate formal solution to the question of representation here, and further permits the text to speak for a much broader swath of the ninety-million-strong global population of refugee camps, concentration compounds, 'illegal' squatters' yards and other modes of spatial prohibition, enclosure and exclusion.[18]

---

[18] '*No Friend But The Mountains* is a philosophical project that raises paradoxes, it raises the problem of isolation and concentration typical in historical motifs of the deserted island, the penal colony, and journalistic portrayals of island detention, while also attending to transnational and cross- cultural travel. It foregrounds the fact that colonial systems of torture and exploitation are global events, threaded between Cairo, Manus, and Sydney, ensuring that we recognise our place in the world, at once irrevocably here and catastrophically there, and further, that we know Australia to be a place of adjectival association, a history we re-tread with each paratext adorning the work.' Dashiell Moore, 'Behrouz Boochani and the Penal Archipelago', *Overland* 239 (Winter 2020): 55 [49–59].

Boochani's allegorical personae are hardly specific to Manus; their generality suggests a global dispensation, a new typology of camp existence, springing as if by default from the identikit spatial forms of 'humanitarian aid' as much as draconian 'offshore detention', irrespective of national origin or cultural complexion.

And yet, for all the tyranny of its exclusion, the island itself, Manus, stages a determinate return over the length of Boochani's great memoir.[19] The one geographical factor that not even the most thoroughgoing carceral production of space can occlude is of course the insistent presence of the tropical sun itself, 'the Manusian sun trying to stifle us all, the Manusian sun trying to incinerate us' (114), so distinct from the 'tender, pleasant grace' of Kurdistan's sun (109): '*But the tropical location of Manus has the most ruthless sun in the entire world/As soon as it gets the chance, it cremates everything*' (110). Natural variations in latitude, longitude, humidity and average temperature create infernal associations for all refugees from more mountainous terrains and sear the psyche with the brand of geographical specificity. Equatorial Manus suspends its sun over the camp like a fierce judgement upon it; and the Kyriarchal System depends upon it, for it is the sun itself that makes the breakdowns of the generator intolerable. But this, along with the Papuan guards, is the thin end of a wedge of locality that not the journalist but the poet Boochani will expand into a seam of lyrical gold in his book and in the associated film, *Chauka, Please Tell Us the Time* (Sarvestani & Boochani, 2019). Lyricism occupies the particular as allegory occupies the generic, and the signal formal success of Boochani's work is his ability to shuttle between both modes with quicksilver grace and assurance: the allegory pushes its central narrating presence up to the bars of his cage where he looks (and eventually leaps) out for lyric traces of a life not lived, a world unacted.[20] 'The prisoner constructs his identity against the concept of freedom. His imagination is always preoccupied with the world beyond the fences and in his mind he forms a picture of a world where people are free' (299):

---

[19] 'Boochani manages to overcome his fear by embracing the generative power of *zoe*' on the island, writes Pilar Royo-Grasa in 'Behrouz Boochani's *No Friend but the Mountains*: A Call for Dignity and Justice', *European Legacy*, 26.7–8 (2021): 757 [750–63].

[20] The full generic complexity of the text is charted in Omid Tofighian, 'Behrouz Boochani and the Manus Prison Narratives: Merging Translation with Philosophical Reading', *Continuum* 32.4 (2018): 523–40.

In the middle of the night it drizzles with rain. For a short time the place is completely abandoned, not a human in sight. I gather the courage to throw myself into the world beyond the fences. With two or three quick leaps I am over the fence. Moments later I am in the dark and among the bushes. It is a form of mutiny, of rebellion, as I discover freedom, as I touch freedom.

Now here I am, a creature outside the prison walls, a creature on the other side of the prison enclosure. And I am now part of the jungle. I am the jungle, like the snakes, like the frogs, like the insects, like the birds. I am the jungle itself. In the darkness of the jungle, on the soft floor of the jungle, groping, fumbling, feeling my way towards the ocean. (301)

The smaller creatures that form such a constant thread of prison writing the world over here attain to a new level of specificity. We learn not of rats or lice or cockroaches, but of crabs, amphibians, serpents and island-specific birdlife, all of which visit the prison not in the invasive way of vermin, but as displaced denizens of an island ecology forced into peripheral status by the imposition of carceral space. On his imaginative escapes from the fences and walls of the detention centre, Boochani revels in an intoxicating becoming-jungle, at one with the local life in a lyrical ambling through the uncolonised precincts of freedom. The crabs are no mere small fry, 'holding their own' against prisoners in the war over fallen mangoes (238); so when his feet 'touch frogs and crabs' on his nocturnal escapades, it is no incidental occurrence, but 'full of marvel, full of delight' (301). Moreover, the island crab is a levelling, undermining, revolutionary figure in Boochani's lyrical logic: '*The elderly crab is gradually digging up the moist earth with its claws/It is calmly excavating the soft dirt that lies beneath the fences/The old crab digs until it penetrates the prison*' (320). And the jungle itself resonates with an exteriority vastly in excess of its merely spatial properties; it is an Outside of the imagination itself, permeated by a surreal, intimidating judgement where the moon holds court with the sun. When the generator fails, this Outside pushes in:

The prison is inoperative, and after a few minutes it regresses even further, regresses into horror. The yelling and screaming finally cease. Just the sound of random, muffled barking can be heard coming out of the depths of the jungle. It seems that the sounds are migrating deep down into the darkest of places, travelling further and further away to the rhythm of some never-ending music, to an eternal rhythm. The sounds continue to drift until a heavy silence creeps in to hold the prison captive. Only the cry of birds remains; they know what is going on around them. (178)

Boochani's enhanced psychogeography locates the limit to Australia's carceral space in this dizzying gulf of unconscious, eternal pulses emanating from the blind heart of things. In this terrible darkness which 'holds the prison captive', one sound above all strikes the fitting note; it is the sound of the Chauka bird, unlike any lark or curlew or crow or pigeon from other prison writings, who gives its name to the torture cell and whose cry sounds the apocalyptic clarion that must finally bring the coming storm of terror, blood and revenge.

> This night, and the nights that follow, the Chauka bird continues to sing that song. Its calling heralds terror. Its calling expresses apprehension, an anxiety for what is ahead. Its calling makes one's hair stand on end.
>
> *Chauka fears the prison/*
> *Sunsets are frightening/*
> *Sunsets deliver the scent of death/*
> *Chauka sings the song of impending death.* (292)

'All of the birds of Manus and the very jungle itself are harmonised in Chauka's voice and flight from the tallest coconut tree on the island into the prison grounds where Chauka unites with a wailing and lamenting human being.'[21] In their grim chorus stirs the necessary next act in humanity's exhausted outrage against a century or more of ruinous incarcerations.[22]

---

[21] Rebecca Hill, 'Chauka's Voice: Resistance in the Art of Behrouz Boochani', *Overland* (9 March 2022), https://overland.org.au/2022/03/chaukas-voice-resistance-in-the-art-of-behrouz-boochani/.

[22] 'As this book illustrates, the prison is everywhere.' Claire Loughnan, Review of *No Friend but the Mountains*, *State Crime* 8.1 (2019): 129 [126–30].

Bibliography

Adorno, Theodor W. *Negative Dialectics*, translated by E. B. Ashton (New York: Continuum, 2007).

Agamben, Giorgio. *Remnants of Auschwitz: Homo Sacer III*, translated by Daniel Heller-Roazen (New York: Zone Books, 1999).

Ahnert, Ruth. *The Rise of Prison Literature in the Sixteenth Century* (Cambridge: Cambridge University Press, 2013).

Alexander, Michelle. *The New Jim Crow: Mass Incarceration in the Age of Colorblindness* (New York: The New Press, 2010).

Aristotle. *The Complete Works of Aristotle*, revised Oxford translation, vol. 2, edited by Jonathan Barnes, translated by B. Jowett (Princeton, NJ: Princeton University Press, 1984).

Attwell, David. 'Writing After the "Poor Little Bomb": Fictionality and Sabotage in Nadine Gordimer's *The Late Bourgeois World*', *ELH* 87.1 (Spring 2020): 273–91.

Auerbach, Erich. *Mimesis* (Princeton, NJ: Princeton University Press, 2003).

Bacigalupo, Massimo. *Ezra Pound, Italy, and the Cantos* (Liverpool: Liverpool University Press, 2020).

Badiou, Alain. *Ethics*, translated by Peter Hallward (London: Verso, 2001).

—. *Logic of Worlds*, translated by Alberto Toscano (London: Continuum, 2009).

—. *Polemics*, translated by Steve Corcoran (London: Verso, 2006).

Badiou, Alain, and Clément Petitjean. 'True Communism is the Foreignness of Tomorrow', *Verso* blog, 26 March 2014. Accessed at: https://www.versobooks.com/blogs/1547-true-communism-is-the-foreignness-of-tomorrow-alain-badiou-talks-in-athens.

Bakhtin, Mikhail. *Rabelais and His World*, translated by Helene Iswolsky (Bloomington: Indiana University Press, 1984).

Baldi, Elio Attilio. '(Meta)Physical Homelessness in Behrouz Boochani's *No Friend but the Mountains*', *Forum for Modern Language Studies* 57.4 (January 2022): 399–416.

Barker, Francis. *Solzhenitsyn: Politics and Form* (London: Macmillan, 1977).

Benjamin, Ruha, ed. *Captivating Technology: Race, Carceral Technoscience, and Liberatory Imagination in Everyday Life* (Durham, NC: Duke University Press, 2019).

Benjamin, Walter. *The Arcades Project*, translated by Howard Eiland and Kevin McLaughlin (Cambridge, MA: Harvard University Press, 1999).

—. *Understanding Brecht*, translated by Anna Bostock (London: Verso, 1998).

Beresford, David, and Peter Maas. *Ten Dead Men: The Story of the 1981 Irish Hunger Strike* (London: Grafton, 1987).

Berkman, Alexander. *Prison Memoirs of an Anarchist*, edited by Jessica Moran and Barry Pateman (Chico, CA: AK Press, 2016).

Bernstein, Hilda. *The World that Was Ours* (London: Heinemann, 1967).

Blake, William. *The Marriage of Heaven and Hell*, edited by Michael Phillips (Oxford: Bodleian Library, 2011).

Boggs, James. *Pages from a Black Radical's Notebook: A James Boggs Reader*, edited by Stephen Ward (Detroit: Wayne State University Press, 2011).

Boochani, Behrouz. *No Friend but the Mountains: Writing from Manus Prison*, translated by Omid Tofighian (Sydney: Picador, 2018).

Brady, Andrea. *Poetry and Bondage: A History and Theory of Lyric Constraint* (Cambridge: Cambridge University Press, 2021).

Brooks, Iolanthe, and Asha Best. 'Prison Fixes and Flows: Carceral Mobilities and their Critical Logistics', *Environment and Planning D: Society and Space* 39.3 (January 2021): 459–76.

Brown, Nathan J. 'Nasserism's Legal Legacy: Accessibility, Accountability, and Authoritarianism', in *Rethinking Nasserism: Revolution and Historical Memory in Modern Egypt*, edited by Elie Podeh and Onn Winckler (Gainesville, FL: University Press of Florida, 2004), 127–44.

Bujalski, Nicholas. 'Narrating Political Imprisonment in Tsarist Russia: Bakunin, Goethe, Hegel', *Modern Intellectual History* 18.3 (2021): 681–707.

Bush, Ronald. 'Poetic Metamorphosis: Ezra Pound's *Pisan Cantos* and Prison Poetry', *Rivista di Letterature d'America* XXIX.126–7 (2009): 37–60.

Carlson, Rachel D. 'The Honey Bee and Apian Imagery in Classical Literature', PhD thesis, University of Washington, 2015.

Carnochan, W. B. 'The Literature of Confinement', in *The Oxford History of the Prison*, edited by Norval Morris and David J. Rothman (Oxford: Oxford University Press, 1995), 427–55.

Carter, Stephen. *The Politics of Solzhenitsyn* (London: Macmillan, 1977).

Cleaver, Eldridge. *Soul on Ice* (London: Penguin, 1999).

Cohen, Uri. 'Consider If This Is a Man: Primo Levi and the Figure of Ulysses', *Jewish Social Studies: History, Culture, Society* 18.2 (Winter 2012): 40–69.

Cook, Steven A. *The Struggle for Egypt: From Nasser to Tahrir Square* (Oxford: Oxford University Press, 2012).

Coyle, Michael J., and Mechthild Nagel, eds. *Contesting Carceral Logic: Towards Abolitionist Futures* (London: Routledge, 2022).

Dante. *Inferno, Divine Comedy*, vol. 1, edited by Robert M. Durling (Oxford: Oxford University Press, 1996).

Davis, Angela Y. *Abolition Democracy: Beyond Empire, Prisons, and Torture* (New York: Seven Stories Press, 2005).

—. *Are Prisons Obsolete?* (New York: Seven Stories Press, 2003).

—. *Autobiography* (New York: Random House, 1974).

—. 'Introduction', in Ruth First, *117 Days: An Account of Confinement and Interrogation under the South African 90-Day Detention Law*, ii–vi.

—. *Selections from the Black: Purple Book* (Jamestown: Jamestown Publishers, 1974).

Davis, Angela Y., and Bettina Aptheker, eds. *If They Come in the Morning: Voices of Resistance* (University Park: Pennsylvania State University Press, 1971).

D'Epiro, Peter. 'Canto 74: New Light on Lucifer', *Paideuma* 10.2 (Fall 1981): 297–301.

di Prima, Diane. *Revolutionary Letters*, 50th anniversary ed., Pocket Poets #27 (San Francisco: City Lights Books, 2021).

Dobson, Miriam, 'Contesting the Paradigms of De-Stalinization: Readers' Responses to *One Day in the Life of Ivan Denisovich*', *Slavic Review* 64.3 (Autumn, 2005): 580–600.

Egan, Frances. 'Resisting Confinement through Translation: Behrouz Boochani's *No Friend but the Mountains*', *Auto/Biography Studies* 36.3 (2021): 523–42.

Eliot, T. S. *The Waste Land* (New York: Boni and Liveright, 1922).

Elkins, Caroline. *Imperial Reckoning: The Untold Story of Britain's Gulag in Kenya* (New York: Henry Holt, 2005).

El Saadawi, Nawal. *Memoirs from the Women's Prison*, translated by Marilyn Booth (London: Zed Books, 2020).

—. 'Translation of the Introduction to the Arabic Edition of *Memoirs from the Women's Prison*', Appendix in Nawar Al-Hassan Golley, *Reading Arab Women's Autobiographies: Shahrazad Tells Her Story* (Austin: University of Texas Press, 2003), 185–8.

Federal Bureau of Investigation HQ File 176–34, section 7 of 10, Report April 13, 1970.

Feldman, Allen. *Formations of Violence: The Narrative of the Body and Political Terror in Northern Ireland* (Chicago: University of Chicago Press, 1991).

First, Ruth. *117 Days: An Account of Confinement and Interrogation under the South African 90-Day Detention Law*, with an introduction by Angela Y. Davis (London: Penguin, 2009).

—. *117 Days: An Account of Confinement and Interrogation under the South African 90-Day Detention Law* (London: Virago, 2010).

Fludernik, Monika. *Metaphors of Confinement: The Prison in Fact, Fiction, and Fantasy* (Oxford: Oxford University Press, 2019).

'Folsom Manifesto for the California Statewide Prison Strike, 1970', *San Francisco Bay View National Black Newspaper*, 26 October 2018. Accessed at: https://sfbayview.com/2018/10/folsom-manifesto-for-the-california-statewide-prison-strike-1970/.

Foucault, Michel. *Discipline and Punish: The Birth of the Prison*, translated by Alan Sheridan (London: Penguin, 1991).

Franklin, H. Bruce. 'The Literature of the American Prison', *Massachusetts Review* 18.1 (Spring 1977): 51–78.

—, ed. *Prison Writing in 20th-Century America* (New York: Penguin, 1998).

Freeman, Thomas S. 'The Rise of Prison Literature', in *Prison Writings in Early Modern Britain*, special issue edited by William J. Sheils and William Sherman, *Huntington Library Quarterly* 70.2 (June 2009): 133–46.

Freud, Sigmund. *Civilization and its Discontents*, translated by James Strachey (New York: W. W. Norton, 1962).

Fuhrmann, Johan, and Stefan Baier, eds. *Prisons and Prison Systems: Practices, Types, and Challenges* (New York: Nova, 2013).

Galip, Özlem Belçim. 'From Mountains to Oceans: The Prison Narratives of Behrouz Boochani', *Biography* 43.4 (2020): 724–35.

Gikandi, Simon. *Ngũgĩ wa Thiong'o* (Cambridge: Cambridge University Press, 2000).

Gilmore, Ruth Wilson. *The Golden Gulag: Prisons, Surplus, Crisis, and Opposition in Globalizing California* (Berkeley: University of California Press, 2007).

Golley, Nawar Al-Hassan. *Reading Arab Women's Autobiographies: Shahrazad Tells Her Story* (Austin: University of Texas Press, 2003).

Gramsci, Antonio. *Selections from Prison Notebooks*, edited and translated by Quentin Hoare and Geoffrey Nowell Smith (London: Lawrence & Wishart, 1971).

Grass, Sean. *The Self in the Cell: Narrating the Victorian Prisoner* (New York: Routledge, 2003).

Grigoryan, Yana, and Kira Bogatyreva. 'Physical Culture and the Process of Human Improvement in Post-Revolutionary Russia', *International Journal of the History of Sport* 39.2 (2022): 127–47.

Grinnell, Richard. 'Shakespeare's Keeping of Bees', *ISLE: Interdisciplinary Studies in Literature and Environment* 23.4 (November 2016): 835–54.

Gugelberger, Georg M. 'When Evil-Doing Comes like Falling Rain', *Comparative Literature Studies* 24.4 (1987): 370–86.

Gupta, Sobhanlal Datta. *Marxism in Dark Times: Selected Essays for the New Century* (London: Anthem Press, 2012).

Haslam, Jason. *Fitting Sentences: Identity in Nineteenth- and Twentieth-Century Prison Narratives* (Toronto: University of Toronto Press, 2005).

Hawser, Harry. *Buds and Flowers, of Leisure Hours* (Philadelphia: Geo. Johnson, for the Author, 1844).

Hegel, G. W. F. *The Phenomenology of Spirit*, translated by A. V. Miller (Oxford: Oxford University Press, 1977).

Heidegger, Martin. *Being and Time*, translated by John Macquarie and Edward Robinson (Oxford: Basil Blackwell, 1962).

—. *The Question Concerning Technology and Other Essays*, translated by William Lovitt (New York: Garland, 1977).

Hill, Rebecca. 'Chauka's Voice: Resistance in the Art of Behrouz Boochani', *Overland* (9 March 2022). Accessed at: https://overland.org.au/2022/03/chaukas-voice-resistance-in-the-art-of-behrouz-boochani/.

Hitchens, Christopher. 'Red Rosa', *The Atlantic* (June 2011). Accessed at: https://www.theatlantic.com/magazine/archive/2011/06/red-rosa/308500/.

Hornsby, Charles. *Kenya: A History Since Independence* (London: I. B. Tauris, 2012).

'Il Tempio di Giove Anxur a Terracina'. Accessed at: https://web.archive.org/web/20120304035917/http://www.italiadascoprire.net/turismo-italia/177/il-tempio-di-giove-anxur-a-terracina.html.

Jackson, George. *Soledad Brother: The Prison Letters of George Jackson* (Chicago: Lawrence Hill, 1994).

James, Joy, ed. *Imprisoned Intellectuals: America's Political Prisoners Write on Life, Liberation, and Rebellion* (Lanham: Rowman & Littlefield, 2003).

Jameson, Fredric. *Brecht and Method* (London: Verso, 1998).

Jenkins, Destin, and Justin Leroy, eds. *Histories of Racial Capitalism*, Kindle ed. (New York: Columbia University Press, 2021).

Kariuki, Josiah Mwangi. *'Mau Mau' Detainee: The Account by a Kenya African of his Experience in Detention Camps, 1953–1960* (London: Oxford University Press, 1963).

Kask, Melanie Margaret. *Soul Mates: The Prison Letters of Eldridge Cleaver and Beverly Axelrod*, vol. 1 (Berkeley: University of California Press, 2003).

Kelly, Michelle, and Claire Westall, eds. *Prison Writing and the Literary World: Imprisonment, Institutionality and Questions of Literary Practice* (London: Routledge, 2021).

Kelly, Molly Robinson. 'Reading Oscar Wilde's Spirituality in *De Profundis*', *REM* 68.3 (Summer 2006): 210–27.

Kenner, Hugh. *Ulysses*, revised ed. (Baltimore: Johns Hopkins University Press, 1987).

Kilgore, James. *Understanding Mass Incarceration: A People's Guide to the Key Civil Rights Struggle of Our Time* (New York: The New Press, 2015).

Kleinfield, Sonny, and Peter Frishouf. 'Hoffman, Dharuba Speak at Square Rally; 180 March on Med School, Disrupt Speech', *Washington Square Journal* (2 April 1970).

Knight, Etheridge. *Black Voices from Prison* (New York: Pathfinder Press, 1970).

Knopp, Fay Honey. *Instead of Prisons: A Handbook for Abolitionists* (Syracuse: Prison Research Education Action Project, 1976).

Langer, Lawrence. 'The Survivor as Author: Primo Levi's Literary Vision of Auschwitz', in *New Reflections on Primo Levi: Before and After Auschwitz*, edited by Risa Sodi and Millicent Marcus (London: Palgrave, 2011), 133–47.

Lefebvre, Henri. *The Production of Space*, translated by Donald Nicholson-Smith (Oxford: Blackwell, 1991).

Lehmann, Vibeke. 'Challenges and Accomplishments in US Prison Libraries', *Library Trends* 59.3 (2011): 490–508.

Levi, Primo. *The Complete Works of Primo Levi, Vol. I*, edited by Ann Goldstein (New York: Liveright, 2015).

—. *The Complete Works of Primo Levi, Vol. III*, edited by Ann Goldstein (New York: Liveright, 2015).

—. *If This Is A Man/The Truce*, translated by Stuart Woolf (London: Abacus, 2013).

—. *The Voice of Memory: Primo Levi – Interviews, 1961–1987*, edited by Marco Belpoliti and Robert Gordon, translated by Robert Gordon (New York: New Press, 2001).

Loughnan, Claire. Review of *No Friend but the Mountains*, *State Crime* 8.1 (2019): 126–30.

Lovelace, Richard. *The Poems of Richard Lovelace*, edited by C. H. Wilkinson (Oxford: Oxford University Press, at the Clarendon Press, 1930).

Lukács, Georg. *Solzhenitsyn*, translated by William David Graf (Cambridge, MA: MIT Press, 1971).

—. *Writer and Critic*, translated by Arthur Kahn (London: Merlin, 1978).

Luxemburg, Rosa. *The Letters of Rosa Luxemburg*, edited by Georg Adler, Peter Hudis and Annelies Laschitza, translated by George Shriver (London: Verso, 2011).

—. *The Rosa Luxemburg Reader*, edited by Peter Hudis and Kevin B. Anderson (New York: Monthly Review Press, 2004).

—. *Rosa Luxemburg: Selected Political Writings*, edited by Robert Looker (London: Jonathan Cape, 1972).

Mallarmé, Stéphane. *Collected Poems*, translated by Henry Weinfield (Berkeley: University of California Press, 1994).

Marx, Karl. *Capital, Vol. 1*, translated by Ben Fowkes (London: Penguin, 1990).

Marx, Karl, and Friedrich Engels. *The Communist Manifesto*, translated by Ben Fowkes (London: Penguin, 2004).

Mathiesen, Thomas. *The Politics of Abolition* (New York: John Wiley & Sons, 1974).

McCarthy, Cormac. *The Road* (New York: Knopf, 2006).

Metcalf, Jerry. 'Prison is a Real-Life Example of the World White Supremacists Want', *The Marshall Project* (24 August 2017). Accessed at:

https://www.themarshallproject.org/2017/08/24/prison-is-a-real-life-ex
ample-of-the-world-white-supremacists-want.

Mills, Nicolaus C. 'Prison and Society in Nineteenth-Century American
Fiction', *Western Humanities Review* 24.4 (1970): 325–32.

Milton, John. *Paradise Lost*, edited by Gordon Teskey (New York: Norton,
2005).

Moore, Dashiell. 'Behrouz Boochani and the Penal Archipelago', *Overland*
239 (Winter 2020): 49–59.

Moran, Dominique, Nick Gill and Deirdre Conlon, eds. *Carceral Spaces:
Mobility and Agency in Imprisonment and Migrant Detention* (Farnham:
Ashgate, 2013).

Nettl, J. P. *Rosa Luxemburg: The Biography* (London: Verso, 2019).

Newton, Huey P. *The Huey P. Newton Reader*, edited by David Hilliard
and David Weise (New York: Seven Stories Press, 2002).

—. *Revolutionary Suicide*, with the assistance of J. Herman Blake (London:
Penguin, 2009).

Ngũgĩ wa Thiong'o. *Decolonizing the Mind: The Politics of Language in
African Literature* (Harare: Zimbabwe Publishing House, 1987).

—. *Detained: A Writer's Prison Diary* (London: Heinemann, 1981).

—. *Devil on the Cross* (London: Penguin, 2017).

—. *Wrestling with the Devil: A Prison Memoir* (London: Random House,
2018).

—. *Writers in Politics: Essays* (London: Heinemann, 1981).

O'Donnell, Samantha. 'Living Death at the Intersection of Necropower
and Disciplinary Power: A Qualitative Exploration of Racialised
and Detained Groups in Australia', *Critical Criminology* 30 (2022):
285–304.

Ogede, Ode. *Intertextuality in Contemporary African Literature* (New
York: Lexington Books, 2011).

O'Hearn, Denis. *Nothing but an Unfinished Song: Bobby Sands, the Irish
Hunger Striker Who Ignited a Generation* (New York: Nation Books,
2006).

Olson, Charles, and Robert Creeley. *The Complete Correspondence*, vol. 1,
edited by George F. Butterick (Santa Barbara: Black Sparrow Press,
1980).

O'Rawe, Richard. *Blanketmen: An Untold Story of the H-Block Hunger
Strike* (Dublin: New Island, 2005).

Pager, Devah. *Marked: Race, Crime, and Finding Work in an Era of Mass
Incarceration* (University of Chicago Press, 2007).

Parry, Benita. 'Perspectives on Rosa Luxemburg 2', *new formations: a
journal of culture/theory/politics* 94 (2018): 49–60.

Pearce, Joseph. *Solzhenitsyn: A Soul in Exile*, revised ed. (New York:
HarperCollins, 1999).

Phillips, Philip Edward, ed. *Prison Narratives from Boethius to Zana* (New
York: Palgrave Macmillan, 2014).

Poletti, Anna. 'Introduction: A Forum on Behrouz Boochani's *No Friend but the Mountains: Writing from Manus Prison*', *Biography* 43.4 (2020): 724–35.

Popova, Zhanna. 'The Two Tales of Forced Labour: Katorga and Reformed Prison in Imperial Russia, 1878–1905', *Almanack* 14 (2016): 91–117.

Pound, Ezra. *The Cantos of Ezra Pound*, fourteenth printing (New York: New Directions, 1998).

—. *Ezra Pound and Dorothy Pound, Letters in Captivity 1945–1946*, edited by Omar Pound and Robert Spoo (New York: Oxford University Press, 1999).

—. *'Ezra Pound Speaking': Radio Speeches of World War II*, edited by Leonard W. Doob (Westport, CT: Greenwood Press, 1978).

Pratt, John. *Punishment and Civilization: Penal Tolerance and Intolerance in Modern Society* (London: Sage, 2002).

Price, Joshua M. *Prison and Social Death* (New Brunswick, NJ: Rutgers University Press, 2015).

Rancière, Jacques. *The Politics of Aesthetics: The Distribution of the Sensible* (London: Continuum, 2004).

Raunig, Gerald. *Dividuum: Machinic Capitalism and Molecular Revolution*, translated by Aileen Derieg (Pasadena: Semiotext(e), 2016).

Reed, Ishmael. *The Reed Reader* (New York: Basic Books, 2001).

Rodríguez, Dylan. *White Reconstruction: Domestic Warfare and the Logistics of Genocide* (New York: Fordham University Press, 2021).

Rose, Jacqueline. *Women in Dark Times* (London: Verso, 2014).

Rothman, David J. 'Primo Levi, Dante, and the Meaning of Reading', *Sewanee Review* 124.3 (Summer 2016): 498–505.

Roussillon, Alain. 'Republican Egypt Interpreted: Revolution and Beyond', in *The Cambridge History of Egypt, Volume Two: Modern Egypt from 1517 to the End of the Twentieth Century*, edited by M. W. Daly (Cambridge: Cambridge University Press, 1998), 334–93.

Roux, Daniel. '"I speak to you and I listen to the voice coming back": Recording Solitary Confinement in the Apartheid Prison', *English Academy Review* 22.1 (2005): 22–31.

Royo-Grasa, Pilar. 'Behrouz Boochani's *No Friend but the Mountains*: A Call for Dignity and Justice', *European Legacy*, 26.7–8 (2021): 750–63.

Sands, Bobby. *Writings from Prison* (Cork: Mercier Press, 1997).

Scammell, Michael. 'Solzhenitsyn the Stylist', *New York Times Sunday Book Review* (29 August 2008).

Schalkwyk, David. 'Chronotopes of the Self in the Writings of Women Political Prisoners in South Africa', in *Apartheid Narratives*, edited by Nahem Yousaf, *DQR Studies in Literature Online*, vol. 31 (Leiden: Brill, 2001): 1–36.

Schept, Judah. *Progressive Punishment: Job Loss, Jail Growth, and the Neoliberal Logic of Carceral Expansion* (New York: New York University Press, 2015).

Scott, Jamie S. 'Space, Time, Solitude: The Liberating Contradictions of Ruth First's *117 Days*', in *Engaging with Literature of Commitment, Vol 1: Africa in the World*, edited by Gordon Collier, Marc Delrez, Anne Fuchs, and Bénédicte Ledent (Amsterdam: Rodopi, 2012), 71–80.

Shakur, Assata. *Assata: An Autobiography* (Chicago: Lawrence Hill Books, 2001).

Shakur, Zayd. 'America Is the Prison', in *Off the Pigs! The History and Literature of the Black Panther Party*, edited by G. Louis Heath (Metuchen, NJ: Scarecrow, 1976), 247–80.

Sharma, Kalpana. 'Egypt's Face of Courage', *The Hindu* online ed. (3 June 2001). Accessed at: https://web.archive.org/web/20041030002518/http://www.hinduonnet.com/2001/06/03/stories/13030786.htm.

Shkovlsky, Viktor. 'Art as Technique', in *Russian Formalist Criticism: Four Essays*, 2nd ed., edited by Lee T. Lemon and Marion J. Reis (Lincoln: University of Nebraska Press, 2012), 3–24.

Sim, Joe. *Punishment and Prisons: Power and the Carceral State* (London: Sage, 2009).

Smith, Caleb. *The Prison and the American Imagination* (New Haven: Yale University Press, 2009).

Solzhenitsyn, Aleksandr. *The Gulag Archipelago: 1918–1956, Parts I–II*, translated by Thomas P. Whitney (New York: Harper & Row, 1974).

—. *The Gulag Archipelago: 1918–1956, Parts V–VII*, translated by Harry Willetts (New York: Harper & Row, 1977).

—. *One Day in the Life of Ivan Denisovich*, translated by Ralph Parker (London: Penguin, 1963).

—. *One Day in the Life of Ivan Denisovich*, translated by Gillon Aitken (London: Sphere, 2005).

—. *One Day in the Life of Ivan Denisovich*, translated by H. T. Willetts (New York: Farrar, Straus and Giroux, 2005).

Soueif, Ahdaf. 'In the Beggars' Cell', *New Society* 15 (August 1986): 23–4.

Steinberg, Jonny. 'Writing South Africa's Prisons into History', in *Prison Writing and the Literary World: Imprisonment, Institutionality and Questions of Literary Practice*, edited by Michelle Kelly and Claire Westall (London: Routledge, 2021), 110–20.

Story, Brett. *Prison Land: Mapping Carceral Power across Neoliberal America* (Minneapolis: University of Minnesota Press, 2019).

Stubbs, Ben. *Creative and Non-Fiction Writing during Isolation and Confinement: Imaginative Travel, Prison, Shipwrecks, Pandemics, and War* (London: Routledge, 2022).

Summers, Joanna. *Late-Medieval Prison Writing and the Politics of Autobiography* (Oxford: Oxford University Press, 2004).

Tempest, Richard. *Overwriting Chaos: Aleksandr Solzhenitsyn's Fictive Worlds* (Boston: Academic Studies Press, 2019).

Tofighian, Omid. 'Behrouz Boochani and the Manus Prison Narratives: Merging Translation with Philosophical Reading', *Continuum* 32.4 (2018): 523–40.

Trotsky, Leon. *The Revolution Betrayed: What Is the Soviet Union and Where Is It Going?* (New York: Pathfinder, 1972).

Trotter, David. 'Saved by the Ant's Fore-Foot', *London Review of Books* 27.13 (7 July 2005).

UNHCR website: https://www.unhcr.org/figures-at-a-glance.html.

Virgil. *The Aeneid*, translated by Robert Fagles (London: Penguin, 2006).

Wacquant, Loïc. *Prisons of Poverty*, expanded ed. (Minneapolis: University of Minnesota Press, 2009).

Waterbury, John. *The Egypt of Nasser and Sadat: The Political Economy of Two Regimes* (Princeton, NJ: Princeton University Press, 1983).

Whalen, Lachlan. *Contemporary Irish Republican Prison Writing: Writing and Resistance* (London: Palgrave, 2007).

Whitman, James Q. *Hitler's American Model*, Kindle ed. (Princeton, NJ: Princeton University Press, 2017).

Wieder, Alan. *Ruth First and Joe Slovo in the War against Apartheid* (New York: Monthly Review Press, 2013).

Wilde, Oscar. *De Profundis and Other Prison Writings*, edited by Colm Tóibín (London: Penguin, 2013).

—. *The Soul of Man under Socialism & Selected Critical Prose*, edited by Linda Dowling (London: Penguin, 2001).

Wood, Alan. *Russia's Frozen Frontier: A History of Siberia and the Russian Far East, 1581–1991* (London: Bloomsbury, 2011).

Woolf, Judith. 'From *If This Is a Man* to *The Drowned and the Saved*', in *The Cambridge Companion to Primo Levi*, edited by Robert S. C. Gordon (Cambridge: Cambridge University Press, 2007), 35–50.

World Prison Brief: https://www.prisonstudies.org/.

Wright, Richard. 'How "Bigger" Was Born'. Accessed at: http://xroads. virginia.edu/~MA01/White/anthology/bigger.html.

X, Malcolm. *The Autobiography of Malcolm X*, as told to Alex Haley (New York: Ballantine Books, 1992).

Žižek, Slavoj. *Sex and the Failed Absolute* (London: Bloomsbury, 2019).

Index